Challenging the
CORPORATE POWER
in Renewable Energy

Also by Dexter Whitfield:

- *Making It Public: Evidence and action against privatisation* (1983)
- *The Welfare State: Privatisation, Deregulation and Commercialisation of Public Services* (1992)
- *Public Services or Corporate Welfare: Rethinking the Nation State in the Global Economy* (2001)
- *New Labour's Attack on Public Services: Modernisation by Marketisation* (2006)
- *Global Auction of Public Assets: Public sector alternatives to the infrastructure market and Public Private Partnerships* (2010)
- *In Place of Austerity: Reconstruction of the state, economy and public services* (2012)
- *Unmasking Austerity: Opposition and Alternatives in Europe and North America* (2014)
- *Public Alternative to the Privatisation of Life: Strategies for decommodification, public ownership and provision* (2020)

Challenging the rise of
CORPORATE POWER
in Renewable Energy

Dexter Whitfield

SPOKESMAN

Cover Image: *Yangphoto/iStock*

Erratum
Page 7 line 20

'totalled US$206,723m'
(not bn)

First published in 2023 by Spokesman
5 Churchill Park
Nottingham NG4 2HF, England
Phone 0115 970 8318
www.spokesmanbooks.org

© Dexter Whitfield

All rights reserved. No part of this publication may be reproduced, stored in a retrieval system or transmitted in any form or by means, electronic, mechanical, photocopying, recording or otherwise, without prior permission of the publishers.

ISBN paperback 9780851249186
ISBN Kindle 9780851249193

A CIP Catalogue is available from the British Library

Printed in Britain
Layout by Kavita Graphics (dennis@kavitagraphics.co.uk)

Contents

Abbreviations   viii

1. **Crisis and opportunities**   1
   Climate crisis context
   Structural flaws
   Objectives and structure

2. **Corporate domination**   11
   Growth of the renewable energy sector
   Liberalisation and privatisation of energy
   Financialisation, private finance and role of the state
   IMF: *"Public Sector must play role in catalysing private climate finance"*
   Theory and practice in primary and secondary energy markets
   Accumulation by dispossession in energy sector
   The political economy of renewable energy framework
   Another version of asset recycling
   State bailouts for Investor State-Dispute Settlement/Energy Charter Treaty claims
   Critique of Environment, Social and Governance

3. **Trading renewable energy assets**   43
   The ESSU Global Renewable Energy Secondary Market Database
   Typology of market participants
   Impact of secondary market
   Shareholders scoop multi-million dividends
   High cost and secrecy of transactions
   Developments in 2022

4. **Wide use of PPPs for renewable energy projects in emerging economies**   63
   Analysis of World Bank PPP renewable energy projects
   Private investment continues despite pandemic
   Debt and the climate crisis

5. **Tax havens and market interventions**   71
   Tax avoidance is widespread in renewable energy
   Global dimensions
   Hedge fund interventions
   Scotland and Norway wind farm ownership comparison
   Negative impact of tax havens

6. **Public ownership and public values** 85
   Scale of public ownership
   Public authorities buy and sell renewable energy assets
   Remunicipalisation of energy
   Public goods
   Core public values framework

7. **The commodification and marketisation of nature and biodiversity** 97
   Flawed economics of biodiversity
   Wall Street's planned takeover of nature
   Decommodification of nature

8. **Equalities - economic, social and environmental justice** 101
   Comprehensive approach essential
   New Zealand's National Adaptation Plan
   Public Sector Equality Duty
   Equality in housing retrofits
   Environmental justice in adaptation and protection

9. **Economic and industrial strategies** 107
   Improving national grids
   Renewable energy zones
   Net-Zero cities
   Manufacturing and industry
   Manufacturing of renewable energy infrastructure
   Decarbonisation of steel, construction and public transport
   Environmental adaptation and protection
   Retrofitting housing, public buildings and business premises
   Future-proofing agriculture
   Jobs and quality employment conditions
   Technological developments in renewable energy

10. Strategic opportunities   137
    Challenging corporate domination of renewable energy
    Opportunities for public ownership
    New public sector organisations
    Community-owned renewable energy projects
    Climate demands to Private Equity
    Other important policy changes are required
    Strategic organising and action

Appendices   149
References   157
About the Author   177
Index   178

Figures

1.	The level of coal, oil and natural gas dependency	5
2.	Global investment in energy transition by sector	23
3.	Growth of world renewable energy generation	13
4.	Political economy of renewable energy framework	34
5.	Increase in climate litigation	39
6.	Private investment in renewables and non-renewables by income group 2012-2020	67
7.	Per capita investment in clean energy concentrated in advanced economies	68
8.	Countries in the Climate Vulnerable Forum	69
9.	The share of Special Purpose Entity (SPE) related foreign direct investment	76
10.	Public sector core values framework	94
11.	The current rate of electrification in the European industrial sector	115
12.	Localised cost of technology	117

Tables

1.	Annual rate of transactions 2019-2021	44
2.	Transactions in selected countries	45
3.	Private Equity's Energy Footprint & Percentage of Assets Under Management	48
4.	Pension fund transactions or renewable energy assets in 2019-2021	51
5.	Transactions by major utility and petroleum companies in 2019-2021	53
6.	Dividends paid to shareholders in 20 renewable energy companies in 2021	56
7.	Second Quarter 2022 profits of fossil fuel companies	57
8.	Renewable energy technology in PPP projects	64
9.	Use of tax havens in renewable energy transactions	72
10.	Global public sector renewable energy assets	86
11.	Renewable energy operated by state owned companies	87
12.	Estimated direct and indirect jobs in renewable energy worldwide	127
13.	USA Offshore Wind Energy Supply Chain: direct and indirect Jobs	129
14.	Wage rates in US Clean Energy Industries	130
15.	Australia's One Million Jobs Plan	132

Appendices

Tables A1:	Result of the Crown Estate ScotWind 2022 auction	149
A2:	Companies often operating through subsidiaries	151
A3:	Examples of publicly owned energy companies	153
A4:	Examples of privately-owned energy companies	155

A Dataset of additional tables are available for download from the ESSU website: https://www.european-services-strategy.org.uk

- ESSU Global Renewable Energy Secondary Market Database 2019-2021 (excel)
- Table B1: Renewable energy assets acquired by publicly-owned companies between 1 January 2019 and 31 December 2021(docx)
- Table B2: Publicly-owned assets sold to private sector between 1 January 2019 and 31 December 2021 (docx)
- Table B3: Transfer of renewal energy assets between public sector companies between 1 January 2019 and 31 December 2021 (docx)
- Glossary of Renewable Energy Terms (docx).

Acknowledgements

I sincerely thank John Spoehr, Australian Industrial Transformation Institute, Flinders University, Richard Whyte, Ursula Murray, Will Haughen, Karen Escott and Andy Mott for their comments and observations. This book would not have been possible without the love, solidarity, analysis and skills of Dorothy Calvert. Sincere thanks to Tony Simpson and Tom Unterrainer of Spokesman Books for their commitment to this project.

Abbreviations

AB	Aketiebolag (limited company or corporation in Sweden)
AES	US energy company
ADB	Asian Development Bank
AG	Aktiengesellschaft (public Company in Germany)
APG	Algemene Pensioen Groep NV (Netherlands)
ARO	Active Retirement Obligation
A/S	Aktieselskab (Public Company in Denmark, Sweden & Norway)
BAE	British Aerospace
BBGI	Bilfinger Berger Global Infrastructure
BP	British Petroleum
B.V.	Besloten Vennootschap (private limited company in Netherlands)
CCC	Climate Change Committee
CCS	Carbon Capture and Storage
CCUS	Carbon Capture, Usage & Storage
CDPQ	Caisse de dépôt et placement du Québec
CEE.	Central and Eastern Europe
CfD	Contracts for Difference
CHP	Combined heat and power
DFI	Development finance institution
DIF	Investment company based in Netherlands
ECT	Energy Charter Treaty
EEG	Renewable Energy Sources Act (Germany)
EDF	Electricite France
EDP	Energias de Portugal
EDPR	Energias de Portugal Renováveis

EIB	European Investment Bank
ENEL	Italian multinational energy company
ESG	Environment, Social and Governance
ESSU	European Services Strategy Unit
ETF	Exchange-Traded Funds
EU	European Union
FDI	Foreign Direct Investment
FIT	Feed-in Tariff
GmbH	Gesellscaft mit beschrankter Haftung (private limited company in Germany)
GND	Green New Deal
GW	Gigawatt
HNWI	High Net Worth Individual
HSBC	Hongkong & Shanghai Banking Corporation
IADB	Inter-American Development Bank
IBRD	International Bank for Reconstruction and Development
IEA	International Energy Agency
IEEFA	Institute for Energy Economics and Financial Analysis
IFC	International Finance Corporation
IFM	Global Infrastructure Fund
IMF	International Monetary Fund
Inc.	Incorporated company
IPCC	Intergovernmental Panel on Climate Change
IPP	Independent Power Producers
INPP	International Public Partnerships
IRENA	International Renewable Energy Agency
ISDS	Investor State-Dispute Settlement
JVC	Joint Venture Company
KKR	Kravis, Kohlberg & Roberts (private equity company)
LLC	Limited Liability Company
LLP	Limited Liability Partnership
LP	Limited Partnership
Ltd	Limited company
MIGA	Multinational Investment Guarantee Agency
MW	Megawatt
MWp	Megawatt peak
NGO	Non-Governmental Organisation
NZE	Net Zero Emissions
NV	Naamloze Vennootschap (limited liability public company Netherlands & Belgium)

NPV	Net Present Value
OECD	Organisation for Economic Co-operation & Development
OFTO	Offshore Transmission Owner
OMERS	Ontario Municipal Employees' Retirement System
OPSEU	Ontario Public Service Employees' Union
PKA	Pensionskassernes Administration A/S (Denmark)
PLC	Public Listed Company
PPA	Power Purchase Agreement
PPIAF	Public-Private Infrastructure Advisory Facility
PPI	Private Participation in Infrastructure
PPP	Public Private Partnership
PRI	Principles for Responsible Investment
PSI	Public Services International
PV	Photovoltaic
REZ	Renewable Energy Zone
RNS	Regulatory News Service
S.A.	Societe Anonyme (public company in France, Spain, Latin America)
S.a.r.l.	Private limited liability company (Luxembourg)
SCSp	Special limited partnership (Luxembourg)
SEC	Securities and Exchange Commission (USA)
SGR	societa di gestione del risparmio (asset management company in Italy)
SICAF-SIF	Specialist investment fund in Luxembourg
SpA	Società Società per azioni (company with shares in Italy)
SPE	Special Purpose Entities
SPV	Special Purpose Vehicle
S.r.l.	Società a responsabilità limitata (a limited liability company)
SSE	Scottish and Southern Energy
TEEB	The Economics of Ecosystems and Biodiversity
TUC	Trades Union Congress
TUED	Trade Unions for Energy Democracy
UAE	United Arab Emirates
UK	United Kingdom
UN	United Nations
UNCTAD	United Nations Conference on Trade and Development
UNEP	United Nations Environment Programme
USA	United States of America
WBG	World Bank Group

CHAPTER 1
Crisis and opportunities

The objective of this book is to demonstrate how corporate interests dominate the renewable energy sector. They range from private investment funds, venture capital funds, private equity funds and subsidiaries of fossil fuel companies which are developers and owner-operators of wind farms, solar parks, storage, hydro and other projects.

These projects are bought and sold in the secondary market with development rights and 'construction-ready status', either as individual projects or as part of a portfolio of operational projects, often located in several countries. The analysis is based on the European Services Strategy Unit Global Renewable Energy Database which contains 1,622 transactions between 1 January 2019 and 31st December 2021.

Several publicly-owned companies in Norway, Sweden, Denmark, France, Germany, China, Romania and the Republic of Ireland are developers and owners of renewable energy assets, but the public sector is in a minority compared to the private sector in a global context.

The long-term impact is likely to be the replacement of multinational fossil fuel companies by multinational renewable energy companies in a system where market forces are dominant. The IMF and vested interests believe the public sector's role should be limited to catalysing private sector finance by taking on risk, funding research and development.

But electricity is a public good, hence it is imperative that not-for-profit publicly-owned companies have a vital role in developing, owning and operating renewable energy projects and distributing energy.

Later chapters chart a way forward in which the public sector can and must have a significant and sustainable role in the provision and ownership of renewable energy projects. This includes the different forms of decarbonisation ranging from retrofitting homes, public buildings and business premises and national planning for environmental adaptations and building resilience, and requires the full application of public values and a core public values framework.

Governments also have a key role in ensuring compliance with equality and equity legislation and economic development initiatives to provide manufacturing and servicing facilities for renewable projects. They must align with the provision of training to maximise the employment opportunities afforded by the renewable energy sector. The decommodification of nature and biodiversity must equally be centre stage.

The corporatisation of renewable energy must systematically be removed and replaced by a new era of not-for-profit publicly owned organisations geared to radically transform the ownership and operation of renewable energy in a way which is participative, with rigorous scrutiny, oversight and democratic accountability.

Climate crisis context

The scientific evidence of a climate crisis overwhelmingly supports the need for decarbonisation to totally replace fossil fuels with renewable energy by 2050 is clear (Intergovernmental Panel on Climate Change, 2021). Forecasts predict the continuing melting of glaciers, rising sea levels, flooding and coastal erosion, the rising threat of extraordinary landscape fires leading to deaths or injuries, power cuts, damage to homes, transport and agriculture.

A follow-up IPCC report examined the vulnerability, adaptation and resilience of human and natural systems and defined three principles of climate justice:

> "...distributive justice which refers to the allocation of burdens and benefits among individuals, nations and generations; procedural justice which refers to who decides and participates in decision-making; and recognition which entails basic respect and robust engagement with and fair consideration of diverse cultures and perspectives" (IPCC, 2022).

Nine additional studies by agencies and research teams have upgraded the threat of rising sea levels; the risk of wildfires; the melting of glaciers; the deadly impact of pollution on the health of millions in communities; the likelihood of missing the 1.5 C target; failure to strand fossil fuel assets in the ground; and the needs of 940m people with no access to electricity and 2.6bn who need space cooling.

> "By 2050, the expected relative sea level (RSL) will cause tide and storm surge heights to increase and will lead to a shift in U.S. coastal flood regimes, with major and moderate high tide flood events occurring as frequently as moderate and minor high tide flood events occur today. Without additional risk-reduction measures, U.S. coastal infrastructure, communities, and ecosystems will face significant consequences" (Global and Regional Sea Level Rise: Scenarios for the United States, National Oceanic and Atmospheric Administration, 2022).

> "A wildfire results from a complex interaction of biological, meteorological, physical, and social factors that influence the likelihood of a wildfire breaking out, its propagation and intensity, duration and extent, and its potential to cause damage to economies, the environment, and society. Around the world many of these factors – climate, land use and land management practices, and demographics – are changing" (Spreading Like Wildfire: The Rising Threat of Extraordinary Landscape Fires, UNEP, 2022).

A new study calculates that, between 2000 and 2019, glaciers collectively lost around 267bn tonnes of ice every year. Assuming that all the water from melting glaciers eventually reach the ocean, this means that meltwater from glaciers alone contributed 0.74mm of sea level rise every year (Hugonnet et al, 2021). Another study found that the Arctic has warmed nearly four times faster than the globe between 1979-2021 (Rantanen et al, 2022).

"Pollution and toxic substances kill more than 9 million people per year, damage the health of billions, and inflict costs measured in trillions of dollars. Everyone in the world is affected by the pervasive pollution that characterizes life in the 21st century, even newborn infants. However, the burden of contamination falls most heavily upon communities that already are vulnerable or marginalized because of race, poverty and other socio-economic factors. This phenomenon is known as environmental injustice" (Boyd and Hadley-Burke, United Nations, 2022).

"There is a 50:50 chance of average global temperature reaching 1.5 degrees Celcius above pre-industrial levels in the next five years, and the likelihood is increasing with time……A single year of exceedance above 1.5 °C does not mean we have breached the iconic threshold of the Paris Agreement, but it does reveal that we are edging ever closer to a situation where 1.5 °C could be exceeded for an extended period" (World Meteorological Organization, 2022).

"We find that developed reserves of oil, gas and coal significantly exceed what can be extracted and burned within the 1.5 ^{0}C budget, a conclusion that is robust to uncertainties in reserves and carbon budgets. Given a rapidly closing window to keep warming below 1.5 ^{0}C, these findings call for urgent policy attention on managing an orderly and equitable phase-out of fossil fuel extraction" (Trout, K. et al, 2022).

Space cooling will become increasingly important to prevent heat-related deaths and reduced productivity with global demand expected to soar 395% from 800 gigawatts in 2016 to 3,350GW in 2050 as temperatures rise and urbanisation increases to 68% of the world population living in urban areas by 2050. 2.8bn people live in hottest parts of the world but only 8% possess air conditioners in contrast to 90% ownership in USA and Japan (OECD/International Energy Agency, 2018, United Nations Environment Programme, 2022).

"…passive building and city design and innovative cooling technologies will be needed to ensure essential cooling for all that minimize environmental damage" (Mastrucci et al, 2019).

"Extreme Danger" (Heat Index above 125 degrees F) will impact about 107m people in the USA in 2053, an increase of 13 times over 30 years thus requiring access to very significant cooling (First Street Foundation, 2022).

Meanwhile,
"...global fossil fuel subsidies were $5.9 trillion or 6.8 percent of GDP in 2020 and are expected to increase to 7.4 percent of GDP in 2025 as the share of fuel consumption in emerging markets (where price gaps are generally larger) continues to climb" (IMF, 2021).

Direct and indirect subsidies comprised under-pricing local air pollution costs (42%), global warming costs (29%), congestion and road accidents (15%), explicit subsidies (8%) and foregone consumption tax revenue (6%). In addition,

"...in 2020 and 2021, the EIB provided almost €2 billion in loans to companies with a high share of coal in their power and heat generation portfolios" (Counter Balance, 2022).

Even more important is the destruction of nation states, the mass killing of people of all ages and deliberate indiscriminate demolition of cities and towns and their public infrastructure of hospitals, schools, public transport, housing and local economies by despots. Others persecute minority groups on an industrial scale. There are current wars or conflicts in Ukraine, Yemen, Sudan, Ethiopia and earlier ones in Syria, Afghanistan, Myanmar, Iraq, Libya, plus civil wars and territorial disputes in several countries.

The Russian invasion of Ukraine in February 2022 led to global financial sanctions and withdrawal from corporate contracts and projects. Germany accelerated implementation of the Renewable Energy Sources Act (EEG) and plans for renewables to account for 80% of its electricity needs by 2030 and 100% by 2035. Russia also blocked the Nord Stream 2 Russian gas pipeline which was designed to double gas supply to Germany.

US Supreme Court 6-3 decision in June 2022 on West Virginia v. Environmental Protection Agency ruled that Agency has very limited powers to regulate power plant emission of greenhouse gases under a provision of the Clean Air Act or to force polluting plants to close. The New York Times described it as:

"...the product of a coordinated, multiyear strategy by Republican attorneys general, conservative legal activists and their funders to use the judicial system to rewrite environmental law, weakening the executive branch's ability to tackle global warming" (Andreoni, 2022). The decision will empower corporations to slow

emission reduction and means the transition process to 2050 will be even more conflictual.

Figure 1 indicates two important realities. Firstly, the high level of regional dependency on coal, oil and natural gas. Secondly, the low level of energy consumption through renewables. Wind and solar power provided 10.2% of energy generation in 2021, exceeding 10% for the first time (British Petroleum, 2022).

The chart exposes the scale of transformation required over the next three decades to meet the climate targets and environmental adaptation and protection. It indicates

Figure 1: The level of coal, oil and natural gas dependency

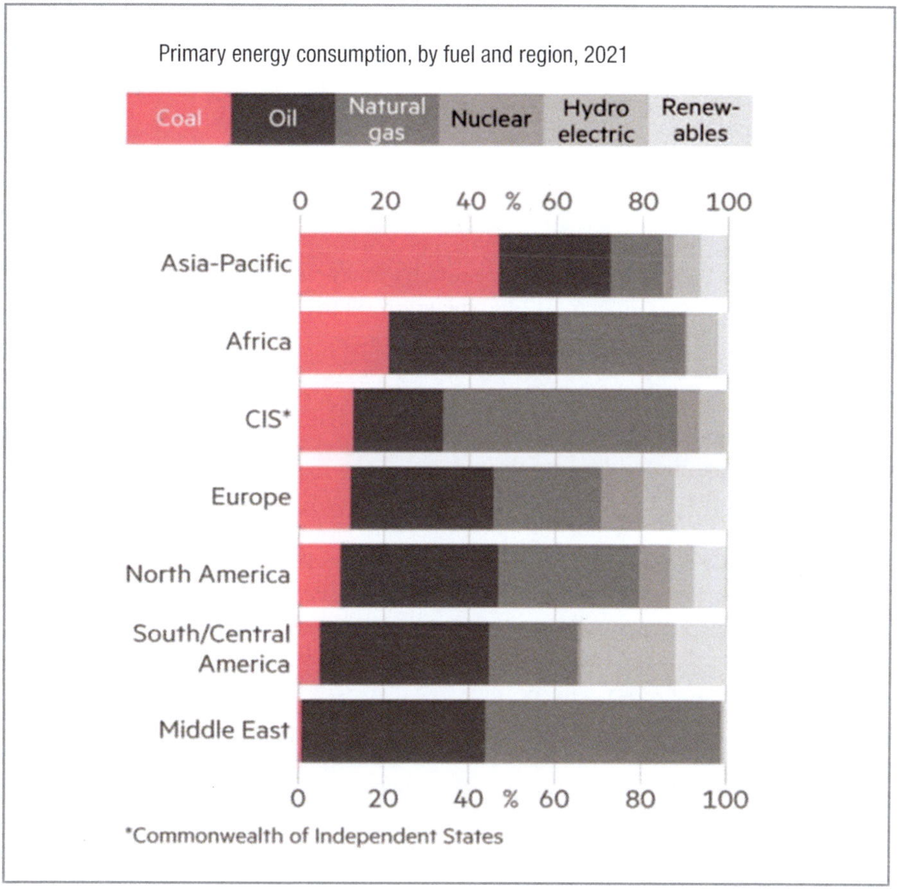

Primary energy consumption, by fuel and region, 2021

Categories: Coal | Oil | Natural gas | Nuclear | Hydroelectric | Renewables

Regions shown: Asia-Pacific, Africa, CIS*, Europe, North America, South/Central America, Middle East

*Commonwealth of Independent States

Source: BP Statistical Review of World Energy 2022 © FT

the limited progress to date and continued reliance on markets, market forces and the corporate sector. More of the same is almost certain to be a disaster with profound climate, environmental, economic and human impacts.

To achieve decarbonisation by 2050 will require 816GW of wind and 632GW of solar installed every year to 2050, plus 257GWh battery storage per annum according to a global forecast (BloombergNEF, 2021). The forecast assumes 49% of electricity will be used to produce large quantities of hydrogen with the remainder by end users in the economy. The forecast implies current investment will have to double – for example annual investment of US$1.7 trillion in 2020 will have to increase to between US$3.1 and US$5.8 trillion every year for three decades (ibid).

In this context it is critically important to identify the structural flaws in the current provision of renewable energy and to map the transformative changes required to achieve the climate targets and an equitable transition.

Structural flaws

The key characteristics of the renewable energy sector are summarised below and are supported by the evidence in the ESSU Global Renewable Energy Secondary Market Database 2019-2021 and analysis in Chapters 2-10.

- There were 1,622 transactions of renewable energy assets in the 3-year period between 1 January 2019 to 31 December 2021; the high level of secondary market sale of wind, solar, hydro, battery, storage, biomass and energy-from-waste projects together with corporate takeovers and partnerships in the development stage of projects. Market ideology and market interests dominate the sector and outsourcing is widespread.
- The twelve major publicly owned renewable energy companies plus three major companies that have a minority public shareholding collectively own 1,671 projects with 98.5GW operational capacity or 3.47% of the global total.
- Public sector organisations bought and sold assets in the secondary market in the same period via 79 acquisitions and 41 sales accounting for 24.6GW. Whilst the acquisitions increased the overall public sector owned GW by 37.9GW, this was countered by the sale of assets by the public sector reducing power generation by 24.6GW. This resulted in a mere 0.46% or 13.6GW increase in public sector renewable energy generating power to 3.93%.
- Private Equity Funds have carved out a pivotal role financing and owning renewable energy assets – they acquired 369 renewable energy assets and sold 178 projects between 2019-2021.
- 41 major renewable energy companies registered in tax havens were involved in 264 transactions to acquire assets whilst a further 47 transactions involved the sale of renewable energy assets. The use of tax havens to avoid or reduce

- corporate taxation increases corporate profits but reduces tax revenue for governments.
- A sample of 20 private renewable energy companies paid their shareholders US$10.7bn in dividends in 2021 alone. In addition, eight fossil fuel multinational corporations had total profits of US$67.71bn in the second quarter of 2022.
- Pension funds have increased ownership of renewable energy assets – 17 pension funds were involved in 39 transactions that acquired renewable energy projects with 43,476MW and 8 transactions that sold projects with 7,213MW.
- Democratic accountability is weak with limited community participation and a lack of scrutiny/oversight and rigorous and comprehensive economic, social and environmental evaluation and impact assessment.
- Environment, Social and Governance (ESG) is widely promoted but is totally inadequate in terms of equalities, employment, social, economic and environmental justice, democratic accountability and transparency.
- Despite the wide criticism and failure of many Public Private Partnership projects, the World Bank and regional development banks continue to promote the PPP model for renewable energy projects in the global south.
- The cost of transactions was disclosed for 504 transactions (31.07%) and totalled US$206,723bn, on the basis that these transactions were a representative sample of all 1622 transactions the total cost was US$671.8bn. Legal and technical transaction costs were estimated to be US$15.0bn, giving the overall cost of the secondary market in renewable energy in the 2019-2021 period to be US$686.8bn.
- The sector is increasingly globalised as many renewable energy companies, developers, financial institutions, constructors and operators traverse nation state boundaries.
- Significant technological advances have been achieved in solar panels, floating offshore wind farms, turbines, battery storage and tidal technology. The rate of innovation and technological development are likely to accelerate leading to new models of renewable energy such as tidal power, more powerful battery storage and efficiency/effectiveness improvements in solar and wind turbines and blades.
- The hedge fund Elliott Management, known for buying the debt of developing economies at knock-down prices and then suing governments for full payment of the debt, targeted three energy companies in 2019-2021 – EDP (Portugal), Duke Energy Corporation (USA) and SSE (UK and Ireland). Elliott acquired company shares and sought to persuade the respective board of directors to sell off subsidiaries or to 'maximise shareholder value' which would benefit Elliott. It failed.

Key objectives

To focus attention on renewable energy generation and the related trends and developments including the trade in assets, mergers and acquisitions, joint ventures and partnerships in the secondary market.

To investigate the global scale of the sale of operational renewable energy assets such as wind, solar, hydro, biomass, energy-from-waste and battery storage projects in the secondary market to reveal the scale of tax avoidance in their planning, finance, construction and operation.

To identify the extensive role of the private sector, particularly private equity funds, in the renewable energy sector and their wide use of tax havens. This has far-reaching implications because the current corporate ownership and control of the fossil fuel industry could be replicated in the renewable energy sector by 2050 or earlier.

To de-commodify and reverse the marketisation, corporatisation and privatisation of the renewable energy sector and to rapidly increase public sector capabilities to plan, develop, own, operate and manage renewable energy projects.

To integrate the continued expansion of renewable energy with an industrial strategy involving local/regional manufacture and production, the manufacture of retrofitting plant and materials together with the equipment and material required for environmental adaptation and protection.

To develop a comprehensive action plan for public ownership, provision and democratic accountability including Net Zero Economic Zones to city scale, industrial hub or local areas, city centres or neighbourhoods, large scale retrofitting, alternative uses for sites and factories to promote local/regional economic development and employment. This will include developing job and skills training for all of these tasks and to plan, coordinate and deliver retrofitting and undertake future repair, maintenance and upgrades.

To expose the limitations of ESG and set out an alternative framework of public values inclusive of the dimensions of equality, social, economic, labour and environmental justice.

To expose the methods that are being adopted to financialise, commercialise and privatise nature and biodiversity and to emphasize the need to focus on sustaining their role and their contribution in sustaining and enhancing their role.

To identify the scope for corporate disruption combined with building alliances of workers and trade unions, community organisations, political parties and NGOs to draw up proposals for renewable energy and retrofitting projects that meet their needs for power under local planning, control and accountability.

To emphasize the need for the integration of nature and biodiversity, sustainable objectives, good quality jobs, regeneration and economic change aligned with equality and public values across the renewable energy and decarbonisation agendas.

To stress the importance for governments, international organisations, political parties and trade unions to use the extensive evidence of the poor performance and impact of PPP projects to make the case for publicly-owned and operated projects in developing economies.

Structure of the book

Chapter 2 discusses the ways in which the renewable energy sector demonstrates many of the attributes of corporate capture, in other words, the dominant role of private finance, private equity funds and private companies that have a key role the finance, development, ownership and operation of the renewable energy infrastructure.

The findings of the three-year ESSU Global Renewable Energy Secondary Market Database 2019-2021 are quantified and discussed in **Chapter 3**. The database contains a summary of 1,622 secondary market transactions which reveal the scale of the sale and purchase of renewable energy assets over a three-year period. It includes a typology of market participants and concludes with an analysis of the use of PPPs for renewable energy in the global south.

Chapter 4 focuses on the wide use of PPPs for energy projects in developing economies. Except for hydro projects the bulk of other energy projects were between 79%-95% privately financed. Equally significant, 1,480 (52.5%) greenfield projects adopted the 'build, own and operate' model which means that under this model, combined with privatisation, 63.8% of PPP renewable energy projects concluded in private ownership.

The extensive use of tax havens by renewable energy companies is highlighted and examined in **Chapter 5** together with hedge fund intervention to change some energy company strategies to benefit recently acquired share stakes. It also examines the scale of tax haven ownership of renewable energy assets in Scotland, UK, Norway and other European countries.

The role of nation states is examined in **Chapter 6** and explains most of the prime reasons for the relatively low level of public ownership. The obsession with Environment, Governance and Social (ESG) is examined and an alternative Public Service Values Framework is proposed as an alternative to ESG and the vagueness of 'global public goods' statements.

To explain how the marketisation of nature and biodiversity is being subjected market forces in parallel to renewable energy. **Chapter 7** discusses the implications of their financialisation and marketisation for environmental protection and the ability to take action against rising sea levels and extreme weather conditions.

Equality and economic, social and environmental justice in renewable energy are discussed in **Chapter 8** which makes the case for a Public Sector Equality Duty as an integral part of the public value framework. Equality issues are rarely part of the retrofit policy, finance or implementation agenda, which must be reversed as a priority. The wider quest for an equitable transition process is also discussed.

Chapter 9 explains why it is important to improve national and international grid networks; the use of area or zonal planning to advance decarbonisation and promote renewable energy; to adopt an industrial and manufacturing strategy to successfully implement policies and achieve the required and sustainable infrastructural change is equally vital. Likewise a holistic approach to retrofitting housing, public buildings and business premises is fundamentally important given that they account for 40% of carbon emissions.

The concluding **Chapter 10** proposes ways in which the corporate domination of renewable energy can be challenged and describes how the public sector must have a key role in direct investment, ownership and operation of renewable energy systems. In effect, translating the objective of global public goods into public policy and operational reality. The third section emphasises the need to combine the different methods of decarbonisation to maximise their impact. The final section focuses on economic growth and technological advances to improve lives, living and working conditions up to and after 2050.

The building of political support will be crucial and must be supported by trade union, community and wider political organising and training.

CHAPTER 2

Corporate domination

Growth of the renewable energy sector

The development of the renewable energy sector was highly influenced, if not determined, by five political economy realities.

Firstly, the dominance of neoliberal ideology in recent decades of free trade, competition, markets, minimal regulation and a focus on outcomes is aligned with attempts to reconfigure the role of the state, justify tax cuts, reduce the cost and power of labour and to marginalise equalities and social justice. This led to market forces prevailing in the renewable energy sector, reliance on private capital and the promotion of entrepreneurship. Inevitably, a secondary market developed with a growing trade in the sale and purchase of renewable energy assets (Whitfield, 2019).

> "Independent power producers own the majority of wind assets built in 2021, following historical trends. Independent power producers (IPPs) own 75% of the new wind capacity installed in the United States in 2021, with the remaining assets (25%) owned by investor-owned utilities" (US Department of Energy, 2022a).

Globally multinational corporations, private equity funds, pension funds and entrepreneurial-led small firms compete for investment opportunities and participate in auctions for contracts alongside several state-owned energy companies. Yet there is a mountain of evidence of the fundamental flaws in the market system for public infrastructure, utilities, services and the welfare state (Whitfield 2016, 2017 and 2020a which cites many others).

The climate crisis finally emerged as a critical public policy around 2000 and a major challenge to the existence of the fossil fuel industry. Renewables (onshore/offshore wind, solar, hydro, biomass, battery storage, energy from waste) are the prime answer. Significantly, this gave capital a clean sheet to start from scratch. Public service principles and values were ignored with the prime focus on private finance and private ownership in a liberalised market. Neoliberal ideology and values remain deeply embedded.

Hence, renewable energy has become the ultimate neoliberal model – markets, private capital, private ownership, competition, state support in procurement/auction programme and funding research, whilst venture capitalists and private equity companies adopt flimsy Environment, Social and Governance (ESG) green washing, offshoring for tax avoidance and operate free trade of capital and companies with limited transparency and accountability.

Secondly, markets are sustained by trade organisations, technical, legal, financial and tax consultants together with political and managerial organisations with collective self-interest in sustaining market forces, minimising regulations and employment rights. They equally campaign to maintain commissioning, outsourcing and privatisation by public sector organisations. International organisations and financial media supply selected market data whilst company donations to political parties, right wing organisations and politicians also sustain market ideology. Renewable energy has developed into a global market in the last thirty years motivated more recently by the impacts of climate change. It was preceded by the liberalisation and privatisation of European energy since the 1980s. Market forces were supposed to increase competition, efficiency and drive down the cost of energy for service users who had the choice to switch suppliers (Weghmann, 2019).

Thirdly, the powerful role of private equity funds, and the earlier privatisation of energy generation and distribution in many countries, created the corporate infrastructure for the renewable energy sector and allowed the fossil fuel companies to continue 'business as usual'. Many began to participate in renewable energy projects and projected a 'greenwashing' image.

Fourthly, a few publicly owned energy companies developed wind, solar and hydro power projects and also acquired projects via the secondary market. However, this led to an assumption that public sector companies had a much larger role in the development, construction and operation of renewable energy projects than they had in reality.

Finally, the financialisation, marketisation and privatisation of public infrastructure and services of the last five decades included the privatisation of many publicly owned energy organisations. Similarly, the adoption of the Public Private Partnership (PPP) model for the delivery of a wide range of public infrastructure, became common in most industrialised economies. The World Bank and Regional Development Banks continue to promote the use of the PPP model for energy and other infrastructure projects in the global south. However, whilst the financialisation and marketisation of renewable energy are extensive, there has been very little privatisation because the bulk of projects originated and remain in the private sector.

The global financial crisis in 2008, and subsequent era of austerity with deep cuts in public spending in many economies, was widely resisted, but the crisis was used to legitimate further privatisation and to widen the use of private finance. A secondary market had earlier developed in trading PPP equity stakes and project ownership in the UK since the early 2000's including the growth of secondary market infrastructure funds (Whitfield, 2010 and 2016). This rapidly extended to a global trade in PPPs.

The significant growth of wind energy projects began shortly before 2000 followed by solar energy (Figure 3). Grid connected solar power grew 60% per annum between 2000-2004 to cover over 400,000 rooftops in Japan, Germany and USA. Wind power increased 28% in the same period with nearly 17GW installed by the end of 2004 (REN21 2005).

Figure 3: Growth of World renewable energy generation

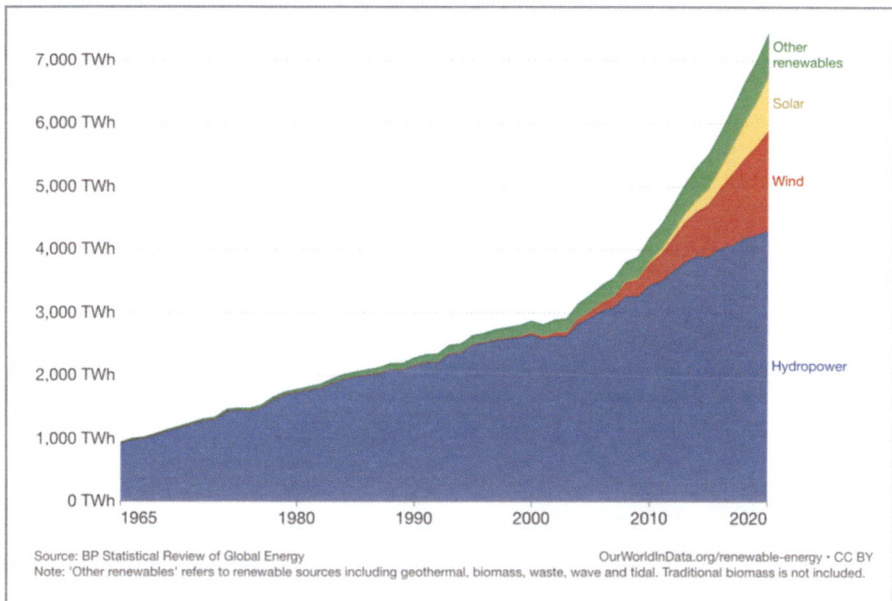

Source: BP Statistical Review of Global Energy — OurWorldInData.org/renewable-energy • CC BY
Note: 'Other renewables' refers to renewable sources including geothermal, biomass, waste, wave and tidal. Traditional biomass is not included.

The sector initially had mainly small companies formed by entrepreneurs and venture capitalists who started within their home country, and soon began to either establish subsidiaries in other countries because they either acquired stakes in other companies, or formed partnerships.

> *"Renewable energy has become big business. Large commercial banks are starting to take notice, and several are "mainstreaming" renewable energy investments in their lending portfolios. Other large investors are entering the renewable energy market, including venture capital investors and leading investment banks like Morgan Stanley and Goldman Sachs. Major investments and acquisitions have been made in recent years by leading global companies, such as GE, Siemens, Shell, BP, Sanyo, and Sharp. Five of the largest electrical equipment and aerospace companies in China*

have decided to enter the wind power business. Combined, 60 leading publicly traded renewable energy companies, or renewable energy divisions of major companies, have a market capitalization of at least $25 billion" (REN21 2005).

"Government support for renewable energy was on the order of $10bn in 2004 for the United States and Europe combined, including direct support ('on budget') and support from market-based policy mechanisms ('off budget'). This included more than $700m per year in research and development spending" (ibid).

The dominant role of private finance, private equity funds, private companies combined with market forces, competition and entrepreneurialism have resulted in the renewable energy sector being under corporate domination. The term 'independent power producers' (IPP) is sometimes used, but this is a neoliberal terminology to describe 'renewable energy companies'. The latter term is used in this study.

In conclusion, these are the prime reasons the corporate sector gained a significant role in the provision of renewable energy. Private capital saw an opportunity in response to the climate crisis together with entrepreneurialism and opportunities for innovation and technological advances on the scale of off-shore wind and solar renewables, and to develop new systems for battery storage and the application of hydrogen.

Growth in hydro, wind and other renewables began to significantly increase in 2004 followed by solar power in 2010 after which all renewables rapidly increased (Figure 3).

"In 2010, solar and wind combined made up only 1.7% of global electricity generation. By last year, it had climbed to 8.7% — far higher than what had previously been predicted by mainstream energy models. For example, in 2012 the International Energy Agency expected that global solar energy generation would reach 550 terrawatt-hours in 2030, but that number was exceeded by 2018. These models often assume that the growth of solar and wind will be linear, but in reality the growth has been exponential" (Jaeger, 2021).

"Falling costs have been the biggest factor in the explosion of renewable energy. Since 2010, the cost of solar photovoltaic electricity has fallen 85%, and the costs of both onshore and offshore wind electricity have been cut by about half. Both of these renewable sources are now cost-competitive with fossil fuel electricity. Costs have fallen so dramatically due to positive feedback loops. The more that renewable energy technologies are deployed, the cheaper they become due to economies of scale and competitive supply chains, among other factors. These falling costs in turn spur more deployment. For example, in the past decade, each time that the amount of solar capacity deployed worldwide has doubled, the price of installing solar

capacity has declined by 34%. As renewable energy technologies are modular and standardized, cost improvements or technological advances made in one place can be quickly copied elsewhere" (ibid).

Financialisation and private finance

The following statements illustrate the source of capital deployed in renewable energy projects in the last decade.

- "The private sector remains the main provider of capital for renewables, accounting for 86% of investments in the sector between 2013 and 2018. Project developers provided 46% of private finance, followed by commercial financial institutions at 22%.
- Project-level equity was initially the most widely used financial instrument, linked to 35% of the investments in renewables in 2013-2016. Since 2017, it has been overtaken by project-level conventional debt, which reached 32% in 2017-2018.
- Public finance, representing 14% of total investments in renewables in 2013-2018, came mainly via development finance institutions. Public financing resources, although limited, can be crucial to reduce risks, overcome initial barriers, attract private investors and bring new markets to maturity" (International Renewable Energy Agency, 2020).

Private finance can be raised from renewable energy investment funds, private equity funds, infrastructure funds, insurance and pension funds, sovereign wealth funds and international organisations such as the World Bank, International Finance Corporation, regional development banks and oversea aid agencies. This includes secondary funds operated by private equity and infrastructure funds that raise capital from investors to specifically engage in buying and selling secondary market renewable assets. Other companies range from public limited companies with shares listed on stock exchanges, privately owned and state or municipal owned companies. Pension funds are increasingly active participants in funding primary and secondary market renewable energy projects, thus reinforcing private sector ownership and operation of renewable energy projects.

> "Pension funds and insurers are less involved in greenfield onshore wind power transactions, suggesting that institutional investors look to the onshore wind sector mainly for the acquisition of existing projects in the operational phase" (OECD, 2019).

The fundamental shift towards financialisation not only increases the role of private capital and financial markets in public policy-making but also increases the power of financial institutions. Global investment markets create new opportunities for accumulation. The growth of secondary market funds by infrastructure funds to specifically finance the acquisition of operational assets has contributed to this process. For example, Ardian Infrastructure announced in April 2022 that its Secondary Fund VIII Infrastructure had raised a record US$5.25bn. The fund was significantly oversubscribed and

> *"...is the largest infrastructure secondaries platform in the world" (Ardian, 2022). The "....platform attracted over 145 investors from 28 countries across the Americas, Europe, Asia, and the Middle East, comprising major pension funds, insurance companies, HNWIs and financial institutions...... The fund is targeting a diverse range of underlying assets, from renewable energy and telecoms to transport and utilities" (ibid).*

New funding mechanisms, such as the World Bank's Sustainable Development Bonds and Green Bonds, promote marketisation and outsourcing. In 2020 investment of US$75bn included the construction or rehabilitation of 2,514MW in energy generation capacity. A total of 2,342MW of wind, solar and hydro renewable energy projects were included in the US$1bn Green Bonds issued in the same year. Both bond programmes were focused on Africa, Asia, Pacific, Europe, Latin America and Caribbean and Middle East regions.

The European Commission launched €250bn of NextGenerationEU Green Bonds for the 2021-2026 period in the 27 Member States which will be funded through bonds issued on the capital markets (European Commission, 2021). The expenditure categories include research and innovation supporting the green transition, digital technologies, energy efficiency, clean energy, climate change adaptation, water and waste management, clean transport and infrastructure and nature's protection, rehabilitation and biodiversity.

The World Bank's Climate Change Action Plan 2021-2025 recognises that public finance will be essential to finance global public goods – adaptation, mitigation and a just transition –

> *"...and build fiscal buffers to prepare for climate-related shocks through domestic public finance (including financing released through asset recycling). The Bank will provide technical assistance to countries to assess the fiscal impact of public-private partnerships (PPPs) for sustainable infrastructure" (Word Bank, 2021).*

The Bank will also work:
> *"...to catalyse and mobilise investment for climate action by (i) supporting upstream efforts to create new, sustainable, and green markets across developing countries that encourage private investment; (ii) expanding access to private capital and green*

finance; (iii) building climate capital markets; (iv) working with development partners and through capital markets to support finance for adaptation and resilience and finance for biodiversity; and (v) enabling the catalyzation of domestic private capital for climate investment" (World Bank Group, 2021).

The Bank's strategic framework for Sustainable Development Bonds and Green Bonds is focused on:

"...creating markets, mobilizing finance for development, and expanding the use of private sector solutions" (World Bank, 2020). This approach will further embed markets and financialise economies by increasing the role of private capital and potentially asset stripping the public sector.

Exchange-Traded Funds pose a new threat. ETF's track a particular index, sector, commodity or other asset and can be purchased and sold on stock exchanges, for example the European solar energy ETF. Global inflows into renewable energy exchange traded funds surged to US$14.7bn in the months to the end of March 2021 compared to US$1.3bn in the same period in 2019-20. Assets in ESG ETFs had a threefold increase from US$59bn at the end of 2019 to US$174bn by the end of 2020 (Johnson, 2021). However, net inflows to ETFs plummeted to US$27.4bn in April 2022 from US$117.4bn in March and the lowest figure since March 2020 (Johnson, 2022).

However, the surge in ETF investment:

"...is beginning to spark concern that retail investors will not be able to differentiate between exchange traded funds that own securities which are easy to trade and those that have illiquid holdings" (Boyde, 2021).

The fundamental shift towards financialisation increases the role of private capital and financial markets in public policy-making and increases the power of financial institutions. Global investment markets create new opportunities for accumulation.

New funding mechanisms such as Social Impact Bonds (Whitfield 2015) and the World Bank's Sustainable Development Bonds and Green Bonds promote marketisation and outsourcing. The design, build, finance and operate PPP infrastructure model similarly accelerates financialisation, marketisation and privatisation.

IMF: *"Public Sector must play role in catalysing private climate finance"*

The International Monetary Fund (IMF) also has a key role in "Mobilizing Private Climate Financing in Emerging Market and Developing Economies" published in July 2022 and a blog on the same subject on 18 August 2022. The report discusses

"...potential ways to mobilize domestic and foreign private sector capital in climate finance, as a complement to climate-related policies, by mitigating relevant risks and constraints through public-private partnerships involving multilateral, regional, and national development banks. It also overviews the role the IMF can play in the process" (IMF, 2022).

"Estimates of global investments required to achieve the Paris Agreement's temperature and adaptation goals range between US$3 to $6 trillion per year until 2050. Global climate finance currently adds to about US$630 billion annually" (ibid).

Under the title Public-Private Risk Sharing in Scaling up Climate Finance Potential ways for the public sector to reduce investment costs include,

"The public sector could play a powerful role in reducing constraints and catalyzing private sector climate financing.

Project-based funding channeling public and private financial resources to infrastructure projects can bring positive climate impacts.

Public equity capital provision and public-private partnership investment imply potentially large public debt increases through the crystallization of contingent liabilities.

The public sector could take equity tranches, which may result in first-loss positions, or provide credit enhancements that would lower the cost of investment by reducing risk to the private sector.

A fund structured with public sector equity and private sector debt provides further scale and diversification benefits.

In addition, public development banks could invest more and help mobilize private sector capital into climate finance.

Debt relief could create policy space for climate related investments, and thus enhance the credibility of emerging market and developing economies mitigation plans but must focus on restoring a sustainable position" (ibid).

The IMF recognises that high fossil fuel investments need to be scaled down but *"...some international investment treaties, such as the Investor State Dispute Settlement system and the Energy Charter Treaty (ECT), which are legally binding, protect fossil fuel investments which can lock in large amounts of emissions, or alternatively expose authorities to legal action for breach of that protection when seeking to adopt regulatory measures to curtail fossil fuel activity. The European Commission is negotiating a modernization of the ECT to better enable regulatory action to be taken to address climate change, and similar steps are needed in relation to other international investment treaties. However, even under the European Commission's proposal, protection of foreign investment in certain natural gas investments is to be kept until as late as 2040"* (ibid).

The IMF completely ignores the potential multi-million cost of payments under ISDS/ECT claims; the significant loss of tax revenue as a result of the use of offshore tax havens which is already rife in the renewable energy sector; and the expected procession of fossil fuel companies seeking public money to finance the closure of plants, stranding of assets and demolition of sites for alternative use. The IMF should be catalysing for public financial resources.

Governments and public authorities

Public organisations have a key role in developing climate action policies and setting renewable energy targets, regulatory frameworks, sanctioning auctions, planning permissions, Power Purchase Agreements and approving financial subsidies or other forms of corporate welfare intended to attract investors. However, they rarely impose: labour standards or monitor them; impose conditions or limitations on outsourcing; prohibit the use of tax havens or require projects to include economic development opportunities in the development, construction and production of renewable energy projects. The state is in effect a facilitator, or agent, for the private ownership and operation of renewable energy (further discussion in Chapter 4).

The World Bank Group have been instrumental in supporting a 'sustainable energy market' in developing economies

> *"...to create a market for solar power generation, mitigate investment risks, or achieve specific national energy policy objectives" (International Bank for Reconstruction and Development and World Bank, 2019). A survey of private investors conducted for the report led to 51 participants and 61 country-specific responses.*
> **"Only 8 percent of the survey responses indicated that direct financing by the public sector in solar generation assets (for example, equipment and civil works) was an important investment consideration, compared to 66 percent which characterized this form of public intervention as nonessential. However, blending public concessional sources of funds with commercial finance has helped develop projects that were not viable on fully commercial terms."** (ibid) [bold in original].

Renewable energy projects in Morocco, Senegal, South Africa, India, Chile, Philippines and Maldives included government or public agency acquisition of land for solar development; provision of infrastructure such as roads and water supply; securing permits; improved distribution grids; grants used for upfront subsidies to private developers; guarantees (multinational development banks are preferred); all of which reduce the risks for private investors and attract finance from national or local banks and bilateral donor agencies (ibid).

European Union taxonomy on sustainable finance

The taxonomy refers to "…reorienting capital flows towards a more sustainable economy" together with mainstreaming sustainability into risk management and fostering transparency and long-termism (European Commission 2020). It establishes six environmental objectives:

- Climate change mitigation
- Climate change adaptation
- The sustainable use and protection of water and marine resources
- The transition to a circular economy
- Pollution prevention and control
- The protection and restoration of biodiversity and ecosystems

The action plan includes creating an EU Green Bond Standard and assessing the extent to which capital flows foster investment in sustainable projects; incorporating sustainability in financial advice; develop sustainability benchmarks; better integrating sustainability in ratings and market research; clarifying asset managers and institutional investors duties regarding sustainability; introducing a 'green supporting factor' in the EU prudential rules for banks and insurance companies; strengthening sustainability disclosure and accounting rule-making; and fostering sustainable corporate governance and attenuating short-termism in capital markets (European Commission, 2020a).

A study was undertaken to test the application of draft criteria for a sample of 101 'green' equity funds based in the EU27 which revealed that only three 'green' equity funds qualified under draft criterion 1 – the extent to which the funds had taken account of the six environmental objectives (European Commission, 2020b). Equally revealing was the fact that 47 of the 101 equity funds were domiciled in Luxembourg, but the study did not comment on the relevance of being domiciled in a tax haven nor the potential impact on tax revenue in the countries in which they operate.

EuroBank investment in renewable energy projects

European Commission 2021: projects in Czech Republic, Hungary, Poland Greece and Croatia €12,757m and 1,300 MW

European Investment Bank 2022: projects in Spain, Slovenia, Denmark, Portugal and Brazil, €445m and 1,145MW (2 missing).

European Bank for Reconstruction and Development 2021: projects in Central Europe, Turkey, Poland and Bulgaria, €129m and 246MW

EU infrastructure fund

The Marguerite Infrastructure Fund manages the 2020 European Fund for Energy, Climate Change and Infrastructure, which was established in 2010 supported by six European public financial institution and the European Commission with €710m to invest in the EU. A successor fund has a further €700m committed. Marguerite's renewable energy transactions in the 2019-2021 period included investments and divestments:

Investments
2020 – 2 solar parks in Merida and Cadiz (100 MWp) to OPDEnergy (Spain)
2020 – solar project in Alcala de Guadaira (50 MWp) to OPDEnergy (Spain)
2021 – investment in Rebi urban heating projects, Spain

Divestments
2019 – 6 solar plants in France to (Tenergie SAS) (France)
2020 – 3 solar parks in Spain (150 MWp) (sell back to OPDEnergy)
2021 – Poznan PPP energy-from waste to PreZero Warszawa (Schwarz Group)

The Marguerite fund manages the Marguerite Pantheon SCSp

"…to acquire what it assessed to be a mature, stable and well diversified portfolio of renewable and concession-based assets across diversified jurisdictions, sectors and technologies in Europe. All assets are fully operational and are currently generating predictable stable cash distributions, underpinned by robust regulatory regimes, feed-in-tariffs, and/or contracted revenues with strong creditworthy counterparties" (Marguerite web site, February 2022).

In November 2017 the Marguerite fund sold a portfolio of operational assets to Pantheon which included equity in two offshore wind farms in Germany and Belgium (614MW) plus 100% of two solar plants in France (72 MWp) plus a 45% stake in a 146km toll road in Spain" (Marguerite Fund, 2022). Although the fund has been a catalyst for greenfield and brownfield infrastructure investments in renewable energy and transport and implemented key EU policies, the Luxembourg-based fund appears to be operating as a private equity fund buying and selling renewable energy assets for financial gain and reinforcing market forces.

Export and import credit agencies and development finance

Many governments provide foreign aid and export credit to companies involved in overseas contracts. UK Export Finance (UKEF) provides direct loans to overseas buyers, of which £2bn has been allocated to support clean growth projects.

The US Export-Import Bank (EXIM) disclosed in 2021 that it had issued US$1.8bn in medium and long-term export credit support in 2020 but admitted it fell significantly below China at $18bn, France at $12.1bn, Germany at $8.6bn, Italy at $8.4bn and South Korea at $5bn (Export-Import Bank of the United States, 2021). Recent projects funded by UKEF, Denmark's EKF and Germany's Private Climate Finance Support are listed below.

The German Federal Government launched a Special Renewable Energies Initiative in 2020 under the governments export credit insurance scheme. Export credit guarantees are available in renewable energy with up to 70% foreign sourced goods or services. There is also the Hermes programme for small or medium-sized enterprises with support to open up difficult markets, offering protection against non-payment, making export financing easier, helping to create a level playing field in international competition and preserving jobs in Germany.

UK Export Finance 2021
- Kalyon Enerji and Hanwha Q Cells joint venture, Turkey, £217m
- Karapinar solar facility 1.35GW to power 2 million households. Finance to support construction with GE Energy Financial Services. Lead lender is J.P. Morgan bank.
- Orsted Taiwan Ltd, and Caisse de depot et placement du Quebec, Cathay Capital Private Equity Taiwan £200m
- Greater Changhua 1 Offshore Wind Farm UK companies – Seajacks and Trellegorg.

Denmark EKF 2019
- Seagreen offshore wind farm, Scotland, £360m
- Scottish SSE plc & Total (France), Norwegian ECA GIEK & 12 commercial banks

The UK Government claimed that financial support to UK exporters in 2020-2021 provided £12.3bn of new loans, insurances and guarantees which supported 107,000 UK Full-Time jobs (58,000 direct and 49,000 indirect). Although the number of jobs supported by buyer credit guarantee, insurance, bond or export working capital support, direct loan or general working capital are provided, the number of jobs supported in each project is not available.

The European Commission (2022a) launched a REPowerEU plan in May 2022 to eliminate Russian energy imports by 2027. It will save €100bn each year on gas, oil and coal imports and increase the EU's renewable energy target from 40% to 45% by 2030 and increase the energy efficiency target from 9% to 13% by the same date (Euractiv, 2022). However, the plan will require short-term new investment in new fossil fuels to facilitate gas and oil imports from other countries.

Annual global investment in renewable energy increased from US$33bn in 2004 to just over US$500bn in the thirteen years to 2017 where it remained for the three subsequent years (Figure 2). Similarly, global investment in other low carbon sectors such as electric heat, electric transport, energy storage, carbon capture and storage and hydrogen increased from about US$30bn in 2004 to just over US$200bn by 2020.

Corporate funding (including venture capital, private equity, debt financing and public market financing of solar projects in 2021) increased to US$27.8bn from 144 deals, a considerable increase on the previous year, reported by a Mercom Capital Group market analysis. Mergers and acquisitions recorded a high of 126 transactions in 2021 which included Adani Green Energy's US$3.5bn acquisition of SB Energy India, and KKR's US$3.3bn acquisition of Sempra Infrastructure Partners (USA).

Figure 2: Global investment in energy transition by sector (US$bn)

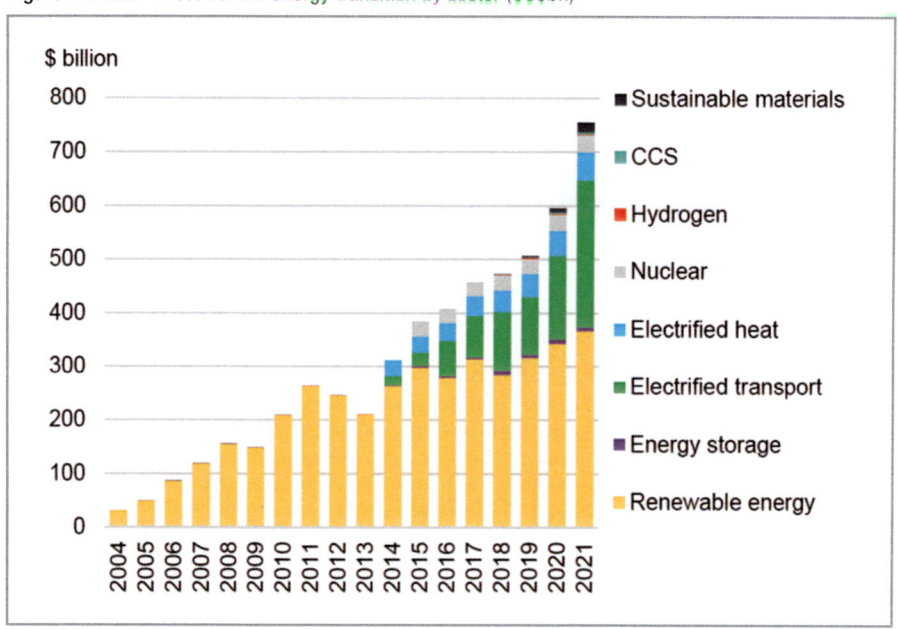

Source: BloombergNEF, 2022

"We recognise that in order to get on a pathway to net zero emissions by 2050 at the latest we will need to provide public financing for renewables as a means of leveraging the required levels of private investment. In this regard, we acknowledge the IEA net zero scenario which suggests that G7 economies invest at least US$1.3 trillion in renewable energy including tripling investments in clean power and electricity networks between 2021 and 2030" (G7 Climate Communique, 2022).

Who is leveraging who and with what impact on ownership and provision by 2050? It requires each G7 economy to invest US$48.1bn per annum for the next 27 years subsidising private investment!

Green New Deals

Proposals for Green New Deals (GND) have been buffeted by the Covid pandemic and economic renewal/transition, the Russian invasion of Ukraine and the subsequent energy crisis together with right wing opposition to the expansion of social policies. Political opposition to the scope and potential public cost of embracing climate and welfare expenditure was a factor in the refocus of the US Green New Deal.

The goals of the Ocasio-Cortez/Markey GND resolution and of the Sanders GND, which is largely based on it, are far more radical and far-reaching. First, the Ocasio-Cortez/Markey GND resolution calls for a "national, social, industrial and economic mobilization at a scale not seen since World War II and the New Deal era" in order to decarbonize the US economy by 2030. Second, it positions addressing structural inequality, poverty mitigation, and neoliberal-driven welfare state retrenchment at its center. The resolution sees the climate crisis as interlinked with deeply entrenched racial, regional and gender-based inequalities in income and wealth and so insists on tackling these with an array of programs that have hitherto been seen as disconnected. By bringing economic wellbeing into the heart of a program to reduce greenhouse gas emissions, the GND promises, "to provide all people of the United States with (i) a "job guarantee with a family sustaining wage" including "high-quality union jobs" that have "adequate family and medical leave, paid vacations and retirement security"; (ii) "high-quality health care"; (iii) "affordable, safe and adequate housing"; (iv) "economic security"; and (v) "clean water, clean air, healthy and affordable food, and access to nature"
(Galvin and Healy, 2020).

"Mr. Biden is pitching his plan as having a big economic return on federal investment – and better roads, bridges and ports could increase productivity. But more than half of his plan is dedicated to reducing CO2, with a goal of eliminating

fossil fuels with a max of federal spending, subsidies and regulation." (Wall Street Journal Editorial Board, 2021).

"His $2.3 trillion infrastructure plan contains enough spending and industrial planning that it amounts to the Green New Deal in disguise" (ibid).

The UK Green New Deal developed by the independent Green New Deal Group was largely adopted by the Labour Party for the 2019 General election but had little traction after the election because the Conservative Party retained power with an 80 seat majority. Subsequent government policies, such as the Green Industrial Revolution, the Net Zero Review and 10 point Recovery Plan, were described as abject failures or wish-lists (Simpson, 2021).

The European Union Green Deal aims to make the EU's climate, energy, transport and taxation policies fit for reducing net greenhouse gas emissions by at least 55% by 2030 compared to 1990 levels (European Commission, 2019). In 2022 the EIB increased funding the REPowerEU Plan with €30bn in loans and equity financing over the next five years to fund "… a wider range of clients and utility companies" (European Investment Bank, 2022).

"Losing that "new" is a signal that the commission does not seek system change through ambitious green macroeconomics and tough regulation of carbon financiers. Rather, it takes a politics as usual, third-way approach that seeks to nudge the market towards decarbonisation.
The macroeconomics of the European Green Deal remains trapped in the black zero logic of austerity. Instead of ambitious green fiscal activism, it mostly reshuffles existing European funds through a logic of seed funding to mobilise private sector money. Public money will be used to take risk out of private business activities and finance a "just transition" mechanism that promises to protect groups like Polish miners after their coal mines close through retraining and reskilling programmes" (Gabor, 2020).

Furthermore,
"….the danger is that the public money the commission plans to put into greening the European economy will instead merely subsidise greenwashing" (ibid).
"In particular, the Sustainable Europe Investment Plan holds a strong bias in favour of the private and financial sector. The focus on bankable projects and leveraging private resources has come at the expense of playing a stronger role in furthering transformative policy orientations. The approach of turning projects into bankable ones ignores the fact that a majority of the needs for ecological transition will simply not be bankable and offer any return on investment……… A new type of public intervention into the economy is needed, one whose primary aim is to de-

financialise the economy by progressively re-absorbing wealth fluctuating on private capital markets" (Sol, 2021).

Political commitment to a comprehensive Green NEW Deal could have ensured a more significant role for the public sector in renewable energy and have avoided the current corporate domination of the sector. It should have set out a role for public sector organisations in retrofitting and a raft of other decarbonisation measures in industry and the public sector, with a radical approach to public management to integrate core public services alongside economic development and employment strategies.

Renewable energy infrastructure as an asset class

The growth of PPPs, and other models of privately financed public infrastructure projects, inevitably led to the promotion of 'infrastructure as an asset class'. This requires a competitive market for infrastructure projects that can be privately financed, valued and priced with stable financial returns for investors. Furthermore, it requires a deal flow of government-backed, legally binding contracts that require a large scale infrastructure investment but have low operating costs.

The Global Infrastructure Hub, established by the G20 member countries in 2014 to promote private infrastructure investment, claim that *"…infrastructure as an asset class is an attractive option for portfolio diversification"* because:

- *"Unlisted infrastructure equities provide high returns at a lower risk than average global equities.*
- *Over a 10-year period, infrastructure debt provided a higher return than 10-year government bonds in developed markets, at slightly higher risk.*
- *Listed infrastructure equities in emerging markets have a relatively high risk and low return profile, but developed markets provide appreciable returns at a lower risk than average global equities and could be preferred for liquidity"* (Global Infrastructure Hub, 2021).

There is a strong preference for a long asset life with fixed-term contracts or concessions, usually 25–40 years, and limited regulatory regimes confined to certain performance objectives that allow the private sector maximum flexibility on financial policies, ownership, control of profits and the management of assets. Availability of surplus or development land or access rights, which may be under-valued, provide scope for additional commercial development and profit.

A secondary market enables equity in projects to be purchased and sold, or entire projects traded, which will, in turn, encourage the formation of infrastructure funds to acquire such assets. Ultimately a secondary market will develop in the purchase and sale of infrastructure funds too (Whitfield, 2016).

The rapid growth of the renewable energy secondary market with at least 1,622 transactions in the 2019-2021 period and the presence of both global and national private equity funds (alongside the investment raising capabilities of established energy companies) make renewable energy a classic infrastructure asset class.

Climate change imposes other policy demands such as retrofitting housing, public buildings, business premises and production plants; environmental seashore protection works against rising sea levels, flooding: and the protection of nature and biodiversity which require significant levels of public and private investment. This raises the threat of further financialisation, marketisation and privatisation of nature (Whitfield, 2020).

Theory and practice in primary and secondary energy markets

Competition between corporate owners and employees generates changes in working practices to increase productivity and thus increased profit. There are different interpretations of the cause of crises in the capitalist economy. Roberts (2018b) cites the tendency of the rate of profit to fall as the general cause of crises. Panitch and Gindin (2013) consider that crises are always historically specific. Harvey (2006) cites overproduction of commodities, surplus and idle capital, surpluses of labour power and the falling rate of profit and emphasised the temporary displacement of surpluses into the built environment (land, transport and communications networks and buildings).

> Lefebvre (2003) described
> *"... the principal circuit - current industrial production and the movable property that results begins to slow down, capital shifts to the second sector, real estate. It can even happen that real-estate speculation becomes the principal source for the formation of capital, that is, the realization of surplus value. As the percentage of overall surplus value formed and realized by industry begins to decline, the percentage created and realized by real-estate speculation and construction increases".*

Gotham (2009) describes how real estate is high risk and can cause crises in the secondary sector such as the provision of affordable good quality housing.

The renewable energy market operates both as a primary and a secondary market. The primary market is normally focused on new capital projects and acquisitions and mergers to strengthen a company's position in the market. The primary market operates via state organised auctions or other procurement processes which require successful bidders to finance, design, construct and operate new renewable energy projects on greenfield sites or pre-determined offshore locations.

The award of contracts for primary sector renewable energy projects, for example, the 17 offshore contracts awarded in the Scotwind auction in early 2022 (Table A1), are therefore excluded from the ESSU Global Renewable Energy Secondary Market Database 2019-2021. Other contract awards or company news statements about primary investment decisions are also excluded.

The market consists of the full acquisition, or equity stake, of operational wind, solar, hydro and battery assets and other renewable energy assets. It includes the sale of development rights and 'ready to construct' projects. This market has enabled developers to acquire a site for a project, obtain planning permission and regulatory approval and to make a financial return by selling the project to another developer who proceeds to construct and operate the project. The sale of construction-ready projects is attractive to large companies seeking rapid expansion and can effectively buy a project 'off the shelf' which shortcuts their development process. It also enables companies to sell operational assets to extract the increased value of an asset or to sell the asset or an equity stake in an under-performing asset or an older project that requires repowering and/or improvement. In effect, the secondary market creates trade in the sale of development rights, financial equity and renewable assets for profit.

The secondary market also includes merger and acquisition transactions in connection with joint ventures or partnerships, strengthening growth position in a particular renewable sector and/or entry into new domestic or overseas markets. Both primary and secondary elements of the renewable energy market have outsourced offshore survey work, servicing of wind and solar assets, the use of consultants and lawyers in project development and due diligence in secondary market transactions.

The secondary market is significant for revealing the relative roles of public and private companies in trading in renewable energy assets. Transactions reflect the sale/purchase of development rights and operational projects which is additional to greenfield capital investment. They also reveal the level of acquisitions and mergers, joint ventures and partnerships. Furthermore, secondary markets make wider use of offshoring than is evident in primary market transactions. They also reveal trends and the valuation of assets, although the latter is frequently not disclosed.

A number of articles and conference reports have appeared in the renewable press recently extolling the success and value of the secondary market. For example, speakers from Greencoat Capital and Octopus Investment discussed the health of secondary markets in Europe at a 2019 London conference. However, a NextEnergy Capital speaker warned of regulatory uncertainty in the Spain and Italy Photovoltaic (PV) markets (Solar Power Portal, 2019).

The sale of equity in the UK offshore wind sector were transacted on a bilateral basis, with the buyer being afforded the opportunity for detailed due diligence negotiations on the nature and terms of the partnership for the development of the assets. However, both Humber Gateway and Doggar Bank A and B were run as competitive auction processes" (LexisNexis, 2021).

This process increased the valuations for the sellers.

An uncritical OECD analysis stated that governments should support primary and secondary markets:

"...much of this secondary market activity is fuelled by increased investor appetite for operational projects. For example, in the renewable energy sector, the increase of equity provision by institutional investors can be traced mainly to the acquisition of operational assets or portfolios for onshore wind deals" (OECD, 2016).

The OECD recognised that a secondary market had developed for renewable energy citing a few transactions and data that revealed transactions increased from US$8.9bn in 2004 to US$93.9bn in 2015. They concluded:

"Corporate asset disposals from utilities and refinancing of projects in operation, coupled with a strong appetite from investors, are contributing to the increase in global secondary market acquisition transactions in the renewable sector" (OECD, 2016).

The OECD also identified:
- *'lack of coherent and sufficiently ambitious climate mitigation policies, such as insufficient carbon prices, inefficient fossil-fuel subsidies and policy uncertainty about renewable energy incentives;*
- *misalignment of broader policies with climate change goals, e.g. within the general investment environment;*
- *inconsistent trade and investment policies that create barriers to cross-border trade and investment in renewable electricity and threaten to fragment rather than optimise global clean-energy value chains, especially in solar PV and wind energy;*
- *fragmentation in electricity markets and the development of electricity infrastructure, favouring fossil-fuel incumbency in the power sector and restricting further integration of renewable electricity"* (ibid)

There was only one mention of public investment in the context of *"...countries need to improve the efficiency of public investment while mobilising private investment at scale and at pace"* (ibid)

However, the OECD concluded:
"Given the considerable need for long-term infrastructure investment, including for renewable electricity and power transmission and distribution, countries need to improve the efficiency of public investment while mobilising private investment at scale and at pace" (ibid).

Auctions

The auctioning of developments for onshore/offshore wind and solar projects has become the dominate mechanism for the supply of renewable energy. The number of countries that have adopted auctions for renewable energy increased from 6 in 2005 to 106 by the end of 2018 (REN21, 2016 and 2019).

In early 2022 the UK government agreed to change the frequency of auctions for funding through the Contracts for Difference (CfD) to be annual instead of biennial. *"CfDs are the government's primary method of supporting renewable energy, driving down the cost of technologies and playing an important role in leveraging £90 billion of private investment by 2030"* (Department for Business, Energy & Industrial Strategy, 2022).

A study on the limits of auctions concluded:

"....while auctions will certainly continue to have an important place in electricity, governments should be more cautious about their use and should be thinking about alternatives; these would include new energy market designs that reflect twenty-first century technologies and economics, especially those reflecting the high penetration of renewables and the more active participation of consumers. A key goal in developing markets for a sustainable future should be to empower consumers as far as possible – and 'one-sided' auctions, at least in their present form, are not necessarily the best tool for this purpose" (Keay & Robinson, Oxford Institute for Energy Studies, 2019).

Many activities connected to renewable energy projects are outsourced such as developer activities, including site investigation, technical and financial advice, planning application and impact assessments. The construction process has its own supply chain specific to the technology, followed by operational management and performance monitoring. A later sale of the asset will require due diligence, legal, technical and financial advice.

Individualisation

The responsibility to take action to address the climate crisis is both a collective and individual responsibility but the financial implications of the high retrofitting costs have yet to be confronted, except for those who have installed solar panels and/or heat pumps. The UK Committee on Climate Change used renewable energy and construction consultants to estimate the cost of Air source heat pumps and ultra-high level of fabric efficiency (equivalent to a space heat demand 15 kWh/m2/yr); passive cooling measures package; water efficiency package of measures, and flood resilience and resistance package of measures, to be £41,900 per dwelling (Committee on Climate Change, 2019).

Dwellings will require different levels of retrofitting, many dwellings will not require flood resilience, public and private sector tenants will not have to bare these costs and the price of heat pumps is falling. The public cost of retrofitting alone was estimated to be £159bn with owner occupiers facing a £590bn cost spread over the next three decades (Whitfield, 2021). The continued reference by many to retrofitting as 'insulation' is myopic and does not take account of the failure of UK Government insulation projects. This does not take account of the personal cost involved in substantial disruption to dwellings, to switch to electric cars and reducing activities that have a negative impact on the climate.

Several other factors are contributing to increasing individualisation, for example the wide use of tax havens, the growth of Exchange-Traded Funds that trade a basket of securities which trade like shares on an exchange. They can be bought and traded by individuals for clean energy and companies in other sectors. Pension funds, ETFs, none of these give any access to express views or to increase collective participation, in fact they operate to prevent and close any channels of communication.

All these developments fuel individualisation ideology (Whitfield, 2020). On the one hand they increase or impose personal responsibility (for example retrofitting homes) or may open new opportunities for individual financial gain, whilst the corporate use of tax havens may induce corporate avoidance of employment regulations and labour rights to reduce costs/increase profits.

A political economy perspective is essential to understanding the climate crisis and to achieving the climate targets, the transition to net zero and the permanent stranding of fossil fuel assets. It is essential to forge a new provision of renewable energy under public democratic control and to secure economic, social, environmental, equality and labour rights. A new future is needed for power generation to meet the way we want to live, supply public goods and services with sustainable manufacturing and industrial economies.

Accumulation by dispossession in the energy sector

A wide range of processes underpinned Marx's description of primitive accumulation which included;

> "...the commodification and privatisation of land and the forceful expulsion of peasant populations; the conversion of various forms of property rights (common, collective, state, etc.) into exclusive private property rights; the suppression of rights to the commons; the commodification of labour power and the suppression of alternative (indigenous) forms of production and consumption; colonial, neo-colonial, and imperial processes of appropriation of assets (including natural resources); the monetization of exchange and taxation, particularly of land; the slave trade; and usury, the national debt, and ultimately the credit system as radical means of primitive accumulation" (Harvey, 2003).

Accumulation by dispossession provides new frontiers for the penetration of capital, allowing it to overcome recurrent crises of over-accumulation. It is also connected to the emergence of struggles over access to land and living space, and to fundamental resources such as water, biomass and energy
(Bohm, Misoczky and Mong, 2012).

Other aspects include the loss of public amenity and the extent of local environmental change caused by wind farm towers and turbines and fields turned into solar parks, although they may be admired by others from a distance. The vast majority are for-profit private projects producing a public good with company shareholders receiving financial gains. The lack of public transparency that the project company is owned by a national or multinational company registered in an offshore tax haven paying little or no annual corporation tax is another dimension of dispossession.

New mechanisms for accumulation by dispossession have been created such as the commodification of nature and biodiversity; decarbonisation and mitigation of climate change; the corporatisation and privatisation of a wider range of public assets and welfare state services.

The increasing role of privately financed infrastructure projects, and the growth of secondary markets in project equity, infrastructure funds, the resale privatised assets and private finance of new PPP models, are the rationale for the inclusion of 'financialisation' as an integral part of private provision (Whitfield, 2016).

Furthermore, 'individualisation' has increasingly had an integral role in the process of financialisation, marketisation and privatisation. This broadens and deepens the definition of the privatisation process.

"Financialisation and individualisation inevitably lead to commodification, marketisation and deregulation and ultimately to commercialisation and privatisation" (Whitfield, 2010).

It is necessary to establish a more comprehensive definition:
"Privatisation is the restructuring, transformation, sale, management, private and for-/non-profit provision of public goods and services; government functions; land and property; nature, biodiversity; and decarbonisation and climate change mitigation. It is interwoven with and co-dependent on financialisation, marketisation, individualisation" (Whitfield, 2020).

Urban growth has changed;
"...from an expression of the needs of industrial producers to an expression of the power of finance capital over the totality of the production process" (Harvey, 1985).

The tertiary circuit of capital includes welfare state expenditure and provision of health, social care, education, welfare benefits and pensions essential for economic and social wellbeing. Whilst many services remain publicly financed, a strategy to increase private ownership and provision remains pervasive.

The political economy of renewable energy framework

Drawing on the above discussion the political economy of privatisation framework in (Whitfield, 2020) is developed specifically for renewable energy. Financialisation, marketisation and individualisation intersect with and reinforce each other and in turn are fundamentally important in setting the terms and ideological framework for the different forms of privatisation to have economic and political legitimacy.

The alternative is for public investment, ownership and operation of renewable energy projects to be achieved by government, city councils or regional authorities acting individually or jointly supported by regulatory controls to safeguard nature and biodiversity and strategic planning.

Another version of asset recycling

The concept of asset recycling developed in the USA and Australia involves public sector leasing of public infrastructure assets to consortia of banks and global corporations for 49-99 years. These contracts are dependent on continuous flow of user charges or tolls, but the attraction of an upfront lump sum payment was sufficient for some state and city governments to proceed. Some even legislated for unsolicited bids, in effect sanctioning the cherry picking of public assets (Whitfield, 2020 and 2021).

The privatisation of renewable energy takes an alternative route to the traditional sale of public assets by share flotation or a trade sale to an existing company. The Crown Estate Scotland's auction of 17 offshore wind sites in 2021/2022 resulted in the successful developer bidders paying £699.2m in option fees to secure the seabed lease rights as they did in earlier auctions (see Table A1 in Appendix). This money will be transferred to the Scottish Government which will increase resources for public expenditure for one year only. This sum reflects the value of the leases, but not the value of renewable energy assets that will be built.

This approach is not the same as asset recycling of publicly owned and operated assets but it is a variation of asset recycling transferring what could have been public assets on publicly owned sea bed rights. It guarantees privatisation in return for a lump sum and pre-empts publicly financed, owned and operated renewable energy. In practice the renewable energy market and auction process ensures that infrastructure assets are privatised, although the state retains ownership of the seabed rights. Wind farms will be financed, constructed and operated by the successful bidders and their subcontractors and will *de facto* become privately owned assets. Public ownership can

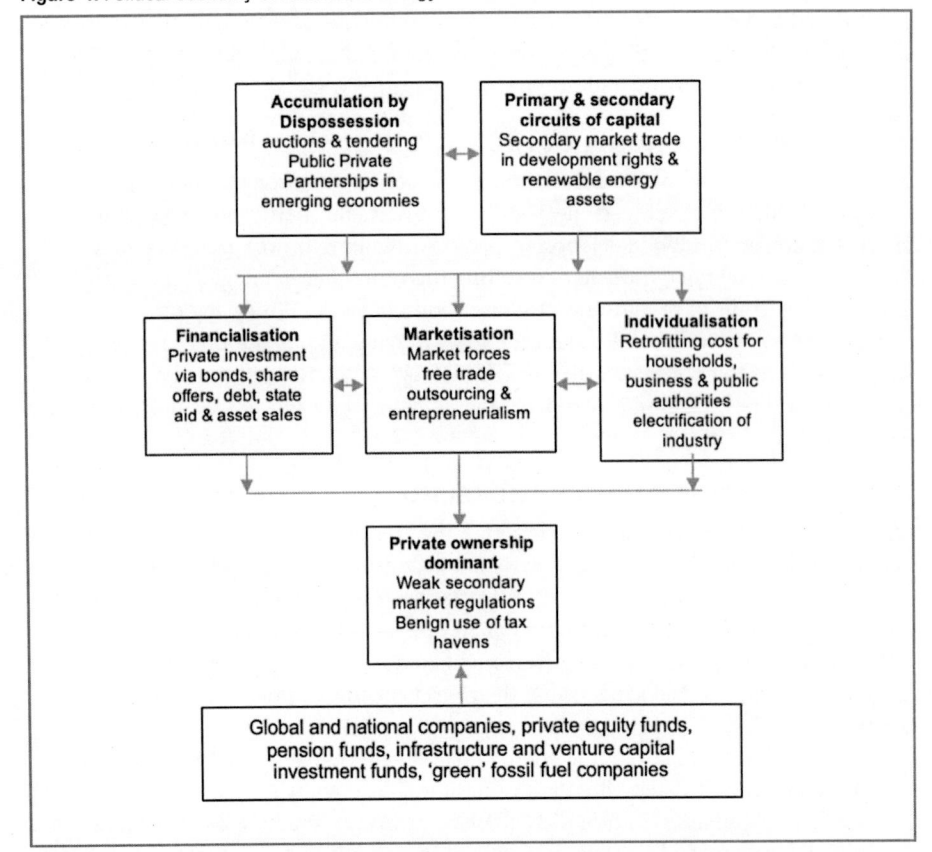

Figure 4: Political economy of renewable energy framework

```
┌─────────────────────────────┐   ┌─────────────────────────────┐
│  Accumulation by            │   │  Primary & secondary        │
│  Dispossession              │◄─►│  circuits of capital        │
│  auctions & tendering       │   │  Secondary market trade     │
│  Public Private             │   │  in development rights &    │
│  Partnerships in            │   │  renewable energy           │
│  emerging economies         │   │  assets                     │
└─────────────────────────────┘   └─────────────────────────────┘
            │                                │
            ▼                                ▼
┌──────────────────┐   ┌──────────────────┐   ┌──────────────────┐
│ Financialisation │   │  Marketisation   │   │ Individualisation│
│ Private investment│◄─►│  Market forces   │◄─►│ Retrofitting cost│
│ via bonds, share │   │  free trade      │   │ for households,  │
│ offers, debt, state│  │  outsourcing &   │   │ business & public│
│ aid & asset sales│   │ entrepreneurialism│  │ authorities      │
│                  │   │                  │   │ electrification of│
│                  │   │                  │   │ industry         │
└──────────────────┘   └──────────────────┘   └──────────────────┘
            │                  │                      │
            ▼                  ▼                      ▼
              ┌────────────────────────────┐
              │  Private ownership         │
              │  dominant                  │
              │  Weak secondary            │
              │  market regulations        │
              │  Benign use of tax         │
              │  havens                    │
              └────────────────────────────┘
                           ▲
              ┌────────────────────────────────────────────┐
              │ Global and national companies, private equity│
              │ funds, pension funds, infrastructure and   │
              │ venture capital investment funds, 'green'  │
              │ fossil fuel companies                      │
              └────────────────────────────────────────────┘
```

only be achieved either by a negotiated sale or nationalisation.

Only two of the 24 companies involved in the ScotWind project are publicly owned Vattenfall (Sweden) and EnBW Energie (Germany) owned by State of Baden 46.75% and an Association of regional & local govt 46.75% whilst the French government has a minority 23% stake in Engie. Most of the other companies are foreign owned (see Appendices Table A1).

Furthermore, some of the these assets may be sold on the secondary market prior to their operational stage. For example, Northland Power (with two ScotWind projects)

> *"...intends to execute a selective sell-down strategy of partial interests of certain of its development projects on or before financial close to allow the Company to:*
> - *manage jurisdictional exposures;*

- crystallize some development profit prior to construction as a result of the de-risking of the project;
- enhance our Adjusted Free Cash Flow and liquidity position; and
- increase project returns, amongst other considerations" (Northland Power, 2022).

A review of 100% Renewable Energy Systems Research in 2022 concluded
"…..*the vast majority of 100% renewable energy systems studies is that such systems can power all energy in all regions of the world at low cost. As such, we do not need to rely on fossil fuels in the future. In the early 2020s, the consensus has increasingly become that solar PV and wind power will dominate the future energy system and new research increasingly shows that 100% renewable energy systems are not only feasible but also cost effective. This gives us the key to a sustainable civilization and the long-lasting prosperity of humankind"*
(Breyer, C. and 23 other researchers in 10 countries).

There are, of course, other fundamental questions about who will own and operate all the renewable energy assets in 2050. A scenario based on the continuation of current trends to 2050 indicates predominately private ownership of renewable energy assets by multinational companies and private equity funds, following a period of sustained consolidation in the 2030-2050 period.

There are certain to be new climate targets in response to changes in climate conditions and ecological threats, millions of climate refugees, food insecurity, water stress and national disasters. Regional migration within nation states is likely to increase as people seek better living conditions.

Technological developments such as green hydrogen, new methods of energy storage and tidal turbines will lead to new renewable energy options before and beyond 2050 for households, public and private sectors.

State bailouts for ISDS and Energy Charter Treaty claims

An investigation into Canada's oil and gas decommissioning liability problem by the Institute for Energy Economics and Financial Analysis revealed:

"Canadian oil and gas companies are failing to make plans to pay for $72 billion in future decommissioning liabilities for oil and gas wells, pipelines, and facilities. The clean-up liabilities, collectively referred to as asset retirement obligations (AROs), are likely to result in future corporate defaults, leaving the Canadian taxpayer to pay to resolve the mess" (Mawji, 2022).

The study included an in-depth analysis of the ten most vulnerable publicly listed oil and gas producers in Canada and concluded that companies "…may be understating AROs through mismanaged accounting and by delaying classification to the Alberta Energy Regulator (AER), which obscures the actual size of AROs" (ibid).

"Like many oil and gas producers in Alberta, the companies are aided by taxpayers through a government subsidy that pays for the abandonment of the wells...... almost $42 million was spent to abandon oil and gas wells in 2021; half, or $21 million, came from taxpayers" (ibid).

"As the global energy system diversifies and transitions towards lower-carbon fuel sources, oil and gas decommissioning liabilities will become a more near-term issue than previously envisioned. The industry, with vigorous government oversight, must take effective and rapid action to avoid defaults and debt impairments that would force the Canadian taxpayer to bail out a broken system" (ibid).

In another example, the government of Guyana is paying ExxonMobil, Hess and the Chinese National Offshore Company 100% of the expected US$3.2bn decommissioning costs of the Liza Field in the next 20 years. In a front-loaded, one-sided contract the oil companies *"...are not required to set aside and use the money to decommission and clean up the project area after production is done. This provision puts Guyana at financial risk and could turn out to be nothing more than a gimmick that enhances the profits of the oil companies"* (Sanzillo, 2022).

Stranded fossil-fuel assets lead to ISDS settlement claims

The present value of future lost profits in the upstream oil and gas sector exceed US$1 trillion according to a new study taking into account expectations about the effects of climate policy (Semieniuk et al, 2022). They identified *"...the equity risk ownership from 43,439 oil and gas production assets through a global equity network of 1.8 million companies to their ultimate owners. Most of the market risk falls on private investors, overwhelmingly in OECD countries, including substantial exposure through pension funds and financial markets"* (ibid).

The financial geography of stranded assets has two impacts. Investors in OECD countries could seek to slow the decarbonisation or lobby for government bailouts. Stranding is likely to be uneven with variable financial risks.

"Even if outright financial instability is avoided, the large exposure of pension funds remains a major concern. In all circumstances, the political implications of loss allocations at each stage are likely to be major. International cooperation on managing and financing the production and stable phase-out of fossil fuels is needed to lessen destabilizing expectation realignments and their social repercussions" (ibid).

Another aspect is the potential threat of Investor-State Dispute Settlement (ISDS) claims when investors claim compensation as states limit or close oil or gas production or close coal-mines as part of their policy response to the climate crisis.

"To date, there have been at least 231 ISDS cases related to fossil fuel investments, which is almost 20% of the total known number of cases across all sectors. The vast majority (92%) of fossil fuel cases are related to oil and gas investments. Fossil fuel investors have been successful in 72% of cases that were decided on the merits where the final award was disclosed. Fossil fuel cases have a high average amount of compensation awarded ($600 million) and asset valuation is complicated by the volatility of oil prices, which are highly sensitive to exogenous shocks such as the pandemic and the war in Ukraine" (Tienhaara et al, 2022).

The Rystad Energy UCube database contains a list of 55,206 crude oil, gas, condensate and natural gas liquid assets in 159 countries with attributes, production status, real or anticipated approval, headquarters of foreign investors, production volume and net present value per investor.

"If countries cancel these projects in line with the Net-Zero Emissions Scenario (International Energy Agency), ISDS claims are possible for at least 10,506 (19%) of these projects across 97 countries, which are currently protected by 334 different investment treaties. This represents 18 to 21% of all crude oil, gas, condensate and NGL assets and 8 to 11% of the total estimated production of all oil and gas projects awaiting a final investment decision. The total NPV of these protected projects is expected to reach $60 billion to $234 billion, depending on future oil prices........This translates to tremendous potential financial losses for countries across income levels if ISDS claims are successful. The five countries with the greatest potential losses from ISDS are Mozambique ($7-31billion), Guyana $5-21 billion, Venezuela $3-21 billion), Russia ($2-16 billion) and the United Kingdom ($3-14 billion)" (ibid).

Boom in renewable energy ISDS claims in Spain

Lawsuits in Spain under the Energy Charter Treaty (ECT) have soared in the last ten years. The ECT is an international agreement reached in 1994 which applies to 53 countries in Europe and Asia. The agreement protects investors foreign energy investments such as compensation for environmental restrictions, bans imposed on oil drilling and any regulatory or policy change that reduces an investor's profits. Spain sought to increase investment in renewable energy projects and introduced overly generous feed-in tariffs, in effect a premium paid on top of the price of electricity.

The incentives were replaced in 2013/14 which led to 51 claims of which 21 were resolved in favour of the investor which cost the Spanish government US$1,257.9bn and US$105.8m legal fees at arbitration tribunals.

> *"In 89% of the cases against Spain the claimant is not a renewable energy company but an equity fund or other type of financial investor, with a direct or indirect stake in companies operating in the sector, including banks"*
> (PowerShift and Transnational Institute, 2022).

Many EU governments (France, Italy, Poland) have withdrawn from the ECT with Spain and the Netherlands considering withdrawal from the ECT because it will obstruct their transition away from fossil fuels (The Guardian, 2022a). For example, two German energy companies, RWE and Uniper, have demanded over $2bn compensation from the Netherlands because the government decided to phase out coal (Peigne, 2022). However, Uniper dropped its case against the closure of coal power plants on 15 August 2022 and a few days later declared a €12.3bn loss in the first-half of 2022 (Financial Times, 2022a and 2022b).

ISDS filed cases since 1987 totalled 1,104 by January 2021 with investors from the United States, the Netherlands and UK having filed the largest number of claims (221) in the last ten years (UNCTAD, 2021). Climate litigation has increased since the 2015 Paris climate agreement illustrated in (Figure 5).

Critique of Environment, Social and Governance

The concept of ESG has been widely promoted by financial and corporate interests. ESG criteria are increasingly used by financial institutions, investment funds and companies to demonstrate they are 'doing good' in their business activities. Rating agencies have adopted criteria that effectively support the share price of companies that claim their business and employment activities produce environmental, social and governance benefits.

But these benefits are defined by private sector activities and thus exclude the much wider public sector policy agenda. For example, 'governance' is focused on private company decision making, and not the decision-making process in local authority, regional and central government.

> *"……governments and regulators have once again succumbed to the siren song of market-friendly mechanisms. The new consensus focuses on financial disclosure because that path promises change without having to deliver it. (It also happens to generate employment for entire industries of accountants, lawyers and business consultants with powerful lobbying arms of their own.) Not surprisingly, the result has been a wave of greenwashing. The financial industry has happily poured trillions of dollars into green-labelled assets that turned out not to be green at all.*

Figure 5: Increase in climate litigation

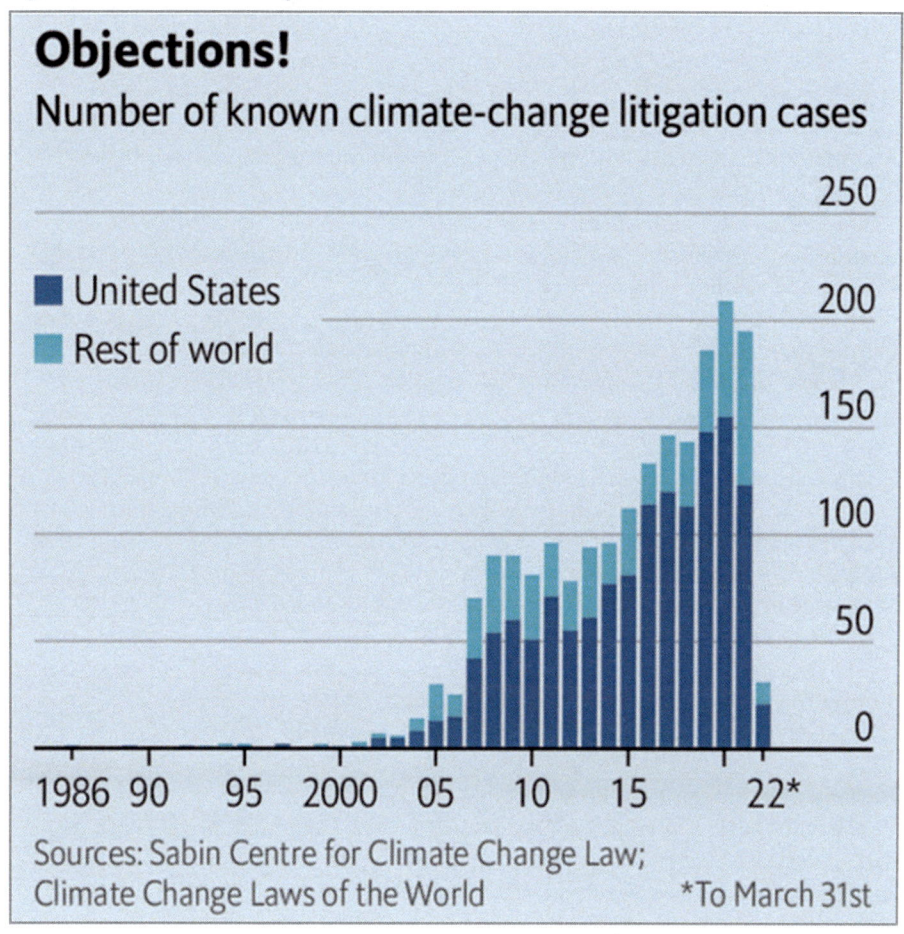

Objections!
Number of known climate-change litigation cases

■ United States
■ Rest of world

1986 90   95   2000   05   10   15   22*

Sources: Sabin Centre for Climate Change Law; Climate Change Laws of the World *To March 31st

Source: The Economist 23 April 2022a

According to a recent study, 71 per cent of ESG-themed funds (those supposedly re-electing environmental, social or governance criteria) are negatively aligned with the goals of the Paris climate agreement (Pistor, 2022).

Greenwashing - flaws in the ESG model

Firstly, there are a wide range of criteria in use which allow advocates of ESG to pick and mix according to their priorities. A study by Doyle (2018) for ESG Ratings

Agencies found disclosure limitations and a lack of standardisation particularly in environment and social disclosures.

Secondly, most of the criteria are very simply stated such as climate change, employment, housing, transparency and accountability which are very broad and not meaningful without details of what element of performance and impact will be assessed. Doyle identified company size bias with companies with higher market capitalisation receiving more meaningful ratings than smaller companies. He also identified a geographic bias, an industry sector bias, inconsistencies between rating agencies and a failure to identify risk (ibid).

Thirdly, there is little reference to the impact of market forces on nature and biodiversity and although environmental issues are often included, environmental justice is usually absent.

Finally, corporate governance usually includes transparency and accountability but should mean more than reporting to ratings agencies and stock exchanges to maintain share values. It must extend to participation of workforces, trade unions and community organisations in the process (Transparency International, 2021).

Management consultants McKinsey (2019) recommended five ways to create

"...a strong environmental, social and governance to value creation in five essential ways: top-line growth, cost reductions, regulatory and legal interventions, productivity uplift and investment and asset optimisation."

This succinctly sums up the ESG approach.

The OECD report Investment Governance and the integration of ESG Factors (2017) makes no reference to 'equality', nor does the G20/OECD/World Bank report on infrastructure as an asset class (2018). The latter report reviews 64 earlier reports by international agencies on ESG, governance and PPP Risks makes only three references to employment.

"Risk Documentation produced by the IMF and World Bank (2019), OECD and the World Bank Group (2015 and 2018) and the Global Infrastructure Hub (2019) are fundamentally flawed because they do not address all the potential risks with few, if any, references to equalities, employment, environment, climate change, or nature and biodiversity. In other words, they have yet to adopt even the basic Environmental, Social, Governance (ESG) agenda" (Whitfield, 2020a).

A study by Vincent Deluard, a global strategist at StoneX, New York, concluded

"*ESG funds are unconsciously worsening the social and political crisis associated with automation, inequality and monopolistic concentration*" (Johnson. 2021). He doubted "*...that the unfolding crises of the 2020s can be averted if the ESG movement's ultimate effect is to funnel more money into tax-avoiding tech monopolies, pharmaceutical giants with few workers, and financial networks.*" Furthermore, "*despite its noble goal, ESG investing unintendedly spreads the greatest illnesses of post-industrial economies. As ESG ratings increasingly determine the allocation of capital, we must pay attention to the kind of companies they reward*" (ibid).

In summer 2021, Tariq Fancy, the former global chief investment officer for sustainable investing at the BlackRock private equity fund blew the whistle on the ESG investment industry (Armstrong, 2021). His criticism included the following:

"*The core mechanism of ESG investing is divestment, but when an investor sells a security in the secondary market, another buys. All the ESG selling may drive down the price at which the buyers buy, giving them an opportunity for juicy returns as the price recovers.*"

"*Giving people the dumb idea that shifting their savings from one investment fund to another is going to help materially with, say, climate change creates a dangerous distraction from solutions that fit the scale of the problem, all of which involve changing the rules of capitalism through regulation.*"

Corporations, and the whole legal and social apparatus in which they sit, were built around the idea that companies exist to maximise shareholder wealth. That's what they are designed to do and are required to do. Thinking that fiddling around in the financial markets is going to make companies fit for a radically different purpose — helping with broad social problems driven by economic externalities and tricky collective action problems — is simply bonkers" (ibid).

The pressure on ESG branded funds increased in 2022 with the European Securities and Market Authority and the US Securities and Exchange Commission proposing to enhance private fund investor protection (U.S.SEC, 2022). The Financial Times cited other planned initiatives to what it described *"ESG as the next mis-selling scandal"* (Agnew, 2022).

Economic, social, equality and environmental strategies must be underpinned by public service principles and values that are significantly absent. Most will claim ESG good practice but meaningful equality, employment, participation and transparency criteria are missing or marginalised.

A random ESSU sample of ESG statements by ten private renewable energy companies of different size in ten different countries were examined by searching for reference to 'equality' and 'employment'. Several documents referred to the UN Sustainable Development Goals and the ten Principles for Responsible Investment. The documents varied from 8 to 65 pages and were published in 2020 or 2021. Six did not refer to 'equality', two referenced 'gender equality', one to 'inequality' and only one referenced the different dimensions of equality. Four companies made no reference to employment, three made one reference and three made several references. This evidence is further proof of the large vacuum that exists between ESG rhetoric and practice. It confirms that it is totally inadequate and should be replaced by the public values framework in Chapter 6.

CHAPTER 3

Trading renewable energy assets

The ESSU developed a major database, the Global Renewable Energy Secondary Market Database, with a total of 1,622 transactions.

It covers the three-year period from 1 January 2019 to 31 December 2021. The annual number of transactions increased from 398 in 2019, 537 in 2020, to 687 in 2021, an increase of 72.6% in the period.

The research and database builds on *Equitable Recovery Strategies: Why public ownership and democratic control must be at the heart of Green and Integrated Public Healthcare Deals,* European Services Strategy Unit Research Report No. 11 (Whitfield, 2020b) and *The Financialisation, Marketisation and Privatisation of Renewable Energy: Strategies for public ownership,* European Services Strategy Unit Research Report No. 12 (Whitfield, 2020c).

The ESSU Global Renewable Energy Secondary Market Database

A secondary market transaction includes the sale/acquisition of renewable energy assets at different stages ranging from the sale of rights, with or without a Power Purchase Agreement, those in construction or operational projects. The database includes transactions with share purchase agreements to acquire equity in renewable energy companies. The formation of partnerships or joint venture companies may ultimately affect the ownership of assets, particularly if one company later wants to sell their stake.

The database excludes announcements of contract awards following an auction or tendering process; investment, planning and regulatory approvals of new greenfield projects; obtaining project finance, commencing construction, orders for turbines, blades or solar panels; Power Purchase Agreements (PPA); the financial close or operational start of new projects; refinancing and/or repowering of operational projects. These events are important stages in the development of renewable energy projects, but do not entail the sale of assets and a change in ownership so are not classified as secondary market transactions.

Each transaction in the database identifies the vendor, purchaser, a brief description of the transaction, the type of renewable energy asset (onshore or offshore wind, solar, hydro, energy from waste, biomass, battery/storage; district heating or grid), the total MW or MWp of the project; the percentage of equity ownership, country location, sale price (where disclosed) and the prime data source.

Renewable energy transactions usually involve the vendor and the purchaser signing a binding confidentiality agreement to; permit an exchange of information and to undertake due diligence; review of the whole life financial model of the project; assess the condition and value of the asset; examine previous and current operational performance; review current contracts; an analysis of risks; and assess employment and equality policies. The transaction is closed (agreed), or the offer is withdrawn, when these processes are completed. The cost of transactions is discussed later.

Table 1: Annual rate of secondary market transactions 2019-2021

Renewable energy asset	Number of transactions			
	2019	2020	2021	Total
Wind	170	177	199	546
Solar	144	238	310	692
Combined wind & solar	30	42	53	125
Hydro	11	18	18	47
Battery/storage	9	14	37	60
Energy from waste	3	6	5	14
Other	31	42	65	138
Annual Total	**398**	**537**	**687**	**1,622**
				MW/MWp
MW/MWp (based on 1,455 transactions)	109,816	245,766	424,946	780,528
Total MW/MWp assuming 100% data				870,154
				Expenditure US$ millions
Expenditure based on 504 transactions	44,485	68,598	93,640	206,723
Expenditure assuming 100% data				671,783

Source: ESSU Global Renewable Energy Secondary Market Transactions Database, 2019-2021. Excludes new transmission contracts but includes 4 secondary market transactions of the sale of equity stakes in grid companies.

Data sources

The primary sources are company press releases and websites, Regulatory News Service notices, annual reports supported by news bulletins from various of renewable energy journals and national/international renewable energy organisations.

There are significant gaps in the data such as the MegaWatt (MW) of projects, the sale price and the failure to identify the company or organisation acquiring or selling the asset. These gaps are entirely due to non-disclosure of information by the companies involved in the transaction. This has little to do with the size of company and their resources because many of the largest private equity companies are very secretive.

Table 2 identifies the scale of acquisitions and sale transactions in 25 countries plus Africa and indicates the level of trade in the secondary market, which includes the sale of

Table 2: Transactions in selected countries

Country	Transactions		Total MW Identified	
	Internal	External	In Country	Overseas
Africa	4	7	830	3,725
Australia	13	31	4,708	11,971
Brazil	27	17	16,962	8,525
Canada	24	6	11,692	5,040
Chile	4	22	1,152	6,065
China	14	2	4,526	579
Columbia	4	5	231	271
Denmark	6	18	1,394	10,672
Finland	6	17	3,757	1,994
France	25	54	6,817	9,168
Germany	47	47	9,315	17,081
India	12	23	14,185	11,631
Italy	25	46	5,446	5,866
Japan	15	13	2,122	2,968
Netherlands	5	31	333	6,268
Norway	20	12	4,212	1,432
Poland	5	43	330	21,591
Portugal	3	20	480	6,750
Republic of Ireland	19	16	1,485	16,324

Table 2: Transactions in selected countries (continued...)

Country	Transactions		Total MW Identified	
	Internal	External	In Country	Overseas
Romania	8	10	232	1,328
Spain	28	103	27,717	45,346
Sweden	10	34	1,916	15,473
Taiwan	4	9	900	5,736
UK England, Wales, N.Ireland	71	33	6,817	10,681
Scotland*	0	34	0	2,733
USA	291	128	177,929	144,442

Source: ESSU Global Renewable Energy Secondary Market Transactions Database, 2019-2021 *Scotland all transactions were to UK or overseas companies.

operational assets and the acquisition of development rights and ready-to-build projects. It does not reflect the full scale of investment in renewable energy in a country. Where a majority of transactions have been with foreign companies, for example Chile had 4 internal transactions and 22 involving foreign companies, this is reflected in the overseas MW column in 18 countries plus Africa. The exceptions were Finland, Germany, India, Republic of Ireland, Japan and England/Wales/Northern Ireland where the distribution of MW data did not correlate with the distribution of transactions.

Typology of market participants

Developers and operators

Renewable energy companies build, operate and maintain onshore/offshore wind, solar, hydro, biomass, battery storage, energy from waste and hydrogen projects. They include subsidiaries of utility and fossil fuel companies, subsidiaries of private equity funds, some are listed on stock exchanges whilst others are private companies that frequently focus on one type of renewable energy, for example, wind, solar or hydro and joint venture companies or partnerships. They outsource many developer, construction and operational functions.

Parent and subsidiary companies

Many companies operate under one or more of their subsidiary company names. They are frequently significant companies with substantial renewable energy assets (see Table 4). The ESSU Global Renewable Energy Secondary Market Database cites the parent company in brackets where a subsidiary has been the purchaser or seller.

Private equity funds

They have a significant role in the renewable energy secondary market. For example, Brookfield Renewable Partners, is active in the renewable energy secondary market, having acquired five new assets and sold two others in the twenty-month period of this research.

Brookfield Renewables referred to having *"…executed our asset recycling strategy, selling a partial interest in mature assets and exiting non-core markets"* (Brookfield Renewable Partners, 2019). The report also cited:

"…capital recycling on an opportunistic basis, and diverse sources of capital. Principal sources of liquidity are cash flows from operation, our credit facilities, up-financings on non-recourse borrowings and proceeds from the issuance of various securities through public markets" (ibid).

"In 2019, we also continued to execute our capital recycling strategy of selling mature, de-risked or non-core assets to lower cost of capital buyers and redeploying the proceeds into higher yielding opportunities. During the year, we raised almost $600 million ($365 million net to BEP) through this funding strategy, allowing us to crystallize an approximate 18% return on our Portuguese and Northern Ireland wind assets and to return more than two times our capital invested in South Africa" (Brookfield Renewable Partners, 2020).

Private equity funds raise capital from wealthy individual investors and institutional organisations such as pension funds, mutual funds, insurance companies and sovereign wealth funds who are seeking a relatively secure and consistent rate of return. The US$19bn capital raising initiatives in late 2021 and early 2022 were discussed in Chapter 2. Capital may also be raised by issuing new shares in the company either by a private placement or by public offer. Investors expect to obtain a return on their capital.

Initially many governments made subsidies available to attract investment in renewable energy projects, but this was replaced by auctions or tendering, which ramped up competition and the award of contracts based on lowest price – a mirror image of the outsourcing of public services.

Private equity funds acquired 369 renewable energy assets in the 2019-2021 period and sold 178 assets, a total of 547 transactions or 33.5% of the total transactions in three years (ESSU Global Renewable Energy Secondary Market Database 2019-2021). This is likely to be an underestimate because a company's private equity fund classification was not always transparent. This data is solely for secondary market transactions and does not account for new investment in wind farms, solar plants, hydroelectric and battery storage and other renewable energy projects.

It is significant that private equity funds had a net gain of 191 acquisitions. The large global firms – BlackRock, Blackstone, Brookfield, Carlyle, Goldman Sachs and KKR reflected this pattern by acquiring 47 assets and selling 20. Similarly, infrastructure funds such as Copenhagen Infrastructure Partners, DIF Capital Partners, Foresight Group, Partners Group and SUSI acquired 51 assets and sold 21.

"The amount of money invested, or waiting to be invested, by private equity funds has swelled from $1.3trn in 2009 to $4.6trn today. This was driven by a scramble for yield among pension funds, insurance companies and endowments during a decade of historically low interest rates in the aftermath of the global financial crisis of 2007-09. Many have more than doubled their allocations to private equity. Since 2015 the ten largest American public-sector pension funds have collectively committed in excess of $100bn to buy-out funds" (The Economist, 2022b).

Private Equity Funds are also deeply involved in fossil fuel projects. Table 3 summarises the fossil fuel investments of 8 private equity funds.

Table 3: Private Equity's Energy Footprint & Percentage of Assets Under Management (AUM)

Company	% of Energy Portfoilo Companies Invested in Fossil Fuels	Number of Fossil Fuel Companies	Energy Portfolio (US $bn)
Carlyle/NGP	76%	42	24
Warburg Pincus	97%	28	10.9
KKR	78%	28	25.6
Brookfiueld/ Oaktree	53%	40	107.4
Ares Management	76%	16	6.7
Apollo	74%	14	6.5
Blackstone	52%	11	34
TPG	25%	2	1.3

Sources: Americans for Financial Reform and Private Equity Stakeholder Project (2022).

Financial institutions

This category includes commercial and investment banks, mostly providing project-level market rate debt to mature technologies such as solar PV and onshore wind, as well as offshore wind. In 2018 alone, solar PV and onshore wind received US$ 21 billion and US$22bn from commercial financial institutions, respectively, while offshore wind received US$14bn.

"In recent years, non-energy-producing corporate actors have played a considerable role in private finance for renewable energy, providing, on average, US$ 17 billion a year in 2017-2018. As opposed to project developers, who produce and distribute electricity as their main business activity, corporate actors most often produce electricity for self-consumption" (IRENA, 2020).

"Public finance contributed an annual average of 14% of total investment between 2013 and 2018. Public finance for the renewable energy sector consists of investments from DFIs, governments and their agencies, and national and multilateral climate funds. Compared to private finance, public finance plays an important role in directing investments toward sectors and regions that are relatively not matured or hard to invest in. These can include, for example, projects to scale up access to affordable clean energy for off-grid households, small-scale hydropower or urban infrastructure investments, e.g. renewable-sourced public lighting in disadvantaged areas." (ibid).

"Out of the total US$ 52 billion invested by the public sector in 2018, US$ 27 billion was provided as project-level conventional debt, US$ 7 billion as project-level concessional debt, US$ 5 billion as balance sheet financing (debt and equity) and under US$ 2 billion as grants" (ibid).

Eight major renewable energy companies and infrastructure funds raised US$13.7 billion in late 2021 and early 2022 to finance new projects and/or growth.

- Actis and Clearway – US$6,750m to fund infrastructure, energy transition and pipeline of projects.
- Ares Management Corporation – US$2.2bn for a new Ares Climate Infrastructure Partners Fund and acquired Landmark Partners LLC experienced in secondary private fund ownership stakes for US$1.08bn in 2021.
- Lightsource BP raised US$1.8bn revolving credit from global banks to fund 20GW new solar by 2025.
- A Canadian Solar share offer raised US$150m to fund battery storage growth.
- Adani Green Energy issued a green bond to raise US$750m to finance projects.

- NextEnergy Capital raised US$663m from insurance companies, pension funds and asset management companies for a new fund backed by UK Infrastructure Bank.
- ib vogt (Germany) raised US$305m from BAE Systems Pension Fund, SCOR Investment & BNP Paribas Asset Management to finance solar and storage projects.

Pension funds

Pension funds acquired 37 assets (43,104MW) in the 2019-2021 period and sold eight assets (7,213 MW). The table does not take account of investment in new renewable energy assets.

A recent article on the Global Infrastructure Hub by a former Minister for Superannuation in Australia and the Director of the World Pensions Council stated:

"The case for institutional investment in infrastructure is being made more forcefully than ever by investors from Blackrock to the Bank of England…. highlight infrastructure's strong position as an asset class and reflect the growing realisation of policymakers that pension powers can play an essential role in building an ESG-driven global economy" (Sherry and Firzli, 2022).

In addition to references about 'the Age of Fiduciary Capitalism' and 'the foundational sectors of the Fifth Industrial Revolution' they recommended:

- *"Guaranteeing the sanctity of property rights and contract law (safeguarding privatised assets and public-private partnerships notwithstanding changes in government) with truly independent judiciary branches.*
- *Being willing to commit to truly long-term privatisation and concession programs (e.g. ports and airports in the US, Latin America, and the EU, where governments need to secure a sufficient number of assets in their privatisation pipelines)"* (ibid).

Scottish public sector pension funds have investments in offshore funds that develop PPPs and renewable energy projects. In May 2018 Strathclyde Pension Fund invested £500m in the JPMorgan International Infrastructure Fund (Cayman Islands). The $14.5bn JPMorgan fund invests in transportation, regulated utilities and contracted power - primarily in the US (37%), Europe (24%) and UK (21%) and is the ultimate owner of Ventient Energy which owns 140 onshore wind farms in Europe. In the same month Strathclyde invested £50m in the Equitix Fund V LP, managed by Equitix GP 5 Limited (Guernsey) adding to an earlier £30m in a similar Equitix fund since 2016 (Whitfield, 2018). There is, or should be, a

Table 4: Pension fund transactions for renewable energy assets in 2019-2021

Pension fund	Acquired		Sold	
	No.	MW	No.	MW
Alberta Investment Managt. Corporation (Can)	–	n/a	1	899
Canada Pension Plan Investment Board	7	7,523	3	193
Ontario Municipal Employees Retirement System	12	13,768	1	1,405
Ontario Teachers Pension Plan	2	*4,780	–	n/a
OPSEU Pension Trust (Canada)	3	3,144	1	4,000
Caisse de depot et placement du Quebec (CDPQ)	1	*605	1	296
Desjardins Group Pension Plan (Canada)	1	202	–	n/a
Universities Superannuation Scheme (UK)	1	4,000	–	n/a
Pensions Infrastructure Platform (UK)	1	n/a	–	n/a
BAe Pension Fund (UK)	1	*861	–	n/a
PKA and Pensam Pension Funds (Denmark)	1	588	–	n/a
Industriens Pension (Denmark)	1	*1,000	–	n/a
APG asset management pension fund (N.lands)	3	733	–	n/a
IFM Global Infrastructure Fund (Aust. pensions)	2	5,630	–	n/a
First State Super (now Aware Super, Australia)	1	*270	–	n/a
Commonwealth Superannuation Corp (Australia)	–	n/a	1	420
Clean Energy Ptners (TIAA American-College Retirement Equities Fund)	2	372	0	0
Total	39	43,476	8	7,213

Sources: ESSU Global Renewable Energy Secondary Market Transaction Database, 2022
*Joint investment with a renewable energy company.

distinction between investing in a specific project and investing in PPP infrastructure funds.

Edinburgh City Council, on behalf of Lothian Pension Fund and Lothian Buses Pension Fund and the Falkirk Council Pension Fund, have investments in the Equitix Fund II LP. The Equitix funds are ultimately owned by Tetragon Financial Group Limited, which is registered offshore in Guernsey (ibid).

Infrastructure funds and asset management companies

Infrastructure funds (such as Antin (USA), Ardian (France), Axium (Canada), Copenhagen Infrastructure Partners (Denmark) and Global Infrastructure Partners (USA) have been active in the secondary market, trading assets as fund managers, although are less likely to develop new projects.

Manufacturers

Manufacturing of renewable energy projects includes the production of turbines, blades, solar panels, energy from waste plants, biomass and hydro project technology. Turbine and some solar panel producers have engaged in equity ownership of some renewable energy projects. There are numerous companies engaged in the manufacturing supply chain and in the support services required, particularly for offshore wind projects.

Technology frontier companies

The renewable energy sector is at the forefront of: technological development in the design and production of solar panels; blades, turbines and foundations of onshore/offshore wind farms; the development of powerful batteries and storage; improving the energy from waste process; and the production of new fuels based on hydrogen. They have been driven by the need to make products more efficient and effective in more challenging geographic locations with extreme weather conditions. Companies that specialise in performance monitoring of onshore and offshore assets have drawn on technological improvements.

Role of utility and petroleum companies

Utility and petroleum companies are under increasing pressure to eliminate fossil fuels and increase power generated from renewable sources. This has resulted in some companies, such as BP and Lightsource, developing renewable energy subsidiaries or partnerships. Several large utility and petroleum companies were engaged in the renewable energy secondary market between 1 January 2019 and 31 December 2021 when they purchased 76 and 38 assets respectively. They sold 61 and 16 assets respectively in the same period (Table 5). EDF (France) was the most active, ending with a net gain of eight assets in this period.

Impact of the secondary market

The secondary market increases the role of markets and market forces in renewable energy and consolidates market interests. The market creates new opportunities for profiteering from the generation of renewable energy. Revenue from the sale of assets accrues to the parent company that owns the equity and does not directly benefit the project, community and local economy.

Table 5: Transactions by major utility and petroleum companies in 2019-2021

Companies	Sold	Purchased
Utility Companies		
American Electric Power	16	3
Dominion Energy (USA)	3	6
Duke Energy (USA)	3	7
EDF (France)	13	21
ESB (Republic of Ireland)	1	5
Iberdrola (Spain)	2	15
RWE (Germany)	8	6
EDP (Portugal)	12	12
SSE (UK & Republic of Ireland)	3	1
Sub total	**61**	**76**
Petroleum Companies		
BP (UK)	5	15
Equinor (Norway)	5	4
Petronas (Malaysia)	0	1
Repsol (Spain)	1	2
Total (France)	5	16
Sub total	**16**	**38**

Source: ESSU Global Renewable Energy Secondary Market Transaction Database, 2020.

Increased the use of tax havens as companies and investment funds seek to minimise or avoid tax liabilities in order to maximise profits.

There is a fundamental lack of democratic accountability because the secondary market operates independently of governments and international agencies (except when regulatory approval is required for a transaction).

Private equity funds have a significant role in the renewable energy secondary market. For example, Brookfield Renewable Partners is active in the renewable energy secondary market having acquired 19 assets and sold 6 in the three-year research period.

"In 2019, we also continued to execute our capital recycling strategy of selling mature, de-risked or non-core assets to lower cost of capital buyers and redeploying the proceeds into higher yielding opportunities. During the year, we raised almost $600 million ($365 million net to BEP) through this funding strategy, allowing us to crystallize an approximate 18% return on our Portuguese and Northern Ireland wind assets and to return more than two times our capital invested in South Africa" (Brookfield Renewable Partners, 2020).

In 2022 Brookfield announced that it was considering spinning of its asset management business reportedly valued at over US$75bn.

The manoeuvre would simplify the structure of the sprawling Toronto-based company, separating the division that manages $364bn in fee-bearing assets across real estate, infrastructure, renewable energy, credit and private equity on behalf of institutional investors from Brookfield's $50bn of directly-owned net assets.

"The financial markets have evolved. What people like are asset-light models," Bruce Flatt, chief executive of Brookfield, told the Financial Times. *"It appears that there is an enormous amount of shareholder value to be unlocked"* (Financial Times, 2022c).

The fact that the secondary market generates additional profits and fees could invalidate the original impact and/or economic/social cost benefit assessments undertaken at the start of the project. Private equity funds, consultants and lawyers have a financial, economic and political interest in sustaining the secondary market.

The flow of capital into the secondary circuit is supported by government investment plans for public infrastructure but their long-term nature can lead to over-accumulation and under-investment (Aalbers, 2016).

Changes in the ownership of assets may alter the priority of certain projects, but it does not increase investment in existing assets except when older assets are acquired for upgrading or repowering. Changing corporate ownership via private negotiation may lead to the weakening of the original environmental and community commitments by the new owners.

The market will mushroom as the rate of renewable energy projects increases, to meet the demands set by climate targets. This will accelerate financialisation, marketisation and private ownership as more and more projects are commodified and traded. Thus public ownership and democratic accountability of power generation will be more difficult to achieve without radical action.

Renewable energy urgently needs a fundamental and permanent shift from the 'market fixing' and 'market shaping' neoliberal ideology which remains pervasive in public policy making. Compulsory competitive tendering of UK local government services and 'market testing' of NHS and social care services were highly damaging for public services and staff. Government and private sector interests colluded to impose regulatory regimes to legitimate market forces. 'Market shaping' implies that market forces can be regulated and restricted and simultaneously produce public goods that continuously sustain public values, but the dominant evidence proves otherwise (Whitfield, 2020a, Cohen and Mikaelian, 2021 and many others). Yet it remains a concept propogated by consultants and academics.

Shareholders scoop multi-million dividend payments

The payment of annual dividends to company shareholders is an indicator of the company's annual profits. Dividends are paid in cash (or the option of additional shares) and are designed to incentivise continued holding of the shares. Privately owned renewable energy companies and the subsidiaries of larger companies (which only pay dividends for the company as a whole), were excluded from the sample.

Annual dividend payments to shareholders in a sample of 20 private renewable energy companies totalled a staggering US$10.7 billion between 2019-2021 (Table 6). The companies were selected from the ESSU Global Renewable Energy Database 2019-2021 as public companies that issue shares to raise capital to fund renewable energy projects and are listed on a stock exchange. They include the privatised National Group plc (1996) which operates the UK Grid and the New York and Massachusetts grid and develops and operates renewable energy projects in several US states.

The profits of private renewable energy companies are increasing too. Recent examples include EDPR disclosing a net profit of US$272m in the first half of 2022, an 87% increase on the previous year.

The major fossil fuel companies reported record profits in the second quarter of 2022 with 8 companies reporting total profits of US$67.71bn (Table 7).

High cost and secrecy of transactions

The ESSU Global Renewable Energy Secondary Market Database 2019-2021 identifies 1,622 transactions in the three year period. The price paid for renewable energy assets is generally highly secretive and was disclosed in only 30.9% of transactions - a total of US$199.9bn. Assuming this figure is likely to be a reasonable reflection of all the transactions, the total expenditure is US$646.0bn.

The widespread lack of disclosure of the prices paid to acquire renewable energy assets, and to a lesser extent their total MW, means that the total value of the transactions relies on an assumption that the cost data for transactions were representative of the transactions that did not disclose financial information. The failure to disclose financial details was common across different types of renewable energy projects.

Table 6: Dividends paid to shareholders in 20 renewable energy companies in 2019, 2020 and 2021

Company	Dividend Payments US$
ABO Wind (Germany)	12,878,611
Acciona Energias Renovables (Spain)	562,110,074
Albioma Group (France)	60,686,630
Aquila Capital (Germany) European Renewables Income Fund	25,140,496
BayWa r.e. (Germany)	175,575,735
Brookfield Renewable Partners L.P. (Canada)	2,389,769,459
Clearway Energy Inc. (USA)	634,000,000
EDPR S.A. (Portugal)	85,035,992
Energiekontor AG (Germany)	23,403,245
Encavis AG (Germany)	187,802,130
Eolus Vind AB (Sweden)	8,288,971
European Energy A/S (Denmark)	9,050,990
Falck Renewables SpA (Italy)	88,535,607
Greencoat UK Wind Plc (UK)	430,178,706
National Group plc (UK/USA)	5,468,733,127
NextEra Energy Solar Fund Ltd (Guernsey)	118,770,191
Octoplus Renewables Infrastructure Trust	33,305,045
Renewable Energy Systems Holdings Ltd (UK)	13,452,773
The Renewables Infrastructure Group Ltd (Guernsey)	358,464,516
US Solar Fund plc (UK)	15,129,252
Total	**10,700,057,777**

Sources: Company Annual Reports 2021 and SEC Form 10-K or Form 20-F in USA. Octopus 15 months 2019/2020: Eolus 16 months for 2019/2020.

Secondary market transactions involve the vendor and the purchaser signing a binding confidentiality agreement to permit an exchange of information. This enables the potential purchaser to undertake a number of functions to provide them with clarity about what they are seeking to acquire and form the basis of negotiations to agree a final price and any additions or amendments to the terms of the original agreement. The functions include due diligence, review of the whole life financial model of the project, asset value assessment, previous, current and potential future operational performance, employment and equality objectives and performance, review of current contracts and risk analysis.

Table 7: Second Quarter 2022 profits of fossil fuel companies

Company	US$bn
BP (UK)	8.50
Chevron (USA)	11.62
Equinor (Norway)	6.76
ENI (Italy)	3.65
ExxonMobil (USA)	17.85
Reposl (Spain)	2.14
Shell UK/Netherlands	11.50
TotalEnergies (France)	5.69
Total	**67.71**

Sources: Company Q2 results statements.

The cost of transactions usually exclude the cost above list functions undertaken by financial advisors, lawyers, accountants, human resource and technical advisors which are even more secretive although there is some evidence on which to calculate these costs. There will be some difference in transaction costs between countries. However, the bulk of transactions occur between European states, between North America and Europe, within the USA, between Europe and Oceania, and between Asia and Europe/North America.

Thrive Renewables (UK) sold two wind farms to Equitix Limited in 2019 for £23.73m and incurred sale costs of £365,130 or 1.54% of the sale price (Thrive Renewables plc, 2020). This sum excluded Equitix's transaction costs which are likely to have been significantly higher than Thrive's because, as purchaser, it would have had higher due diligence, legal and technical costs.

The cost of transactions involving UK Private Finance Initiative infrastructure projects was frequently not disclosed, but there was reasonable evidence to assess costs based on a 2% fee for transactions with a 3% fee for larger and more complex transactions (Whitfield, 2016). A similar calculation has been used to estimate the transaction costs for the 1,622 renewable energy transactions based on the 3% rate applying to transactions which cost over US$500m.

The analysis first identified 504 transactions (31.07%) which disclosed their cost, a total of US$208.7bn. On the basis that these transactions were a representative sample of all 1622 transactions the total cost would be US$671.8bn. It identified 117 transactions that cost over US$500m and represented 23.2% of the 504 transactions which disclosed the selling price of the assets.

Therefore, 23.2% of US$671.8bn is US$155.8bn and a 3% transaction cost will be US$4.7bn. Likewise, 76.8% of US$671.8bn is US$515.9bn and a 2% transaction cost will be US$10.3bn. Combining the two costs gives the transaction cost of US$15.0bn.

Therefore the estimated total cost of the secondary market in renewable energy in the 2019-2021 period was US$671.8bn plus US$15.0bn = US$686.8bn.

Developments in 2022

The need to accelerate investment in renewable energy in response to the climate crisis, the lack of progress in abandoning fossil fuels, the Russian invasion of Ukraine and the international response to terminate European reliance on Russian gas and oil, has led to a spiralling increase in the cost of fuel and food. It has also led to recognition of the need to accelerate investment in renewable energy. This section identifies key transactions in the first nine months of 2022 involving fossil fuel companies, new joint ventures and partnerships, private equity fund investments and other renewable energy companies. Whilst binding agreements have been signed, many of the transactions had not been concluded at the time of writing.

The following include primary and secondary market investments in renewable energy.

Fossil fuel company renewable energy investments increase

Shell plc and the Brazilian steel company Gerdau agreed a 50/50 joint venture for the development, construction and operation of a 260MWp utility-scale solar park in the state of Minas Gerais (Shell, Gerdau joint venture, 2022).

British Petroleum acquired a 40.5% stake in Asian Renewable Energy Hub to develop 26GW wind/solar/hydrogen in Western Australia. The $30bn project covers a 6,500 square kilometre site in the Pilbara mining region with partners Macquarie, CWP Global and Intercontinental Energy (Financial Times, 2022d).

Shell plc acquired solar developer Sprng Energy from Actis LLP with a 2.9GWp portfolio of projects and a 7.5GWp pipeline project in India for US$1.55bn (Shell, 2022).

TotalEnergies (France) acquired a 25% interest in India's Adani New Industries Limited which plans to produce one million tonnes of green hydrogen annually by 2030 with 30GW renewable projects (TotalEnergies, 2022a). TotalEnergies had earlier acquired a 20% stake in solar developer Adani Green Energy in 2021.

TotalEnergies also formed a strategic partnership with Global Infrastructure

Partners (GIP) in which it acquired 42% in GIP's Clearway Energy Group (USA) for US$1.6bn whilst GIP obtained 50% of Total's 51% stake in SunPower Corporation. Total added a further 5.4GW of renewable assets in the USA by acquiring Core Solar for an undisclosed cost (TotalEnergies, 2022b).

Repsol (Spain) sold a 25% stake in its renewable energy company to Credit Agricole Assurances and Energy Infrastructure Partners for US$948m (Repsol, 2022).

The Austrian utility Verbund AG acquired a 4.5GW portfolio (operational/greenfield) of wind and solar sites in the Iberian peninsula from the Q-Energy Group (Verbund, 2022).

Norway's Equinor ASA acquired 100% of East Point Energy LLC, Virginia, with a 4.1GW pipeline of battery storage projects on the US East Coast (Equinor, 2022).

New joint ventures and partnerships

Sembcorp Industries (China) signed a collaboration agreement with Bamboo Capital Group to jointly develop a pipeline of 1.5GW of wind and solar projects in Vietnam to contribute to the national power plan for 21.4GW solar and 12.5GW wind by 2030 (Sembcorp Industries, 2021).

Canadian Solar and north-east England based Windel Energy expanded their current working relationship by signing an agreement to co-develop 1.5GW of Battery Energy Storage Systems in the UK. Windel will develop projects to the 'ready-to-build' stage with the batteries provided by Canadian Solar (Windel Energy, 2021).

A consortium of Macquarie Asset Management, the British Columbia Investment Management Corporation and Munich Ergo Asset Management GmbH acquired the French solar developer Reden Solar in a US$2.5bn transaction. Reden has 762MW operational projects and 15GW pipeline projects in France and Spain (Macquarie Asset Management, 2022).

The Ontario Teachers' Pension Plan Board formed an alliance with Corio Generation, part of Macquarie's Green Investment Group to develop 9GW of offshore wind projects (Green Investment Group, 2022).

The Kerpen municipal utility (west of Cologne) signed an agreement with RWE Renewables in December 2021 to jointly develop two wind farms in a rezoned area along the A4 motorway in Germany (RWE, 2021).

Private equity fund investments

Brookfield Renewables closed US$15bn funding of the Brookfield Global Transition Fund to finance decarbonisation projects. The fund has already deployed or allocated US$2.5bn for the acquisition of U.S. and German solar power and battery developers, with a combined renewable power development pipeline capacity of approximately 25,000 MW; an investment in a carbon capture and storage developer to fund the rollout of the company's critical technology across energy and industrial facilities in North America; and a development partnership with a U.K. battery storage provider to roll out up to 1,200 MW of capacity alongside 200 MW of co-located solar power (Reuters, 2022).

Brookfield Renewables announced a US$1bn takeover of Scout Clean Energy in September 2022 with the potential to invest an additional US$350m to support business development. The same day as the Scout acquisition was announced, Brookfield also closed the acquisition of Standard Solar for US$540m (Brookfield Renewables, 2022).

Quinbrook Infrastructure Partners (US, UK and Australia) acquired 100% of Scout Clean Energy for US$6m in 2017 as a start-up renewable energy company with 1,600 MW of wind projects. Over the next five years Quinbrook invested a further US$470m into Scout Clean Energy so that it became a developer, owner and operator with 1,200 MW wind projects in four states and a pipeline of 22 GW of wind, solar and storage in 24 states (Businesswire, 2022). Consequently, Quinbrook shareholders made a return of over 200% on the sale of Scout Clean Energy to Brookfield (Infrastructure Investor, 2022).

Another private equity fund, Blackstone Inc. closed a US$650m deal via its credit portfolio company, ClearGen LLC, to fund solar energy systems in commercial and industrial properties by solar developer Wunder Capital – the monetising of rooftops (UrbanLand, 2022). ClearGen also concluded a US$150m deal to fund Verdant Microgrid LLC which supplies solar power, energy storage, combined heat and power systems, backup generators and other technologies to commercial and industrial premises. ClearGen also began a US$500m partnership with Schneider Electric and Huck Capital to provide similar renewable energy microgrid systems.

Blackrock Real Assets led consortium invested US$525m for a 10.53% interest in Tata Power Renewables which has 4.9GW of operational assets in India (Blackrock & Mubadala, 2022).

KKR agreed a deal to acquire French renewable developer Albioma with 1GW biomass, solar and geothermal plants in metropolitan France and overseas territories plus Brazil, Turkey and Canada (KKR, 2022).

Blackstone Inc., invested US$3bn in Invenergy Renewables Holdings Llc owned by the Canadian pension fund, Caisse de dépôt et placement du Québec (CDPQ) to fund further expansion of its 30GW of wind, solar and storage projects (Blackstone, 2022).

Exus Management Partners acquired 20 solar parks (1GW) in north east Brazil in a US$686m deal buying 100% of the shares of Riacho da Serra Energia and the Brazilian project-related assets from Decal Renewables (Italy) and Upside Value Renewables (UK).

Private equity Carlyle Group and GIC (Government of Singapore) invested in Eneus Energy (UK and USA) to develop a 14GW+ pipeline for the green hydrogen economy (Carlyle and GIC, 2022).

Other transactions

Infrastructure Investments Fund Holding LP, the Cayman Islands fund advised by JP Morgan and owners of Ventient Energy, purchased a 60% stake in Falck Renewables S.p.A. following a binding agreement in late 2021. Falck has 1,408MW operational projects and manages 4,800MW (Falck, 2022).

Canadian Solar sold a 70% interest in two solar plants of 738MWp in the Brazilian states of Piaui and Ceara to SPIC Brasil, a subsidiary of the State Power Investment Corporation of China (Canadian Solar, 2022).

Greencoat Renewables acquired a 50% stake in the Borkum Riffgrund 1 offshore wind (Germany) for US$350m from Kirkbi A/S & Demant Healthcare (Greencoat Renewables, 2022).

The California Public Utilities Commission (CUPC) approved plans in February 2022 for 25,500 MW new supply-side renewables and 15,000 MW of new storage in the next decade. In addition, 23 projects costing US$2.9bn were approved to enhance reliability of the state's transmission network (CPUC, 2022).

A large renewable energy and green hydrogen project is planned in the Gippsland Renewable Energy Park in Victoria, Australia beginning with 500 MW of solar and 500 MWh of battery storage. The Federal Government's green bank is contributing A$8.5m (AusNet update, June 2022).

EnBW (Germany) agreed to acquire 800MW of solar projects from Procon Solar GmbH (EnBW, 2022).

Aker Horizons ASA (Norway) acquired a 75% stake in Mainstream Renewable Power (Ireland) in 2021 followed by the Japanese Mitsui Corporation agreeing to invest US$585m and a 27.5% stake in 2022, reducing Aker's stake to 54.4%, leaving Irish investors with a 18.1% stake (Mainstream/Mitsui 2022).

Octopus Group launched US$10bn renewable energy funds and acquired the 333MW Darlington Point solar farm, New South Wales, Australia's largest operational solar project (pv-tech, 2022).

Quinbrook Infrastructure Partners has planning permission for a AU$2.5bn data centre campus in Brisbane adjacent to high voltage transmission connections (Quinbrook, 2022).

The French Government announced on 19 July that it would acquire the remaining 16% of Electricite de France (EDF) which it does not already own thus achieving 100% ownership and control (EDF 2022).

Orsted A/S acquires German and French onshore wind platform Ostwind with 678MW operational or advanced development projects and a 1GW pipeline in a US$690m transaction (Orsted, 2022).

Other significant transactions include US solar developer selling its development unit with a 8.4GW solar and 6.4 energy storage pipelines to Emerging Capital Partners, the African private equity fund (Mainstream and Actis, 2022).

RWE AG (Germany) acquired Con Edison Clean Energy in a US$6.8bn transaction to acquire 3GW operational projects, 90% of which are solar, and a 7GW development pipeline (RWE Press Release, 2022).

The plethora of private sector investments, new ventures, partnerships, private equity fund and other transactions make effective monitoring, scrutiny/oversight and democratic accountability even more difficult.

CHAPTER 4

Wide use of PPPs for energy projects in emerging economies

The World Bank Group, including the International Finance Corporation (IFC) and the International Bank for Reconstruction and Development (IBRD), have been instrumental in supporting a 'sustainable energy market' in developing economies. The objective has been to *"...to create a market for solar power generation, mitigate investment risks, or achieve specific national energy policy objectives"* (IBRD and The World Bank, 2019). They concentrated on providing legal, policy, and regulatory framework; planning, technical and operational capacity; government-sponsored guarantees; and investment in enabling infrastructure with direct and indirect financing having a marginal role.

Analysis of World Bank PPP renewable energy projects

The World Bank Private Participation in Infrastructure Database was accessed (8 March 2022) and a separate database for research purposes compiled of electricity PPP projects since 1997 in the six regions of East Asia and Pacific, Europe and Central Asia, Latin America and the Caribbean, Middle East and North Africa, South Asia and Sub Saharan Africa. The database had 3,767 entries but 315 coal, 277 Natural Gas, 245 diesel and two nuclear projects were excluded because the focus is on renewable energy projects.

It is significant that such a large number of fossil fuel PPP projects were still being commenced until very recently. The Private Participation in Infrastructure 2001 half year report indicated that all of Bangladesh's newly added power generation capacity (307MW) was from coal but it planned to cancel several new coal fired power projects. It intends to focus on gas and renewable energy in future (World Bank, 2021).

The exclusions reduced the database to 2,928 entries which included 22 projects which had been cancelled, 4 which had been concluded and 5 that were classified as being 'distressed'. Privatisation occurred in 322 (11.3%) projects with a third being full divestiture and the remainder classified as partial privatisation.

Equally significant, 1,480 (52.5%) greenfield projects adopted the 'build, own and operate' model which means that this model, combined with privatisation, means that 63.8% of PPP renewable energy projects concluded in private ownership. The 'build, operate and transfer' model accounted for 31.2% of contracts and 60 projects were management, lease or rental contracts mainly in the Europe and Central Asia region. The relevant data was missing from 90 projects.

Hydro, wind and solar generation accounted for over two thousand projects followed by biomass and waste projects but the data in Table 8 is limited because 491 projects were unclassified. Total investment was US$467.7bn between 1997-2021, but investment data was missing from 231 entries.

Table 8: Renewable energy technology in PPP projects since 1997

Renewable energy technology	Number of projects
Solar	696
Wind	686
Hydro (small)	402
Hydro (large)	250
Biomass	193
Waste	127
Geotherm	41
Biogas	22
Other	20
Unclassified	491
Total	**2,928**

Source: World Bank Private Participation in Infrastructure Database.

A World Bank/PPIAF (2019) study of public and private investment in infrastructure used the Private Participation in Infrastructure database covering 28 years of project data, combined with an analysis of projects sponsored in 2017. It included a sector analysis of energy projects in electricity generation, transmission and distribution. It concluded:

Electricity generation
- Wind **95% private investment,** 2% public and 3% state-owned entity
- Solar **85% private investment,** 4% public and 12% state-owned entity
- Waste **79% private investment,** 2% public and 19% state-owned entity
- Hydro **10% private investment,** 24% public and 57% state-owned entity

"…**wind and solar power projects are predominantly privately funded** led by projects in Brazil, China and Mexico. These are more attractive sub-sectors for private investors, because of relatively shorter construction periods and reduced capital costs (particularly for solar)."

"Public infrastructure-project investments in the renewable-energy sector were comprised mainly of investments in hydropower projects in China, Nigeria and Pakistan. Capital intensive and with long gestation periods, hydropower projects carry high risks for private-sector sponsors and, as such, are traditionally carried out by the public sector" (World Bank and PPIAF, 2019).

Multilateral and bilateral support

The level of multilateral and bilateral support for PPPs, primarily via loans and guarantees, varied significantly between regions, and 72.6% of projects had neither type of support. The Asian Development Bank (2017), International Finance Corporation, European Bank for Reconstruction and Development had a key role in multilateral loans and to a lesser extent equity and guarantees. The World Bank's Multilateral Guarantee Agency provided over US$4bn guarantees to nearly 60 projects. A number of funds and agencies provided bilateral loans.

The renewable energy PPPs in the 1997-2021 period had a total of 262,835MW. However, the actual total will be higher because over 470 (16%) project entries did not provide MW data. The database has 243 'large hydro' projects which each can generate up to 1000MW and a further 410 'small hydro' projects with very variable levels of MW.

Projects in Morocco, Senegal, South Africa, India, Chile, Philippines and Maldives provide examples of how a renewable energy strategy has been implemented. It included government or public agency acquisition of land for solar development; provision of infrastructure such as roads and water supply; securing permits; improved distribution grids; grants used for upfront subsidies to private developers; guarantees (multinational development banks are preferred); all of which reduce the risks for private investors and attract finance from national or local banks and bilateral donor agencies (ibid). Little surprise that corporate welfare is established in renewable energy.

PPP secondary market

A broad-based PPP secondary market grew rapidly both in the UK (under the Private Finance Initiative) and internationally since 2003 but was distinctly different to the renewable energy secondary market in several aspects. Projects were developed by the public sector with assets transferred to public ownership at end of the contract so there was no trade in development rights; projects were mainly financed by bank debt; a majority of transactions were equity stakes rather than full ownership; and a host of secondary market infrastructure funds emerged to build portfolios of equity stakes and were subject to takeovers by other funds (Whitfield, 2010, 2016, 2017, 2018). There was wide use of tax havens.

The high level of profiteering and use of offshore tax havens in the UK secondary market were a key factor in the recommendations of the House of Commons Public

Accounts Committee (2011 and 2018) and the House of Commons Treasury Committee (2011). The Government finally abolished the Private Finance Initiative in late 2018 (HM Treasury, 2018).

The ESSU PPP Equity Database 1998-2016 identified 462 transactions involving 1,003 projects in the UK with an estimated total value of £10.3bn (Whitfield, 2017). The average rate of return obtained in PPP transactions was 28.7% i.e. infrastructure funds have acquired PPP equity at a price that reflects this rate of return. These funds in turn aim to provide their shareholders with a 7%-8% rate of return (Whitfield, 2018).

Private investment continues despite pandemic

"Private investment in infrastructure within the secondary market has seen a trend increase over time, almost quadrupling the levels seen at the beginning of the decade. This reflects the growth of infrastructure as an asset class and the increasing trend towards active portfolio management across all private markets, with the secondary market servicing changing investor needs and preferences over time, particularly considering the long holding periods of infrastructure assets.

Secondary private investment in infrastructure rose by 25% in 2020, to US$412 billion across 927 transactions in 2020. This mainly reflects the needs of investors for more mature investments, particularly in a context where primary transactions are facing economic uncertainty" (Global Infrastructure Hub, 2021). Renewable energy projects accounted for 25% of expenditure in 2020.

A recent OECD working paper undertook an econometric analysis of the impacts of climate mitigation policies and the quality of the investment environment on investment and innovation in renewable power in OECD and G20 countries. The study avoided the secondary market despite it having grown from US$8.5bn in 2004 to US$146.2bn in 2017 (Frankfurt School-UNEP Bloomberg New Energy Finance, 2020) on the grounds that:

"The investment flows considered by the project include both domestic and international flows of new investment in greenfield (i.e. newly built) infrastructure assets. They include: asset finance; corporate debt; venture capital (VC) and private equity (PE). Asset finance represents the majority of flows considered by the study.

Since the analysis here focuses on the impact of policy on new investments rather than buying and selling existing projects and companies, the analysis disregards deals for mergers and acquisitions as well as for public markets. The exclusions of flows from mergers and acquisitions and public markets also safeguard against the possible risk of double-counting" (OECD, 2017).

Electricity demand increased 22% in the last seven years in the key ASEAN economies of Indonesia, Malaysia, the Philippines, Thailand and Vietnam but only 4% was sourced from wind and solar in 2021. Electricity demand is forecast to continue to rise with demand outpacing the supply of clean electricity with reliance on increasing generation by fossil fuels resulting in increasing CO_2 emissions (Ember, 2022).

Investors are twice as likely to invest in renewable energy in developed markets

Total private investment in energy generation projects in 2020, renewables represent 91% in high-income countries and just 45% in middle and low-income countries (Figure 6).

"In 2020, while the value of private investment in non-renewable projects outstripped that in renewables in middle-and low-income countries, the number of renewable projects was 5 times the number of non-renewable projects – indicating a clear appetite for renewables even in emerging markets. It is again notable, however, that in high-income countries, this figure was almost 20 times higher" (Global Infrastructure Hub, 2022).

The growing gap between clean energy investment in advanced economies and those in developing nations is further highlighted in Figure 7.

Figure 6: Private investment in renewables and non-renewables by income group 2012-2020

% of total private investment in energy generation projects, 3-year moving average

Source: Global Infrastructure Hub, 2022.

"...the relative weakness of clean energy investment across much of the developing world is one of the most worrying trends revealed by our analysis" (International Energy Agency, 2022).

"Much more needs to be done to bridge the gap between emerging and developing economies' one-fifth share of global clean energy investment, and their two-thirds share of the global population. ……If clean energy investment does not rapidly pick up in emerging and developing economies, the world will face a major dividing line in efforts to address climate change and reach other sustainable development goals" (ibid).

Debt and the climate crisis

Countries in the global south spent US$372bn on servicing debt in 2020 alone but extreme climatic events have increased indebtness (Jubilee Debt Campaign (2018 and 2021).

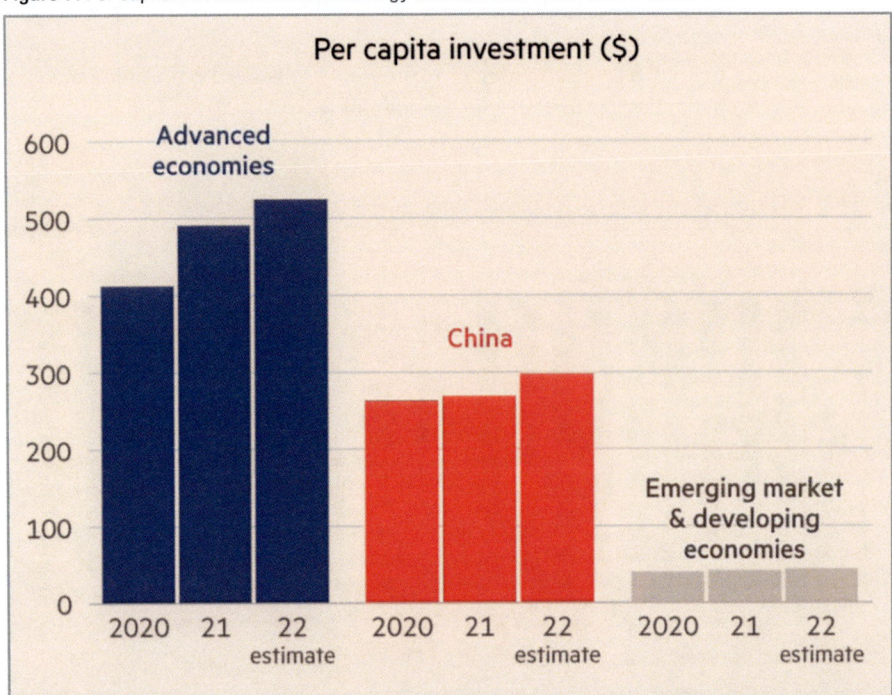

Figure 7: Per capita investment in clean energy concentrated in advanced economies

Sources: IEA – 2021 prices. Financial Times, Williams & Campbell.

In several empirical studies that were replicated by the IMF and others, we showed that physical climate vulnerability is driving up the cost of capital of climate-vulnerable developing countries. As financial markets increasingly price climate risks, and global warming accelerates, the risk premia of these countries, which are already high, are likely to increase further. There is a danger that vulnerable developing countries will enter a vicious circle in which greater climate vulnerability raises the cost of debt and diminishes the fiscal space for investment in climate resilience (Volz, 2022).

"*Climate vulnerability has already raised the average cost of debt in a sample of developing countries by 117 basis points. For every ten dollars paid in interest by developing countries, an additional dollar is spent due to climate vulnerability.*"

"*Countries that have not contributed to climate change effectively end up paying twice: For the physical damage their economies face & through higher costs of capital. 40 Members of the Climate Vulnerable Forum have paid US$40 billion in additional interest payments over the past 10 years on government debt alone. We estimate the additional interest payments attributable to climate vulnerability to increase to between US$146 – US$168 billion over the next decade*" (Volz, 2022).

A strategy for debt relief for a green and inclusive recovery was developed by a consortia of the Centre for Sustainable Finance (University of London), Global

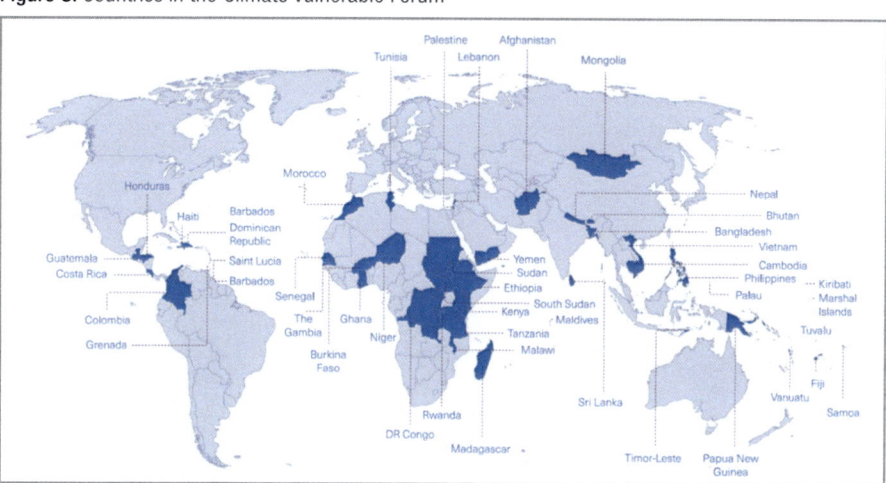

Figure 8: Countries in the Climate Vulnerable Forum

Sources: Climate Vulnerable Forum, 2022.

Development Policy Center (Boston University) and the Heinrich Boll Stiftung (Volz et al, 2021). It requires a revised Debt Sustainability Analysis accounting for climate risks and investment needs in resilience and the achievement of Agenda 2030 indicates need for debt restructuring. A debtor government develops a Green and Inclusive Recovery Strategy with public, transparent consultations with stakeholders, including national parliaments and civil society, academia, bilateral and private creditors, IMF, World Bank, Multilateral Development Banks, and UN agencies. The government revises the Green and Inclusive Recovery Strategy and agreement on Debt Relief for Green and Inclusive Recovery between debtor government and steering committee. This is followed by a five stage process:

> "1. New Green and Inclusive Recovery Bonds with credit enhancement are swapped with a significant haircut for old debt held by private creditors; commensurate debt relief from bilateral creditors; debt relief by multilateral institutions only for International Development Association-eligible countries.
> 2. Guarantee Facility for Green and Inclusive Recovery managed by the World Bank secures Green and Inclusive Recovery Bonds.
> 3. Countries implement Green and Inclusive Recovery Strategy.
> 4. A portion of the restructured repayments are channelled into a Fund for Green and Inclusive Recovery (or an already existing national fund that could be used for this purpose) that is used by the government for investment in Sustainable Development Goals and Paris-aligned spending.
> 5. Ongoing monitoring, reporting, and verification to assert that the policy commitments are being implemented and that money from the Fund for Green and Inclusive Recovery is spent by the debtor government according to its Green and Inclusive Recovery Strategy" (Volz et al, 2021).

It is vitally important that a debt relief strategy is implemented as a matter of urgency.

CHAPTER 5

Tax havens and market interventions

Tax avoidance is widespread in renewable energy

The use of tax havens to shift profits to low tax countries as a means of avoiding or reducing taxation is common in renewable energy companies. It not only means a loss of tax revenue for countries with renewable energy projects, but also increases corporate secrecy and reduces democratic accountability.

The extent to which renewable energy assets are owned or financed through tax havens is summarised in Table 9. The ESSU Global Renewable Energy Secondary Market Database identifies 43 companies registered in tax havens engaged in 264 transactions that acquired renewable energy assets and 47 that sold assets. The 310 transactions account for 19.1% of the database transactions. This is likely to be an under-estimate because it has not been possible to undertake a detailed analysis of every transaction and company corporate structures. If a parent or subsidiary company is registered in a tax haven, this does not always imply that all its transactions are undertaken via a tax haven.

The tax havens most frequently used by renewable energy companies disclosed in the ESSU database are Luxembourg, Jersey, Guernsey, Bermuda and the Cayman Islands which rank 6th, 8th, 17th, 2nd and 3rd respectively in the Tax Justice Network's Corporate Tax Haven Index 2021.

The OECD/G20 is taking measures to reduce tax avoidance globally with 141 countries signed up to the 'base erosion and profit shifting (BEPS)' initiative and include the tax havens referenced in the ESSU database and Table 9.

Tax Justice Network rankings
1. British Virgin Islands
2. Cayman Islands
3. Bermuda
4. Netherlands
5. Switzerland
6. Luxembourg
7. Hong Kong
8. Jersey
9. Singapore
10. United Arab Emirates

Source: Tax Justice Network Corporate Tax Haven Index 2021

Corporate tax rates in tax havens

Companies that are regarded as resident in Jersey for tax purposes will be subject to the current corporate income tax rate of 0%. Dividends on ordinary shares, together with the sale of ordinary shares, are tax exempt. Stamp duty is not levied on the issue or transfer of ordinary shares (except in the case of death), nor does Jersey levy taxes on capital, inheritances, capital gains or gifts. Companies registered in **Guernsey** are also exempt from paying taxes on income, profit and capital gains. Under EU regulations SICAF-SIF is a limited liability investment company with variable share capital that is exempt from paying income and/or capital gains taxes in **Luxembourg**. A company is, however, liable to annual subscription tax of 0.05% of its net asset value computed and payable quarterly.

Bermuda imposes no taxes on profits, income, dividends, or capital gains, has no limit on the accumulation of profit, and has no requirement to distribute dividends. Corporate income, capital gains, payroll, or other direct taxes are not imposed on corporations registered in the **Cayman Islands**. The **British Virgin Islands** has no corporate tax, capital gains tax, wealth tax, or any other tax applicable to a British Virgin Islands company (Table 9). These companies are exempted from income taxes and stamp duties regarding all instruments or deeds relating to company business, including the transfer of all property to or by the company and its securities transactions.

Table 9: Use of tax havens in renewable energy transactions

Major Companies	Sell	Buy
Luxembourg		
Actis LLP (ultimate parent in Guernsey)	2	5
Aquila Capital	3	17
Antin Infrastructure Partners		3
B Capital Partners Lux SICAV_SIF	3	4
Beaufort Investments s.a.r.l.	1	
China Three Gorges (Europe) Co. Ltd.		3
Chorus Infrastructure Fund SA		1
Conquest Asset Management		1
Credit Suisse Energy Infrastructure Ptners		2
DIF Management Luxembourg S.a.r.l.	5	12
Ellomay Luxembourg Holdings	2	1

Table 9: Use of tax havens in renewable energy transactions (continued...)

Major Companies	Sell	Buy
Luxembourg (continued...)		
Envavis AG (Encavis Infrastructure S.a.r.l	4	30
European Solar Energy		2
FP Lux Investments S.A. SICAV-SIF		5
Fontavis Forte Hydro S.a.r.l.	1	
In Control SA	1	
Foresight Energy Infrastructure Partners		13
LongWing Energy France SA	1	
Luxcara GmbH		7
Marguerite Pantheon SCSp	3	2
Meridiam Infrastructure		3
Mirova SA	1	3
NovEnergia Holding Co.	1	
Onex Renewables S.a.r.l.		1
Prime Capital AG	1	2
SUSI Partners (adviser Sustainable S.a.r.l)		13
Jersey		
Altor Fund V		1
3i infrastructure fund		2
Quinbrook Infrastructure Partners (Jersey)		3
Guernsey		
Bluefield Solar Income Fund		4
Equitix (Tetragon Financial Group)		6
NextEnergy		12
The Renewables Infrastructure Group		12
International Public Partnerships		1
Foresight Energy Infrastructure Partners		1

Table 9: Use of tax havens in renewable energy transactions (continued...)

Major Companies	Sell	Buy
Bermuda		
Brookfield Renewable Partners LP	7	21
CGN New Energy Holdings Co. Ltd	1	3
Cayman Islands		
Capital Dynamics Clean Energy & Infra LP	2	16
Ventient Energy Ltd. ultimate parent is IIF Holding LP, JP Morgan Asset Management		5
Sonnedix Power Holdings (Luxembourg 7, Bermuda 1)	1	39
Xinyi Energy (BVI) Limited (Xinyi Solar)		1
Zheneng Jinjiang Environment Holding Company Ltd		1
Total	47	264

Sources: ESSU Global Renewable Energy Secondary Market Transactions Database, 2019-2021 and The International Consortium of Investigative Journalists Offshore Leaks Database.

Multiple use of tax havens

Some companies operate by being registered in more than one tax haven. For example, National Grid plc operates the National Grid in England and Wales and Eastern states in the USA and has subsidiaries registered in Netherlands, Luxembourg, Hong Kong, Jersey, Republic of Ireland and Isle of Man, which are ranked 4th, 6th, 7th, 8th, 11th and 20th in the Tax Justice Network Corporate Tax Haven Index 2021.

Global dimensions

It is important to understand the international links to tax havens and the ultimate ownership of companies. Three examples, Ventient Energy, Sonnedix Power Holdings and Brookfield Renewable Partners LP illustrate these issues.

Ventient Energy operates 135 onshore wind farms in six European countries with installed capacity of 2.6 GW and signed a purchase agreement for an additional 443 MW in Spain in late 2021. The company was launched in November 2017 by merging the Zephyr and Infinis wind assets in the UK.

It now operates from three tax havens. A new holding company, Ventient Energy UK Holdco Limited, acquired 100% of the share capital of Ventient Energy in 2019 and has an immediate parent company, Mobius Renewables Midco registered in Jersey. Ventient Energy S.a.r.l. is registered in a second tax haven, Luxembourg, for the consolidation of financial statements.

A third tax haven hosts the ultimate parent company:

'IIF International Holding LP, is an entity 100% owned by institutional investors and so there is no ultimate controlling party. IIF International Holding LP is a Cayman Islands exempted limited partnership advised by JP Morgan Investment Management, a registered investment advisor regulated by the US Securities Exchange Commission and which is wholly owned subsidiary of JP Morgan Chase & Co."
(Ventient Energy Holdco Limited, Annual Report 2020).

Sonnedix Power Holdings has a global platform of renewable energy projects with 6.6 GW installed capacity, 359 MW under construction and a 4.4 GW development pipeline in Europe, Chile, Japan, South Africa and USA. Sonnedix UK Holdings Limited's immediate parent is Sonnedix BV registered in the Netherlands with the ultimate parent company registered in Bermuda.

Sonnedix was acquired by institutional investors advised by J.P Morgan in September 2016 and had global investment of €4.5 billion by 2020. The Company's shareholders are IIF Solar Investment Ltd and Solar Global Holdings Ltd. The ultimate parent company is IFF Holding LP, a Cayman Islands fund for institutional investors advised by J.P. Morgan Asset Management.

Brookfield Renewable Partners LP has 45,900MW operational assets and development pipeline in the USA; 20,800MW in Europe, 12,800MW in South America and 10,400MW in Asia Pacific. It operates hydroelectric, wind, solar and storage facilities in North America, South America, Europe and Asia. Brookfield Renewables sold 7 assets and acquired 20 in the 2019-2021 period (Table 13). Brookfield is a global, diversified company with a high level of liquidity (US$3.4bn in August 2020) which enables finance opportunities as they arise including use of asset recycling. The US$598m investment and commitment to increase its shareholding in TransAlta Corporation, a major hydro-electric operator in Alberta, is an example.

Brookfield Renewables is registered in Bermuda together with the infrastructure, property and business services companies that are part of the Canadian based Brookfield Asset Management with US$690bn of assets under management.

Special Purpose Companies

A large proportion of measured foreign direct investment can be flows going in and out of a country on their way to a final destination via Special Purpose Entities

(SPEs). Every renewable energy or PPP project has a 'special purpose company' and frequently a holding company.

> "SPEs are legal entities set up to obtain specific advantages from a host economy, in which they have little to no employment, physical presence, or production. They are usually set up to benefit from low taxes but can be established for other reasons such as easier access to capital markets, financial services, and skilled workforces. Because they have little to no impact on the economy, these financial flows can distort the true picture of economic activity provided by foreign direct investment numbers. Directly measuring flows from SPEs helps resolve this" (IMF, 2022).

A new IMF database for the first time measures cross-border flows and positions of SPEs resident in 26 participating economies, based upon an international definition. Foreign direct investment positions channelled through resident SPEs are remarkably high, in Luxembourg they are 45 times the size of its economy, it's 30 times in Mauritius, and 28 times in Bermuda (IMF, 2022).

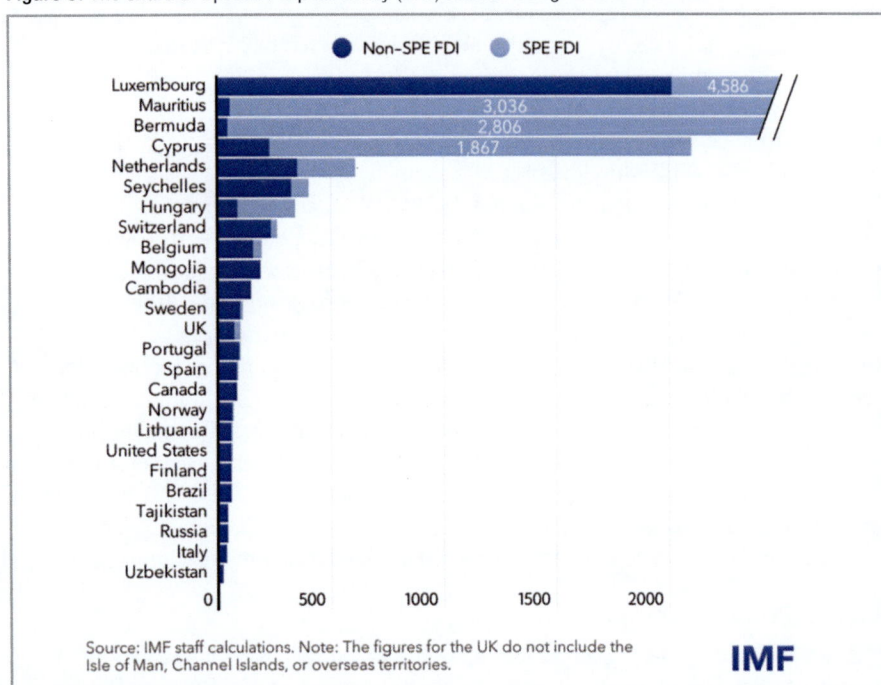

Figure 9: The share of Special Purpose Entity (SPE) related foreign direct investment

Source: IMF staff calculations. Note: The figures for the UK do not include the Isle of Man, Channel Islands, or overseas territories.

Lost taxation

Offshoring has been common in PFI/PPP projects – for example the five largest listed offshore PPP infrastructure funds made a total profit of £1,828.3m in the five-year period 2011-2015. They paid a total of £11.1m taxes or a tax rate of 0.61%, but when £19.4m of tax credits was included, they paid ZERO tax for five years. This was a loss of an estimated £400m in UK tax revenue had these companies been registered in the UK (Whitfield, 2016).

It is very difficult to determine the level of tax losses from renewable energy companies located in tax havens for several reasons. Firstly, financial information for companies registered in tax havens is very difficult and time consuming. Secondly, company accounts usually cover a range of activities and transactions making identification of renewable energy transactions difficult to separate and quantify from other activities. Thirdly, it is difficult to determine if some or all renewable energy transactions in a company are processed through a tax haven.

Five companies listed in Table 11 are also listed in Table 9 and paid US$3.1bn dividends between 2019-2022. In other words, these companies were profitable and would be liable to taxation if they were registered onshore. Therefore, the 41 companies in Table 11 represent a loss in government tax revenue of several billion US dollars over the 2019-2021 period.

Share offer in tax haven for renewable energy company

Azure Power Global Limited is a major renewal energy company with over 7GW of solar projects in India and listed on the New York Stock Exchange. It decided to raise US$250m capital by an equity share issue and published a prospectus on 10 December 2021. It subsequently sought subscribers for 15.8m shares at $15.79 per share. By the end of the share offer on 24 January 2022 12.4m shares (78.4% of the offer) had been subscribed. Azure required capital to fund projects and to repay a $100m credit facility with HSBC bank which had a maturity date of 2 February 2022 (Azure Power Prospectus, 2021). HSBC was a joint Deal Manager for the share offer.

The remaining 3.4m shares were purchased under the Backstop Commitment Agreement at the share offer price by CDPQ Infrastructures Asia Pte. Ltd (2.05m shares) and OMERS Infrastructure Asia Holdings Pte. Ltd. (1.37m shares). Although both pension funds acquired additional Azure shares they paid a premium of US$2.18 per share or a total of US$7.4m because the shares were trading at US$13.16 on the New York Stock Exchange at the time of the transaction (Azure Power Stock Information, 27 January 2022).

Caisse de dépôt et placement du Québec (CDPQ) and Ontario Municipal Employees' Retirement System (OMERS) are two of the largest Canadian public pension funds. On 23 December 2021 they respectively held 50.2% and 19.3% of

Azure's share capital. CDPQ acquired its stake in three transactions in 2018, 2019 and 2020, whereas OMERS acquired its stake in July 2020.

> "We have chosen to pursue a rights offering because holders of Equity Shares have pre-emptive rights under the laws of Mauritius, and the rights offering gives existing holders of Equity Shares the opportunity to participate on a pro rata basis and, if all holders of equity exercise their rights, avoid or limit dilution of their ownership interests in the Company." (Azure Prospectus, page 3).

Mauritius is a leading corporate tax haven ranked 14th on the Tax Justice Network's Corporate Tax Haven Index (Cobham, 2019). Although it is a small player in global terms.

> "...its policies are very aggressively focused on undermining corporate taxation in other countries by attracting profit shifting" (Ibid).

It is also one of the most secretive jurisdictions globally.
> "The island, which sells itself as a 'gateway' for corporations to the developing world, has two main selling points: bargain-basement tax rates and, crucially, a battery of 'tax treaties' with 46 mostly poorer countries. Pushed by Western financial institutions in the 1990s, the treaties have proved a boon for Western corporations, their legal and financial advisers, and Mauritius itself — and a disaster for most of the countries that are its treaty partners" (International Consortium of Investigative Journalists, 2019).

Hedge fund interventions

Elliott Management is always looking for opportunities to buy shares in a company to gain a seat on the board and then propose to break the company up by selling key assets. It is ruthless, aggressive and arrogant in acting in its own interests by combining the practices of hedge and private equity funds. Its track record in the Argentina 15 year debt dispute netted $2.4bn "..a 392 percent return on the original value of the bonds" it acquired (Kolhatkar, 2018). Elliott earlier bought defaulted debt in the Congo Republic and Peru and then sued the government to pay the full face value of the bonds.

Elliott targeted three energy companies in 2019-2021 – EDP (Portugal), Duke Energy Corporation (USA) and SSE (UK and Ireland). Elliott opposed China Three Gorges (Europe) SA bid to take control of EPD in May 2018. Elliott's letter to the EDP board stated

> "EDP's ability to pursue growth opportunities has been considerably restricted, depriving the Company and its shareholders from accelerating investment in high return opportunities available in EDP's core markets." (Elliott Management, 2019).

Elliott proposed the sale of EDP Brazil and the sale of a 49% stake in EDP's Iberian Electricity Distribution – the same tactics that would financially benefit Elliott Management but not improve public services or public values.

Elliott proposed that Duke Energy be split into three separate regional companies 'to maximise shareholder value'. The Letter to the Duke Board claims 'Near-Term Valuation Upside' on the assumption that the regional companies will have a combined value of $90bn - $93bn which exceeds Duke's equity market capitalisation of $78bn (Elliott Management, 2021). The focus is entirely on creating shareholder value and is bereft of power generation to meet the needs of residents, businesses and the public sector.

Elliott Management proposed that SSE separate or sell its renewables, another focus on shareholder value and nothing relevant to improving and extending renewable energy. It rejected the break-up option in late 2021 (Thomas, 2021). Elliott targeted Taylor Wimpey, Britain's third largest home builder in later 2021 by building a share stake and with another scathing attack on the company's performance and demanding a new chief executive from outside of the organisation.

The Communications Workers of America and the Strategic Organizing Center Investment Group, a coalition of four unions representing over four million members, recently produced a detailed impact assessment of the performance of Elliott Management Funds and the impact on companies they have targeted. Their findings include:

"Consistent with research on activist hedge funds broadly, we find that while Elliott's interventions produce a short-term improvement in some performance measures, over the three-year period following intervention, Elliott's portfolio companies' total market return relative to risk, revenue, earnings, leverage, debt coverage, and return on assets underperform an objectively identified set of control companies.

Because Elliott's targets are widely held, Elliott's limited partners bear this negative, long-term impact on their own public equity portfolios. Since most pension funds allocate more assets to public equity than hedge funds, the negative long-term effect Elliott and other activist hedge funds have on public companies may dwarf any benefit pension funds receive as a limited partner.

Also consistent with established research, increased bond yields (and falling bond prices) at companies following an Elliott intervention further indicate that public market investors bear costs from Elliott's intervention that rival or exceed the benefit they may enjoy as an Elliott limited partner, if they are also invested in the bonds." (CWA and SOC Investment Group, 2021).

Everwood's financial dealings

Everwood Capital (Spain) was founded by two former bankers at Goldman Sachs, Merrill Lynch, Morgan Stanley, UBS and at consultants McKinsey&Co. In September 2019 Everwood sold three portfolios with 21 solar plants (25 MW) in Spain to Reden Solar, owned by two French-based private equity funds Infravia Capital Partners and Eurazeo. The sale process was handled by accountants Price Waterhouse Coopers (PwC) and the international lawyers Garrigues.

The three portfolios were financed by three Everwood investment funds which "...*achieved annual returns for the owners of the capital managed by Everwood Capital of between 17.8% (Fund I), 18.6% (Fund II) and 33.1% (Fund III) net IRR after the success fee. Fundamentally, high net worth individuals managed by Andbank, the investor that has bet the strongest on this renewables project.*" Furthermore, the "...*funds have recovered between 155% and 170% of their investment in less than three years. In addition, Everwood Capital had already returned 66% and 44%, respectively, of their investment in Funds I and II prior to the sale*" (Everwood Blog, 12 September 2019).

Two weeks later another Spanish renewable company, Univergy, sold two solar projects (50MW and 25MW) at the development stage to Everwood.

"*Everwood Capital sold these portfolios to Infravia and Euraeo for over 150 million euros. This led to Andbank clients, the entity committed to the project and which placed this investment for its clients, obtaining returns of up to 33% per annum, after managers success fees*" (Everwood Blog, 27 September, 2019).

Everwood Capital later sold 100% of the Desafio Solar plant (50 MW) in Escatron, Zaragoza, to the Italian firm Falck Renewables S.p.A. in March, 2021. The deal involved a payment of €22m plus Falck "...*taking over the outstanding project financing*" and the deal was completed less than a month later on 20 April 2021 (Falck Renewables, 2021). Everwood reported sources in the sector stating a total cost of €43m.

"*This represents a new returns milestone, which Everwood Capital places at more than 50% in two years. In other words, it achieved an annual IRR greater than 25%. ..Everwood Capital once again enriches its clients, mainly private banking investors from Andbank and Santander....the profit of this operation will be invested in other plants and the capital gains will be distributed among the private banking investors of the fund*" (Everwood, 2021).

In December 2021 the European Investment Fund (part of the European Investment Bank) closed an investment commitment of €50m to the Everwood

Renewables Europe V FCR fund to invest, construct and operate new solar assets in southern Europe (European Investment Fund, 2021).

Given that Everwood already had four funds which had successfully raised capital and had obtained large returns on solar project transactions, they were hardly in need of €50m from the European Investment Fund!

Civil fines for Global Infrastructure Partners

Global Infrastructure Management were required to pay a US$4.5m fine by the Securities and Exchange Commission (SEC) in December 2021 which related to deficiencies and violations in three Global Infrastructure Partners funds. GIF owns ACS Renewables, Clearway Energy, Eolian and Borkum Riffgrund 2 offshore wind. They also had to voluntarily repay US$5.4m to private fund clients affected by the deficiencies (Compliance Week, 2021). The SEC found two cases where Global had overcharged investors in two funds for advisory services. Between December 2009 and March 2019 investors in Fund 1 were charged $12.4m in fees but the fund only owned 41.9% of the portfolio company. In the other fund director fees should have been credited 100% against fund-level management fees but this was miscalculated (Securities & Exchange Commission, 2021).

Tax haven deal-making

Ventient Energy became one of Europe's largest renewable energy companies following a series of deals beginning in 2017 when Terra Firma Capital Partners private equity fund sold the Infinis Group's 20 operational UK onshore wind farms (409MW) to institutional investors advised by JP Morgan Asset Management (J.P. Morgan Chase & Co).

A month later Infracapital Partners LP sold its 33.3% stake in Zephyr Investment's 17 wind farms to institutional investors advised by J.P. Morgan. Ten years earlier Infracapital and 'an investment entity' advised by J.P. Morgan had jointly bought the 50% share stake in Zephyr from Arcapital Bank, a Bahrain based investment bank.

Ventient Energy was launched in November 2017 by merging the Zephyr and Infinis assets to create the UK's third largest wind renewable energy company, again advised by J.P. Morgan.

The following year Ventient Energy succeeded in two large acquisitions. Firstly, Vortex Energy (EFG Hermes, Egypt) launched the sale of its 49% stake in a 998MW portfolio of 56 wind farms in Spain, France, Portugal and Belgium to institutional investors in late 2018 advised by J.P. Morgan. The €800m sale to Ventient Energy was completed in late March 2019. The next month EDP Renewables (Portugal) decided to sell its 51% stake in the same 56 assets to Ventient Energy advised by J.P. Morgan. Ventient completed the acquisition of Iberwind (Portugal) from CK Infrastructure Holdings Limited (Hong Kong) in October 2020 adding 31 wind farms and 730MW.

Ventient Energy Limited has its headquarters in Edinburgh but it is a subsidiary of Ventient Energy Sarl, Luxembourg, and as I noted above, is ultimately owned by IIF in the Cayman Islands. In effect, Ventient is J.P Morgan's European wind energy platform.

Sonnedix Power Holdings shareholders include IIF Solar Investment Ltd and Solar Global Holdings Ltd. The ultimate parent company is the same IFF Holding LP, a fund for institutional investors advised by J.P. Morgan Asset Management. Sonnedix operates through over 500 subsidiaries (with 100% ownership in the vast majority) in 16 countries including mainly France, Italy, Spain and USA and 41 in British Virgin Islands, 7 in Luxembourg and 1 in Bermuda.

The Sonnedix Board of Directors includes a Managing Director and an Investment Principal for the Infrastructure Investment Group at J.P, Morgan. Sonnedix arranged a €202m shareholder loan from IIF in 2019 as an advance on equity which was converted to contributed share capital and share premium on 1st January 2020 (Sonnedix Power Holdings Limited Annual Report, 2019).

The JP Morgan Chase bank is the biggest global lender to fossil fuel companies and was fighting four shareholder petitions related to climate change in early 2022 (Financial Times, 2022e).

Scotland and Norway wind farm ownership comparison

Thirty-nine of **Scotland**'s largest 50 wind farms are ultimately owned outside Scotland in England, Spain, France, Germany, Norway, China and elsewhere. At least 16 of the 50 wind farms have owners *"…with verifiable links to the Cayman Islands and Luxembourg, as well as to the islands of Guernsey and Jersey"* (The Ferret, 2021).

Another investigation revealed that five companies that part-own the transmission cables from 24 offshore wind farms have links to Luxembourg, Guernsey, Jersey or the Cayman Islands (The Ferret, 2022). The transmission contracts worth £7.7bn were awarded by Ofgem, the UK energy regulator following an auction under the Offshore Transmission Owner regulations.

This is clear evidence that wind farms and transmission lines are awarded by government agencies in full knowledge that a significant percentage of successful bidders are registered in tax havens.

In **Norway** 40% (16) of wind turbines in operation in 2021 were owned or financed through a tax haven. 61.7% of wind power was in foreign ownership with 32.9% publicly owned (Tax Justice Norway, 2021). Foreign ownership can increase the risk of profit shifting which results in less income for the host economy.

"One of the most common methods of profit shifting in a group. It involves placing a lot of debt in a company in the group structure that is registered in countries with higher tax rates, as in Norway. The interest rates give this company higher costs, which in turn reduces tax profit. Interest income often goes to a company in a

country with little or no tax in interest income. This way, the group's total tax bill can be minimised" (ibid).

The average equity ratio for Norwegian companies across all sectors was 47.2%, about the same as debt, but in the renewable energy sample the equity ratio was on average 60.8%, ie companies have on average more equity than debt. The equity ratio for companies wholly owned overseas was 32% compared to the 78% for wholly owned Norwegian companies.

The Tax Justice Norway investigation revealed that foreign-owned renewable energy plants had higher financial costs as a share of operating revenues compared to Norwegian-owned plants.

"These costs are naturally higher with higher debt ......But with debt-based profit shifting, one would also expect to see the use of higher interest rates than elsewhere in the market, and thus the costs can be higher even with the corresponding size of debt".

"The wind turbines in the sample had on average annual financial costs in the order of 3.1% of their debt. But here too there are big differences between the Norwegian-owned companies and the foreign ones. The average for the Norwegian-owned was 2.5%, while for the wholly or partly foreign-owned the financial costs were 3.6% of the debt amount (a difference of as much as 42%)".

"Another and related indicator of the risk of profit shifting is how much of the companies' operating revenues go to financial costs ie primary costs of servicing interest on debt....The trend line shows that the foreign-owned power plants have higher financial costs as a share of operating revenues, compared with the Norwegian-owned ones. For six wind power companies, where we can connect ownership or financing to tax havens, the average was even higher, with annual financial costs of 4.8% of the debt amount (a difference of 88% from those Norwegian-owned wind power companies)" (Ibid).

As we saw above, the UK's five largest listed offshore PPP infrastructure funds made a total profit of £1,828.3m in the five-year period 2011-2015. They paid a total of £11.1m taxes or a tax rate of 0.61%, but when £19.4m of tax credits is included, they paid no tax for five years. This represented a potential loss of an estimated £400m in UK tax revenue had these companies been registered in the UK (Whitfield, 2016). Four of the companies - HICL, 3i infrastructure, John Laing and INPP - had investments in renewable energy whilst BBIG was focused on social infrastructure.

Although the focus is on the use of tax havens for secondary market transactions it must be remembered that tax havens may also be used for primary market transactions for new wind farms, solar plants, hydroelectric projects battery storage, energy from waste, transmission line and grid projects.

Negative impact of tax havens

- Secrecy imposed on company activity, performance and financial investments.
- Lack of democratic accountability
- Profit shifting as explained in the Norwegian example above.
- Participation of community organisations and trade unions in corporate strategies and plans is usually non-existent.
- Local economy issues are marginalised.
- Evidence of progress to reduce inequalities and improve social justice are difficult to verify.
- Increased focus on financial returns within renewable energy companies.
- Loss of national tax revenue in the countries in which companies operate and thus have lower level of public expenditure.
- The financial benefits of tax haven status are exclusive to investors and shareholders and are rarely, if ever, shared by service users and the workforce.
- Makes a mockery of Environment, Social and Governance claims.

The ESSU Global Renewable Energy Secondary Market Database 2019-2021 reveals gaps in disclosing the project MW or MWp, the sale price and the name of the company selling or acquiring renewable energy assets. This reflects 'commercial confidentiality' induced by market forces and tax haven status.

Increased regulations

Bids in procurement processes or auctions should confirm that the company and its subsidiaries are not registered in a tax haven, nor should the company have a holding company in a tax haven, nor engage advisory, financial, accounting or technical support from a company or consultancy registered in a tax haven..

Renewable energy companies should publicly express support for the OECD's initiative against the role of tax havens.

CHAPTER 6
Public ownership and public values

Electricity is critical for people living their lives, communications, leisure, public services, industry, business, entertainment and welfare states. This section examines the critical role of nation states in providing capital investment via regional agencies and via export/import credit finance. It identifies the current state of public ownership of renewable energy companies and assesses the current obsession with Environment, Social and Governance (ESG) issues and the fundamental shortcomings in this approach. There is an alternative focus on 'global public goods' which is an important principle although often vague in practice. The section concludes with a core public values framework as a way forward to specifying more clearly what should be valued in investment strategies.

Community renewable energy is focused on the residential sector with little mention that the energy needs of health and social care, schools, universities, public transport, social and welfare services and the benefits systems also rely on a sustainable and secure provision of power. Businesses (industry/factories, offices, banks, retail, hotels, leisure and entertainment) and other workplaces are equally dependent on access to electricity.

Scale of public ownership

Governments and public authorities are involved in renewable energy policy making, auctions of project sites, approving planning applications, subsidies and guarantees intended to attract private investment in renewable energy. The World Bank, the International Finance Corporation, regional development banks and overseas aid agencies provide direct finance or loans to similarly attract private investment in the global south. This investment model is a repeat of the corporate welfare role which became common in other sectors over the last 40 years. The roots of the renewable energy market lie in the privatisation of utility and fossil fuel companies in many countries in the last forty years culminating, for example, in the UK, with the sale of the UK's Green Investment Bank to Macquarie Group in 2017.

As Table 10 shows the degree of state ownership varies enormously. Statkraft (Norway), Vattenfall (Sweden), China Three Gorges Corporation and Masdar (UAE) are 100% state-owned companies (Table A3). In addition there are six companies in which the state has between 96.10% and 50.10% ownership followed by those with a minority stake. Currently the French and Italian governments have minority stakes of 23.64% and 23.58% in Engie and ENEL respectively. Institutional shareholders own 86% of RWE (26% based in Germany). China Three Gorges owns 21.55% of EDP (Portugal) with BlackRock private equity holding 5% with the latter holding similar stakes of 7.13%, 7%, 5.16% and 3.51% of SSE, RWE, EDP and Engie respectively (2019/2020 data). The Qatar Investment Authority owns 8.69% and 2.27% of Iberdrola and EDP respectively (Table A4).

The total global installed renewable energy capacity in 2021 was 2,838.8GW. Wind accounted for (743GW), solar (760GW), hydropower (1,170GW), bio-power (145GW), geothermal (14.1GW), concentrating solar thermal power (6.2GW) and ocean power (0.5GW) (REN21, Global Status Report, 2021).

Table 10: Global public sector renewable energy assets

Company	Projects	MW
Statkraft (Norway)	412	17,815
Vattenfall (Sweden)	121	16,878
China Three Gorges Corp.	32	1,431
CGN Energy (China)	47	2,039
CGN Europe	23	2,653
CGN Brazil	8	1,182
Masdar, Mubadala Investment Co. (UAE)	33	2,681
EnBW Energie Baden Wurttemberg AG	134	4,400
Electricity Suppl Board (Republic of Ireland)	4	639
EDF (France)	386	16,889
Hidroelectrica (Romanian)	187	6,422
CEZ group (Czech Republic)	73	3,124
Equinor ASA (Norway)	7	553
Orsted (Denmark)	21	13,000
Partial public ownership		
ENI (Italy - 30.33 public)	23	345
Engie (France – 23.64% public)	160	8,463
ENEL (Italy – 23.6% public)	n/a	11,814
Total		
	1,671	98,514

Sources: Company Annual Reports and websites 2021. Excludes projects at development stage.

Publicly-owned companies buy and sell renewable energy assets

The twelve major publicly-owned renewable energy organisations/companies, plus three major companies that have a minority public shareholding, own 1,671 projects with 98,514MW operational capacity or 3.47% of the global total (Table 10).

Further analysis of the ESSU Global Renewable Energy Database 2019-2021 is provided in three tables available on the ESSU website. Table B1 identifies 79 transactions in which 37.9GW was acquired by public sector companies. However, Table B2 lists 41 transactions in which 24.6GW were sold by the public sector to private companies resulting in a net gain of only 13.3GW for the public sector. Table B3 identifies 20 transactions and 9.27GW which involved the sale of assets between public sector companies with no overall gain.

The impact of these transactions is summarised in Table 11. Public sector acquisitions increased their share by 37.9GW or 1.33% but the sale of assets to the private sector led to a reduction of 24.6GW or -0.87%. The net impact was a gain of 13.3GW or +0.46%.

I noted above that public sector companies owned 3.47% of the global GW which increased by +0.46% to 3.93%, as a result of the transactions in Tables B1 and B2. Thus, the public sector owned 4% of global renewable energy GW in December 2021.

The funding renewable energy projects by public investment banks, infrastructure funds, foreign aid and export/import credit agencies (see Chapter 2) has not been quantified on a global scale and should be added to the public sector data.

Municipally-owned renewable energy projects are understated in the list of publicly-owned energy companies (Table 10). Four municipal acquisitions in the

Table 11: Public sector acquisition and sale of renewable energy assets 2019 - 2021

Renewable energy asset	Number of countries	Number of public sector transactions	Total GW in transactions	% Impact GW
Global renewable energy			2,838	
Acquisitions by public authorities	21	79	+37.9	1.33
Sale of assets by public authorities	13	41	-24.6	-0.87
Sale of assets between public authorities	10	20	9.3	0.0
Net impact		+38	+13.3	+0.46

Source: ESSU Global Renewable Energy Secondary Market Database, 2022. MW not provided in 18 transactions.

ESSU secondary market database 2019-2021 (2,259 MW) and about twenty energy examples in the Transnational Institute re-municipalisation database will only have a marginal impact on the 3.93% figure since many were transactions to acquire distribution networks rather than power generation projects.

The dominance of the corporate sector in renewable energy is evident, so claims that the public sector has a significantly larger role in owning and operating renewable energy projects are false and distort reality. For example:

> *"the overwhelming majority of renewable energy has been developed by public sector or non-profit organisations, not by private companies [...]. Moving to public ownership therefore makes it easier to develop renewable energy systems, rather than using public money to offer financial 'incentives' for private companies to choose investments in renewables sold through a dysfunctional market system."* (Sweeney and Treat, 2017)

Remunicipalisation of energy

Three studies of remunicipalisation have identified the scale, constraints and advantages of the remunicipalisation of public services, particularly energy. Busshardt's (2014) study of remunicipalisation in OECD countries concluded *"The desire to utilise the electricity grids and the public utility as a means of producing renewable energy, thus combating climate change and supporting the energy transformation in Germany, was especially outstanding."* It identified Hamburg, Berlin, Tübingen, Münsterland, Schönau and Umkirch as particularly representative.

Wagner and Berlo (2015) identified 72 new municipal power authorities between 2005-2013 in nine clusters in the west of Germany.

> *"Municipal power utilities are usually not just the local grid operator. They are characterised by a commercial involvement along the entire value chain and have as their main activity generation, transmission, distribution, trading and supply of energy"* (ibid).

The power utilities were part of the one hundred and fifty-two new local Stadtwerke established in Germany between 2005-2016 (Wagner et al, 2021).

The Stadtwerke (municipal utilities) are majority owned by one or more municipalities and had four goals and had to demonstrate public value to individual citizens, the local and regional economies:

1. *"Democratisation of energy supply with a stronger focus on public value than traditional energy companies;*

2. *achievement of environmental goals and implementation of the Energiewende at a local level;*
3. *establishment and/or improvement in the local supply chain and the support of local market partners;*
4. *increased awareness among the local community of the requirement for social responsibility in the provision of energy"* (ibid).

However, the municipal utilities have been opposed by:
"…the triopoly of E.On, RWE and EnBW dominates the distribution grid business for power and gas", unfair competition, legal challenges and "obstructive behaviour" (Berlo, Templin and Wagner, 2016).

The Traill, Cumbers and Gray (2021) study of European municipal energy transition reported:

"Ninety-two per cent of municipalities (88 out of 96) are involved in producing their own renewable forms of energy. However, the precise data supplied on renewable energy in the survey by individual cities is quite erratic".

Most municipal authorities were involved in solar power (83.4%), biomass (52.5%) and hydro (40%). The authors were forthright in concluding:

"Getting a clear picture of the extent of action taken at a municipal level across Europe is itself a difficult task. Accurate, up to date and extensive macro-level data (both quantitative and qualitative) on actions being taken, on implementation, and on outcomes towards transitioning to low or zero carbon energy solutions are not readily available. Many documents are written with the purpose of encouragement, demonstrating possibilities and trajectories through focusing on the successes of key municipalities" (ibid).

The ESSU Global Secondary Market Database 2019-2021 includes five transactions involving Stadtwerke in München (acquired a 132MW wind farm), Tübingen (three solar plants, 13.3MW) Hamburg (district heating system and energy from waste) in Germany and the Vienna Stadtwerke Group (Austria) which acquired a 367MW wind farm.

The Hamburg projects were acquired from Vattenfall (Sweden) whilst three projects were acquired from German renewable energy companies. This is positive evidence that the vast majority of municipal authorities in Germany are developing and retaining their renewable energy assets.

Public goods

The growing discussion of global public goods is important. This section identifies the key attributes of public goods and demonstrates the connection with Core Public Values Framework discussed below.

Public goods have several key attributes:

1. Non-rival (consumption by one user does not reduce the supply available to others).
2. Non-excludable (users cannot be excluded from using public goods) and use by one individual does not reduce the amount available to be consumed by other individuals.
3. It is not possible to charge for their consumption, for example street lighting, except where they require a production process (electricity) where minimum charges should be cost-based and equitable.
4. They derive from social, environmental, climatic, health and economic needs and seek to eliminate or minimise collective public risks.
5. Some public goods, such as health care treatment and childhood education, require early intervention.
6. They originate through collective choice (voting) and are funded through taxation.
7. They should be publicly owned and operated (private delivery often has profound implications for service users because reduced quality of service is common and frontline workers are confronted by wage cuts and significant reductions in other terms and conditions compared to public sector employment).
8. Public goods should be provided to meet collective needs, rights, standards, equality and social justice, not to realise surplus revenue or profit.

Natural goods: Air, water and land are natural goods; air is a natural good; clean air is a public good as is biodiversity. Land is a natural good; national parks are public goods. (Public goods are created to protect and preserve natural goods).

Global public goods: Three dimensions cover countries in more than one region: they benefit a broad spectrum of countries and a broad spectrum of the global population; and meet the needs of present generations without jeopardising those of future generations (Kaul et al, 1999 and Anand, 2004).

Public infrastructure: The transport, utility and communications networks, facilities, buildings and equipment required to sustain and improve the economy and quality of life. Public works refers to the maintenance and improvement of a city's public buildings, highways and drainage systems. It can include maintaining traffic lights, street cleaning, waste collection and disposal, and utilities.

There is increasing recognition that an economistic definition of public goods is flawed (Orchard and Stretton,1994, Deneulin and Townsend, 2006).

"Orthodox economic theory, and Samuelson's 1954 definition ignore the reality that public goods derive from social as well as economic forces. In reality, public goods originate through collective choice (voting) and are funded by collective payment (taxes). Government produces them because the market does not or because a society decides that all citizens should have access to them regardless of ability to pay because their social or economic benefits are so important" (Sekera, 2014).

The recognition and identification of public goods is important together with the concept of 'basic public services' but the debate is frequently general and circular. We need to make clear how we define and value the criteria that constitute a public good to provide a working framework so that public goods can be operationalised. In effect to move on from limited 'feelgood' rhetoric to provide a framework by which public goods can be assessed and valued for what they provide and how they are delivered.

Public service principles

The following principles should underpin all the functions and services provided by the public sector.

1. Universal public provision and delivery and funded through progressive taxation and public investment.
2. Committed to gender, racial, economic, social and environmental equality and social justice.
3. Early intervention and prevention.
4. Integrated, responsive and flexible local public services that meet economic, social and community needs and strive to increase innovation and effectiveness.
5. Sustainable development that takes account of global, national and local economic and environmental standards and impacts, and conserves natural resources and minimises waste.
6. A clean energy economy with emission reduction objectives and successes, prioritises renewable energy and a comprehensive adaption programme to retrofit homes and public buildings.
7. Rigorous economic and social cost benefit analysis together with economic, social, health, equality and environmental impact assessment.

8. Quality employment with good terms and conditions, pensions, equalities and diversity, training, workforce development, the right to organise and an industrial relations framework.
9. Continuous monitoring and democratic scrutiny with implementation of lessons learnt.
10. Democratic accountability, participation and transparency with citizen/user/employee participation in the planning, design and delivery processes supported by freedom of Information (Whitfield, 2019).

Core public values framework

The framework (Figure 10) has been developed from research, analysis and impact assessments for a wide range of public policies and alternative proposals with community, trade union, regional and local authorities, health and social care organisations in the UK and many other countries. It has often involved detailed involvement with service users and frontline workers assessing current policies and service provision, research and developing plans and strategies for their improvement and the implementation of radical changes

The Core Public Values Framework is based on five key pillars - quality, effectiveness, equality, efficiency and sustainability – that are essential in providing public infrastructure and services to meet social, economic and environmental needs and human rights. Not only are the five pillars inter-dependent but they are also dependent on inputs, working methods, impacts and outcomes, outputs and monitoring and evaluation. For example, quality is not only dependent on inputs but also working methods, impacts and outcomes, outputs and on monitoring and evaluation (Figure 10).

The five pillars in turn rely on public service innovation and improvement plans that engage service users and employees in developing local service delivery plans which rely on public policy legislation and rights, regulation and standards, public funding, employment, training and industrial relations together with strategic planning and investment.

Six key policy functions of national, regional and local government are:

- Public ownership and integrated in-house provision
- Equality, social and environmental justice
- Climate targets/retrofits environmental protection, nature and biodiversity
- Economic policies, sustainable development and tackling inequalities
- Welfare state, early intervention, anti-poverty and promote wellbeing
- Public management, economic and social cost benefit analysis

These functions are implemented in local and regional economies which generate economic activity, supply chains, repair and maintenance of equipment and buildings together with the improvement and renewal of infrastructure. These activities generate direct, indirect and induced employment.

They are shaped by democratic governance, accountability, participation and scrutiny at the base of the pillars. Equally, they have responsibility for the achievement of public value. The vertical and horizontal connections within the framework are critically important.

These connections are crucially important because each has a direct impact on the implementation process and the achievement of public values. The framework exposes the limitations of the myopic neoliberal obsession with outcomes which lead to the marginalisation of inputs, working methods and outputs and other important public values and standards (Whitfield, 2019).

The framework includes many important issues that are essential preconditions:

1. How service users and potential users are respected and opportunities to express their views about policies and practices and have opportunities to participate in the planning and design of services and infrastructure.
2. How the workforce is respected, has good terms and conditions and opportunities to participate in the planning and design of services and infrastructure.
3. Equality rights, policies and impacts are an essential core value in all elements of the framework inclusive of human, labour, economic, environmental, ecological rights and social justice.
4. Monitoring, review and scrutiny of services and functions must be continuous, rigorous and transparent otherwise it will not be accountable nor will intelligence be shared and lessons be learnt to make them more effective in future.

The selection of a singular element such as 'outcomes' or 'efficiency' must be avoided because this will produce a very narrow perspective and exclude other important elements that have a key role in the planning, design, delivery, monitoring and evaluation of public services and infrastructure. The objective is to produce a holistic and integrated approach which will significantly improve the quality of public management and the planning, design and delivery of public services.

The history of public services reveals a direct relationship between the quality of employment and the quality of service. Staffing levels, training and skills have a direct impact on the quality of care and patient outcomes. Increasing the skills of staff is associated with more effective services. Job satisfaction has a significant impact on service quality and organisational effectiveness.

The following methods can be used individually or in combination to assess the effectiveness and impact of the elements of the public service core values framework or the framework as a whole.

- Community and workforce participation in service planning
- Comprehensive and rigorous social, economic, health, and environmental impact assessments
- Equality and social justice audits
- Economic, social and environmental cost benefit analysis
- Capability reviews and skills needs assessments
- Monitoring and performance reviews, scrutiny and oversight

All of the above are critical to ensure public sector organisations delivering renewable energy have continuing capabilities to implement and review the Public Service Core Values Framework.

Figure 10: Public sector core values framework

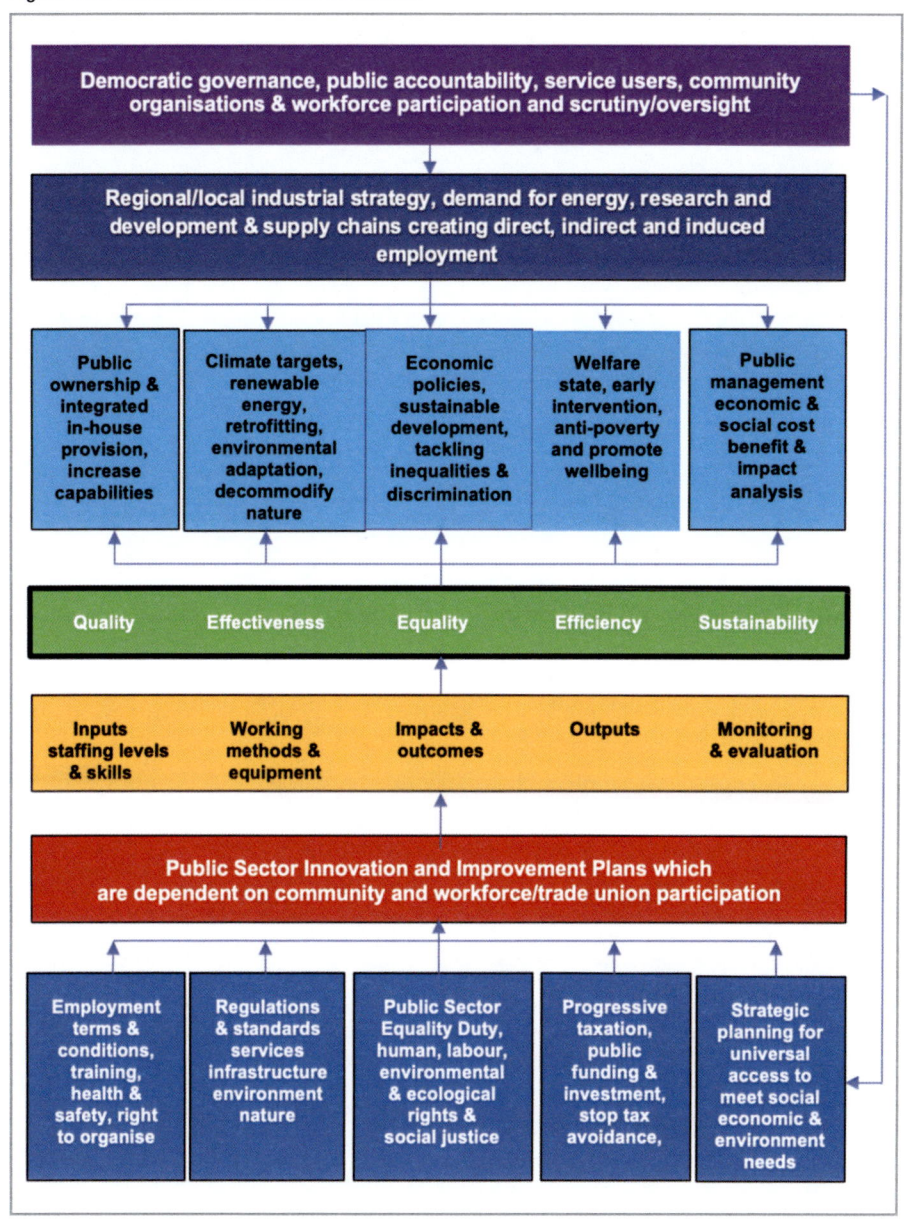

```
┌─────────────────────────────────────────────────────────────────────────┐
│ Democratic governance, public accountability, service users, community  │
│ organisations & workforce participation and scrutiny/oversight          │
└─────────────────────────────────────────────────────────────────────────┘
                                    ↓
┌─────────────────────────────────────────────────────────────────────────┐
│ Regional/local industrial strategy, demand for energy, research and     │
│ development & supply chains creating direct, indirect and induced       │
│ employment                                                              │
└─────────────────────────────────────────────────────────────────────────┘
```

| Public ownership & integrated in-house provision, increase capabilities | Climate targets, renewable energy, retrofitting, environmental adaptation, decommodify nature | Economic policies, sustainable development, tackling inequalities & discrimination | Welfare state, early intervention, anti-poverty and promote wellbeing | Public management economic & social cost benefit & impact analysis |

| Quality | Effectiveness | Equality | Efficiency | Sustainability |

| Inputs staffing levels & skills | Working methods & equipment | Impacts & outcomes | Outputs | Monitoring & evaluation |

Public Sector Innovation and Improvement Plans which are dependent on community and workforce/trade union participation

| Employment terms & conditions, training, health & safety, right to organise | Regulations & standards services infrastructure environment nature | Public Sector Equality Duty, human, labour, environmental & ecological rights & social justice | Progressive taxation, public funding & investment, stop tax avoidance, | Strategic planning for universal access to meet social economic & environment needs |

Source: Whitfield (2022).

Challenging the rise of Corporate Power in Renewable Energy

CHAPTER 7

The commodification and marketisation of nature and biodiversity

The ownership and provision of renewable energy by the private sector is a product of neoliberalism, specifically financialisation, marketisation and private provision. This has ensured that public ownership and provision has been marginalised.

The privatisation of nature and biodiversity is accelerating as governments adopt the United Nations Environment Programme 'The Economics of Ecosystems and Biodiversity' (TEEB, 2010) the mantra for commodifying and marketising 'ecosystem services'.

This is fuelled by global estimates of the annual financial value of 'ecosystem services' which run into trillions of dollars, pounds, euros or other currencies. For example, goods and services in the 'traditional economy' have been estimated to value US$90 trillion compared to goods and services in 'nature's economy' valued at US$125 trillion (Intrinsic Exchange Group, 2022).

Sullivan (2014) discussed the use of the term 'natural capital' as a category embodying all of 'external nature' within the disciplines of environmental and ecological economics and the tendency to conceive of nature as a 'bank of (natural) capital' as business and financial interests are involved in 'green' policy debates.

"Increasingly, it seems, 'nature' is actually money. The contemporary moment of global crisis in both ecological and economic spheres is thus also the moment wherein 'nature' is being consolidated, metaphorically and literally, as 'natural capital'"(Sullivan, 2014).

Flawed economics of biodiversity

Predictably, the UK Conservative Government commissioned a study of the economics of biodiversity from Sir Partha Dasgupta supported by a government appointed Advisory Panel which consisted of "...a select elite including financiers, bankers and professors" (Spash and Hache, 2021).

"In fact, there is nothing new in The Review's orthodox economic 'solution' for loss of biodiversity, namely, putting a price tag on Nature so that businessmen and financiers can recognize its existence in their accounts, capture its value and profit from trading. Neither is there anything new about an economist claiming he can direct environmental policy by correctly pricing Nature to optimize resource management. However, Dasgupta does not stop there.

Human health, education and population are also to be monetized and treated like man-made capital. Together three forms of capital – natural, human and produced – are taken to represent the 'inclusive wealth' of humanity. In this way, all social, ecological and economic aspects are equated, allowing their aggregation and integration into national accounting systems. Conflicting objectives and interests are assumed commensurable via reduction to monetary equivalents that support financial wealth accumulation

While pricing, trading-off and optimizing are traditional economic fare, the political vision here involves a far-reaching public policy agenda, promoting the total domination of non-financial aspects of life by finance" (ibid).

Furthermore, the concept of 'natural capital' and 'eco-system services' would require large scale marketisation which would dwarf the outsourcing of public services. Advocates clearly chose to ignore the poor performance and decline in quality in outsourced health, social care, education, public transport and many other public services, the exploitation of labour and the high public cost of procurement and managing contracts in the last four decades (Whitfield, 2020a).

Despite wide opposition to the commercialisation of nature and biodiversity, most governments and many NGOs, public authorities and the media largely appear to have accepted the concept simply because it is in tune with neoliberal ideology. They falsely and dangerously conclude that the commodification and monetisation of nature and biodiversity is inevitable.

Wall Street's planned takeover of nature

Shortly before the COP 2021 conference, the New York Stock Exchange (NYSE), the Intrinsic Exchange Group (IEG) and the Rockefeller Foundation announced they were:

"…jointly developing a new asset class of publicly traded assets called Natural Asset Companies….that hold the rights to ecosystem services produced by natural, working of hybrid lands" (The Rockefeller Foundation, 2021).

IEG's investors include the Inter-American Development Bank, Aberdare Ventures (private equity fund) and the Rockefeller Foundation. Selected Partners include World Wildlife Fund, Birdlife International, Amazon Conservation and Conservation International. They claim that Natural Asset Companies (NACs) will be a new form of corporation which will enable:

"…the conversion of natural assets into financial capital" (IEG). The IEG began *"… seeking regulatory approval to bring the first natural asset transactions to the capital*

markets. Our vision is to bring to market hundreds of Natural Asset Companies representing several trillion dollars' worth of natural Assets" (IEG, 2021).

"...the NAC is merely the issuer while the potential buyers of the natural asset the NAC represents can include institutional investors, private investors, individuals and institutions, corporations, sovereign wealth funds and multilateral development banks" (Webb, 2021).

The IEG is focused on 'Natural Areas' and is proposing:
"...a transformational solution whereby natural ecosystems are not simply costs to manage, but rather an investible productive asset which provides financial capital and a source of wealth for governments and its citizens" (IEG, 2021).

It claims to be working with the Costs Rica government to explore the creation of a Natural Asset Company. 'Working Areas' (converting agriculture to restorative practices) and 'Hybrid Areas' (comprising natural, working and built environments) are equally vague (Intrinsic Exchange Group, 2022). The implications are far reaching:

"Thus, NACs open up a new feeding ground for predatory Wall Street banks and financial institutions that will allow them to not just dominate the human economy, but the entire natural world. In the world currently being constructed by these and related entities, where even freedom is being re-framed not as a right but "a service," the natural processes on which life depends are similarly being re-framed as assets, which will have owners. Those "owners" will ultimately have the right, in this system, to dictate who gets access to clean water, to clean air, to nature itself and at what cost" (Webb, 2021).

Monetizing public land

Management consultants McKinsey & Company are claiming that public land could 'unlock private investment' for green infrastructure. Current publicly financed incentives to attract private investment include grants, loans, equity and credit guarantees. Others include tax concessions, subsidised utilities or regulatory concessions. Fiscal pressures may restrict the use of these incentives. "There is a fifth incentive policy makers often under-utilise: land portfolios" (McKinsey 2022).

"As things stand, many governments have large portfolios of untapped real-estate assets that can be monetized as equity or through leasing at preferential cost" (ibid). They suggest land could be *"government's equity contribution to a project, leased at a discount to the private sector or land given as a grant to the private sector"* (ibid).

Same old story – give away public assets to encourage private investment when public investment will be cheaper, more effective, and democratically accountable and more likely to meet public objectives and public values.

Decommodification of nature

The elimination of market forces and outsourcing from nature and biodiversity and so-called ecosystem services is essential. Therefore, the TEEB programme should be abolished by the United Nations Environment Programme and by all the governments which blindly adopted the TEEB proposals. Decommodification MUST include:

- Dismantling of all initiatives to promote 'natural capital' and 'ecosystem services';
- Removal of competition and procurement process for 'ecosystem services' and all other forms of commercialisation such as outsourcing existing services;
- Ensuring user charges should be minimised and relate to actual costs;
- Reviewing the role and performance of arms-length companies and trading organisations to consider potential benefits of transfer to in-house provision;
- Adopting a policy of in-house provision;
- Preparing service innovation and improvement plan for each group of services;
- Abolishing commissioning and integrate purchaser and provider functions;
- Intensifying monitoring and review of existing contracts;
- Preparing the case and justification for terminating contracts.

CHAPTER 8

Equalities - economic, social and environmental justice

The climate crisis takes different forms and impacts as outlined in Chapter 1. To achieve an equitable transition to renewable energies and permanently phase out all fossil fuel assets will result in differential impacts that will potentially deepen existing inequalities and create new ones.

A comprehensive approach essential

This chapter outlines the equalities, rights and forms of environmental, economic, social, labour, democratic and public service justice that must be safeguarded and radically improved in the transition. The following aspects of equality will be central to overseeing investment and delivery of renewable energy projects.

Environmental justice must ensure that class/geographic differential treatment is avoided in the allocation of funding and/or prioritisation of projects for coastal/river erosion; housing and business premises retrofitting; and in decisions regarding relocation from flood plains and/or levels of compensation or valuation of assets written off in relocation or demolition. It also includes access to clean water and sanitation, a pollution-free environment and the protection of nature and biodiversity.

Climate justice and renewable energy should be inclusive of a series of rights of access to heating and cooling and broadband/telecommunications at an affordable cost.

Social justice requires that a Public Sector Equality Duty assess the impact of public policies and plans on nine equality groups - namely between persons of different religious belief, political opinion, racial group, age, marital status or sexual orientation; men and women; persons with a disability and persons without; and persons with dependants and persons without. Impacts must be assessed and demonstrate how negative impacts can be eliminated or mitigated.

Democratic accountability and the right to participation in planning, regeneration and public policy making process including strategic and local plans and in the design and delivery of public services, right of access to public services and achievement of public values. It includes disclosure of the performance of public services and participation (including giving evidence) in scrutiny/oversight.

Economic rights include the right to develop alternative proposals for the use of factories, plants or depots that are closed during the transition process up to and beyond 2050; to have access to national, regional and/or local economic development support and finance; and to have proposals fully evaluated and subjected to the full democratic due process.

Labour rights include equality of access to training and jobs, equitable terms and conditions of employment, the right to organise and to have industrial relations negotiating machinery.

New Zealand's National Adaptation Plan

New Zealand launched a draft National Adaptation Plan in early 2022 to tackle the forecast impacts of climate change such as rising sea levels, extreme weather, drought, projected changes in north-easterly airflows which will change rainfall patterns, and the risk of wildfires (New Zealand Ministry for the Environment, 2022). The Plan sets out a series of critical actions such as reform of the resource management system; pass legislation to support managed retreat; reform of institutional arrangements for water services; modernise the emergency management system and review of the future of local government.

In addition, the plan included supporting actions such as: establishing a foundation to work with Maori on climate actions; set national direction on natural hazard risk management and climate adaptation through the National Planning Framework; implement the National Disaster Resilience Strategy; develop the emergency management workforce; and establish central government oversight and coordination for implementing the National Adaptation Plan.

New Zealand's first National Adaptation Plan - 'Adapt and thrive: Building climate-resilient New Zealand' was produced by the Ministry for the Environment in 2022. This section draws on their approach and scope.

> *"Some New Zealanders are more vulnerable than others*
> *Māori as tangata whenua are particularly sensitive to climate impacts on the natural environment for social, economic, cultural and spiritual reasons. Many Maori depend on primary industries for their livelihoods. In some places, climate change may alter patterns of use of mahinga kai (food gathering sites) or rongoā crops (medicinal plants) and coastal impacts could disrupt access to marae or wāhi tapu.*
>
> *Different groups experience extreme events and disaster responses differently. Older people may be more reluctant to evacuate their homes, because of income and accessibility and/or mobility issues, and may suffer from the loss of cultural and*

social networks. Ethnic minorities are more vulnerable in disaster responses due to language and integration barriers.

If communities need to shift, low-income groups have less choice about where to relocate and are less able to move elsewhere. Mobility-compromised and disabled people have specific needs that can be overlooked in the planning of new community locations and accessible housing.

Some groups feel the psychological and physical impacts of climate change more than others. Young people and children are more prone to psychological impacts from extreme events, while women are more vulnerable to domestic and sexual violence, which can increase in times of disaster. The mental health of members of farming and rural communities can be affected by the disruptions to livelihoods and of social cohesion.

Those with poorer health outcomes, such as Māori and Pacific people, children and older people, may also physically suffer more from increased heat and disease.

New Zealanders are already experiencing the impacts of climate change. As these impacts increase, there is a risk that existing vulnerabilities will deepen.

An equitable transition for all New Zealanders is important. To ensure that our transition is equitable, fair and inclusive, we will need to:
* Uphold Te Tiriti o Waitangi, work in partnership with Māori to address climate risk, maximise opportunities and avoid disproportionately affecting Māori or locking in existing inequalities;

- work inclusively with affected groups to understand their needs;
- take opportunities to reduce inequalities and support communities and regions to promote resilience in line with local objectives;
- prioritise support to those most affected and least able to adapt, particularly lower-income households;
- set clear, stable policies that provide predictability for communities and businesses, allowing them time to plan, respond and seize opportunities;
- support workers to adapt by transitioning to quality jobs at lower risk from the effects of climate change;
- ensure adaptation decisions balance the need to avoid abrupt and disruptive changes with the need for early action to address near-term risks, reduce costs over time and avoid an inequitable burden on future generations."
(New Zealand Ministry for the Environment, 2022).

This national comprehensive approach sets an important model that can be drawn on in other countries and adapted for other minorities.

Public Sector Equality Duty

A Public Sector Equality Duty is an important part of an equity framework. A comprehensive framework became law in the Northern Ireland Act 1998 as part of the Good Friday Agreement. Section 75 of the Act requires that a public authority shall, in carrying out its functions relating to Northern Ireland, have due regard for the need to promote equality of opportunity between nine equality groups (Equality Commission for Northern Ireland, 2010). The Northern Ireland legislation is much more comprehensive than the legislation in England, Wales and Scotland in 2010, but was weakened even more by later governments. It included a Public Sector Equality Duty that requires public authorities to:

"...have due regard to the need to eliminate discrimination, advance equality of opportunity and foster good relations between different people when carrying out their activities" (UK Government, 2015).

It is vital that a Public Sector Equality Duty is applicable in all renewable energy projects irrespective of whether they are publicly or privately financed. Furthermore, rigorous impact assessment and socio-economic cost benefit analyses are essential to identify the potential impact of a renewable energy project so that negative impacts can be eliminated or mitigated to significantly reduce their impacts.

The criteria to assess the impact on each equality group should, for example, include size, age and gender of population; socioeconomic factors; urban/rural differences in needs and cost differences; existing utilisation and unmet needs; factors which could lead to the nine groups being affected differentially; the extent to which any groups suffer multiple disadvantage; misallocation of resources within and between budgets.

Economic justice includes employment, economic development, regeneration when comprehensive economic, social, equality and environmental impact assessments and cost/benefit analysis with the same scope should be a requirement for all projects and be subject to public disclosure and participation. The findings and key criteria should be used publicly at the later stage of assessing the implementation process and final review. Similarly workforce monitoring should identify that working practices comply with the original standards. A systematic reduction in inequalities and poverty could be achieved by better planned and integrated public services and infrastructure, with specific objectives and targets to reduce service and employment inequalities. This will require strengthened legislation, regulations, enforcement and best practice guidance, coupled with comprehensive impact assessments and a public service ambition. (See p418-422, Whitfield, 2020a for the scope and application of equality and social/economic impact assessments).

Equality in housing retrofits

The planning and delivery of retrofitting, access to grants, monitoring building work and installation of heat pumps, claims of damage and/or failed installations, arrangements made for tenants/owners with existing health conditions to be protected from building works, and the quality and accountability of contractors raise equality issues.

Local authority, social housing and private tenants will have retrofitting financed and carried out by their landlord. However, it is vital that tenants are involved in the planning and retrofitting processes to ensure equality and quality objectives are sustained. Owner occupiers will be able to access grants but will have to arrange for the work to be carried out.

The UK government set a target for all social housing - local authority (council) housing and Registered Social Landlord housing (including Housing Associations) - to be 'decent' by 2010. The Decent Homes Standard defined a 'decent' home as one that is in a reasonable state of repair and has reasonably modern facilities and services – including a reasonably modern kitchen, bathroom that is appropriately located, adequate insulation against external noise (where this is a problem) and adequate size and layout for public/common spaces and provides a reasonable degree of thermal comfort – with effective heating and insulation.

The Decent Homes Standard was upgraded in 2006 (Department for Communities and Local Government, 2006) but made no mention of climate change, heat pumps, wind or solar energy or retrofitting. A Social Housing White Paper published in November 2020 announced a review of the Decent Homes Standard to understand if it is fit for the social housing sector today.

Private landlords in tax havens

An investigation by 'The Ferret' investigative journalists revealed that 4,000 homes in Glasgow are currently let by overseas landlords with 1,460 linked to landlords registered in the top ten corporate tax havens ranked by the Tax Justice Network (Tibbitt, 2022).

This has major implications for repairs and maintenance with more profound implications in the case of the retrofitting of housing and how this is carried out and the impact on rents, tenants access to charging of electric vehicles, and the landlords potential installation of solar panels and access to them. A clear example of inequality in the Decent Homes standard.

The planning of a programme of works, tenant involvement and the need for coordination of health and social care support in the retrofitting process are vitally important to prevent further inequalitie being created.

Environmental justice in adaptation and protection

Environmental justice must ensure that class/geographic differential treatment is banished in the allocation of funding and/or prioritisation of projects for coastal/river erosion; housing and business premises retrofitting and in decisions regarding relocation from flood plains and/or levels of compensation or valuation of assets written off or demolished.

Decarbonisation and the switch to the production of renewable energy combined with the closure of coal mines, oil and gas extraction and distribution, and the secure stranding of assets is critical to ensuring equitable transition to renewable energy and decarbonisation. The latter will require constant monitoring and a rapid response to any attempts to gain access to stranded assets.

The ESSU Research Report No 11 Equitable Recovery Strategies made a number of recommendations on the managed decline of fossil fuel energy production and jobs, increased renewable energy projects and job creation. It also called for national and local support and public financing of conversion projects together with a Code of Practice for Quality Employment.

The report detailed sources of increased finance and stressed the need for democratic accountability and transparency together with the implementation of equality and environmental justice (Whitfield, 2020b).

Strategic issues for the stranding (leaving coal, oil, gas permanently in the ground) of fossil fuel assets must include national, regional and municipal authorities establishing a monitoring and inspection system to ensure the private sector meets its legislative requirements to finance the closure of fossil fuel assets and is responsible for the continued security of stranded assets and take immediate action to prevent attempts to access the assets. The monitoring of the economic and supply chain impact on local firms plus the environmental and employment impact of the stranding process, and to take action to mitigate any negative effects, should be a priority.

CHAPTER 9
Economic and industrial strategies
Introduction
This chapter explains why it is important to improve national and international grid networks; use area or zonal planning to advance decarbonisation and promote renewable energy; adopt an industrial and manufacturing strategy to successfully implement policies and achieve the required and sustainable infrastructural change that is equally vital. A holistic approach to retrofitting housing, public buildings and business premises is fundamentally important given that they account for 40% of carbon emissions. An equitable transition process is another fundamental requirement.

Continuing the current corporate model in renewable energy to 2050 will further consolidate private ownership of renewable energy generation and distribution among a small number of powerful global companies. Multinational fossil fuel companies could be replaced by green-washed multinational renewable energy companies adopting 'business as usual' practices.

A combined public sector approach is required to enable the expansion of renewable energy to be implemented with an equitable transition from fossil fuels; maximising the economic benefits of an industrial and manufacturing strategy; undertaking the extensive environmental adaptation and protection works required to tackle rising sea levels and flooding resulting from more extreme weather conditions; and reversing the commodification of nature and biodiversity.

Improving national grid networks
Renewable energy projects in many countries face long delays to access national grids. *"The amount of new power generation and energy storage projects in so-called 'interconnection queues' seeking to connect to the grid across the US continues to rise dramatically, with over 1,400 (GW) of total generation and storage capacity now seeking connection to the grid"*
(Lawrence Berkeley National Laboratory, 2022).

Welton (2021) makes the case that
"...it is time to re-evaluate the United States' functionally privatized mode of electricity governance, to make it work for an era in which regulatory priorities are shifting in response to climate change. U.S. electricity law suffers from a gaping and growing accountability gap, in which neither Federal Energy Regulatory Commission nor states have the authority needed to make electricity markets bend to democratically established prerogatives that harm industry incumbents.

He concludes:
"Reforms in this sector must be calculated, swift, and decisive if the United States is to achieve anything close to the clean energy transition demanded by atmospheric physics"

"An expansion of public utility law to new sectors could help to curb the extreme corporate domination of this second Gilded Age. But before embracing this strategy, the modern potential of public utility must first be reclaimed within the electricity sector, which will either embrace the existential challenge of climate change or take us all down with it" (ibid).

The Building a Better Grid Initiative was launched by the US Department of Energy in January 2022 with a $20bn federal funding to strengthen the grid against wildfires, extreme weather and other natural disasters by improving reliability and increasing resilience and reducing power failures (DOE, 2022b). Four months later the Federal Energy Regulatory Commission (FERC) published documents on building for the future through electric regional transmission planning, cost allocation and generator interconnection including proposed rule changes to regional transmission planning (U.S.FERC 2022).

The U.S. Department of Energy launched the Interconnection Innovation e-Xhange (i2X) programme in June 2022 to bring together grid operators, utility companies and renewable developers to connect more clean power generation to the grid, and to reduce the three-year waiting time and connection costs (U.S. Department of Energy, 2022c).

National grids in England, Wales and Scotland, Australia and more recently Greece (49% stake sold to Macquarie Infrastructure) and three US grids, the Eastern, Western and Texas interconnections, are privately owned. The privatised UK National Grid also owns and operates the electricity distribution networks in New York, Massachusetts, New Hampshire, Rhode Island and Vermont (National Grid, 2022). Belgium's grid operator Fluvius, owned by 11 municipalities, is adding 30,000 kilometers of low-voltage grid and 6,000 kilometers of medium-voltage grid over the next decade (Bellini, 2022). Italian grid operator Terna will invest US$10.45bn to improve the transmission grid and build cross border interconnections to increase stability of the network and improve resilience in extreme weather conditions.

"The idea that the performance of an infrastructure system as vital as the National Grid can be treated as a problem of market design, in which private firms operate under the guidance of a technical regulator, is a nonsense. When the system fails, governments will inevitably be held accountable. Under the current system, with no capacity for systematic public management of the grid, the response will inevitably be one of short-term panic" (Quiggin, 2017).

Renewable energy projects in the UK currently face up to a six to ten year delay to gain access to the national grid, plus significant costs. Targets to add 50GW of offshore generation in 2030, 70GW of solar energy by 2035 and 24GW of nuclear energy by 2050 could delay renewable energy projects and/or increase grid connection waiting times (Plimmer, 2022).

Three west London Boroughs, (Ealing, Hillingdon and Hounslow) were informed by the Greater London Authority in July 2022 that

"...major new applicants to the distribution network electricity from the regional grid would not be available to housing developments, commercial premises and industrial activities until up to 2035" (Financial Times, 2022f).

New data centres built in the area had captured existing capacity. However, significant additional demand will arise from the network of charging points for electric vehicles and the switch from gas to electric heating associated with the retrofitting of existing housing (The Economist, 2022c). Demand for power will also be driven by digitalisation and automation in industry and public services; wider installation of air conditioning in homes, workplaces and public transport; and charging of equipment and gadgets.

In Ireland, 8% of wind power could not be used from January to August 2021 due to lack of capacity of the grid. EirGrid is publicly owned and operates independently of the state-owned Electricity Supply Board which incorporates the Electricity Transmission System for Northern Ireland and the East West Interconnector linking electricity grids between Ireland and UK.

"The EirGrid 2030 scenario expects that only an additional 1,300 MW of onshore wind will be connected from today to the end of 2030. In reality 700 MW is already under construction, an additional 1,000 MW with full planning permission is set to compete in the renewable energy auction opening this year and many more projects are in the pipeline" (Wind Energy Ireland, 2021).

Ireland's Climate Action Plan is based on 80% renewable electricity by 2030, which will impose additional demand on EirGrid (EirGrid, 2021). A subsea 700 MW high-voltage Celtic Interconnector is planned between the southern coast of Ireland and the northwestern coast of France. The European funded €530m project is planned to be operational by 2026.

A 1.4GW high voltage cable is planned between Fedderwarden, Germany and the Isle of Grain in south east England, which reached financial closure in July 2022 with completion planned for 2028. The European Investment Bank (EIB) has agreed €400m support for the €2.8bn NeuConnect project, which has a consortium of

Meridiam, Allianz Capital Partners and Kansai Electric Power. Other funders of the 725 kilometre cable include UK Infrastructure Bank and the Japan Bank for International Cooperation (Meridiam, 2022).

South Australia privatised its grid in 2000 with the formation of ElectraNet and separation of the distribution network to SA Power Networks. ElectraNet is now owned by the State Grid Corporation of China (46.6%) and Australian Utilities Pty Ltd (53.4%), which comprises the Utilities Trust of Australia and the Australian Retirement Trust, who acquired an additional 33.5% stake in ElectraNet from YTL Corporation, a Malaysian infrastructure group, in February 2022 for AU$1.03bn.

ElectraNet has formed a joint venture with Transgrid, the privatised New South Wales grid, to build a AU$2.3bn high-voltage interconnector route between the two states with a spur into Victoria. The objective is to improve energy security and accelerate access for renewable energy projects. The project will install over 9,000 kilometres of cabling, build 1,500 transmission towers with 30,000 tons of steel (Carroll, 2022a). New South Wales has over 50 large-scale renewable energy projects of 16GW capacity in the planning system with a AU$1.2bn Transmission Acceleration Facility with new transmission lines over the next decade (Scully, 2022).

Ninety percent of the 311 worldwide examples of re-municipalisation have occurred in Germany, notably:

"Stadtwerke, municipal organisations, now supply half of all electricity to households in Germany and 80% of the distribution networks are now owned and run by regional and municipal public authorities" (Weghmann, 2019).

Strategic challenges facing national grids include:
- Public investment is urgently needed to significantly increase the capacity of national and regional grids to increase accessibility for renewable energy projects.
- Public investment should be tied to gaining an equity stake in privatised grid companies and a step towards public ownership.
- Development of national networks of fast recharging points for electric vehicles located in safe public places.

Renewable energy zones

The preparation of national and local plans is vitally important drawing on different examples. The Republic of Ireland published a *National Retrofit Plan* as part of its Climate Action Plan based on four pillars of driving demand and activity, financing and funding models, supply chain, skills and standards and structures and governance (Department of the Environment, Climate and Communications, 2022). About US$8bn is allocated for residential retrofit between 2022-2030.

***NetZeroCities* Pilot Cities Programme** is a European Union project to create 100 climate-neutral and Smart Cities by 2030 funded by the EU Horizon 2020 Framework Programme.

"The Pilot Cities are expected to test and implement innovative solutions, or groups of solutions, at city or district level over the duration of the pilot project, surfacing explicit lessons learnt from the innovative trajectories, with knowledge, capacity and capabilities developed at city level. A clear set of innovative solutions ready to be implemented, scaled and/or replicated should be identified by the end of the pilot project. This could include new business models, policy initiatives, governance innovation, funding or financing models, and replication or scaling strategies" (NZC Consortium coordinated by EIT Climate-KIC)

Stadtwerke Berlin – the municipal utilities company commenced a programme of installing 300 roof-top solar systems on schools (23MW) and has installed similar systems on other public buildings as part of *'Master Plan Solarcity'* to generate 4.4GW within the city (Berliner Stadtwerke, 2021).

The creation of **Net Zero Economic Zones** could vary between national economy-wide net zero emissions and city scale, industrial parks or local areas, city centres or neighbourhoods. Open spaces, parks and areas of natural significance and biodiversity could also be designated to maximise and demonstrate the benefits of implementing decarbonisation. Net Zero Zones could be established for industrial parks, housing areas, city centres and areas or for schools and colleges and significant parks and open spaces and sports centres.

Eurowind Energy launched a plan for five **Energy Parks** in Denmark where it already has wind and/or solar projects which will be expanded so that each centre has wind, solar, battery storage and hydrogen production.

"These will be major centres where green energy is produced and processed on a very significant scale" (Eurowind Energy, 2022).

The company has agreements with landowners for the use of land in all five centres which will have a total capacity of 2.5GW. The planning process has commenced in Aalborg and Bronderslev.

The United Nations Industrial Development Organisation (UNIDO) programme of **Eco-Industrial Parks** 2012-18 was piloted in 22 parks in 7 countries (Columbia, Peru, Morocco, South Africa, India, Vietnam and China). An analysis of 18 parks with 180 participating companies identified 1,685 resource efficient and cleaner production synergy opportunities with 991 implemented; annual 59,800 metric tonnes CO_2 Greenhouse Gas reduction; 20,939 tonnes per annum solid waste reductions and 1,962,218 cubic meter water savings per annum with overall financial savings of US$7.1m per annum (UNIDO, 2017b).

The Republic of Ireland plans to develop its first dedicated renewable energy business park on Bord na Mona peat production land at junction 3 of the M6 motorway in Westmeath. The land provides access to 400, 220 and 110kV grid network.

The Australian Energy Market Operator (AEMO) identified the scope for *Renewable Energy Zones* (REZ) with good access to transmission capacity and potential zones that required increased transmission capacity (AEMO, 2018). Three years later it identified 35 candidates and 4 Offshore Wind Zones. The REZ concept is based on

> "...high-quality resource areas where clusters of large-scale renewable energy projects can be developed using economies of scale. As coal-fired power stations retire, significant investment in renewable generation will be required, with a resulting need for network expansion to unlock REZs across all National Electricity Market (NEM) regions" (AMEO, 2021).

In 2022 the Illawarra Renewable Energy Zone in New South Wales (NSW) received proposals for 44 projects for 10 wind, 5 solar, 16 energy storage, 4 pumped hydro and 4 hydrogen production and 2 hydrogen electricity generation projects - a total generation of 17GW and investment of AUD$43bn or US$29.4bn. The state-owned Energy Corporation will now evaluate the proposals and consult with industry, local governments and local communities. Applications to other REZs have also been very successful – Hunter Central Coast received 40GW, South West 34GW, New England 34GW and Central West Orana 27GW (Energy Corporation of NSW, 2022).

Sendai City, Japan, conceived the *Green Community Tagonishi* as a Reconstruction Plan for a model eco-town following the 2011 Great East Japan Earthquake. The City is constructing 176 apartments in four medium-rise buildings centered around an inner court, a network of houses connected by pathways and open spaces. The community will have high-voltage grid access, solar power and batteries that utilize both direct current and alternating current, sharing of power sources by multiple homes to maximise energy efficiency. The system will be disaster-resilient to maintain a certain degree of life continuity in the event of a power failure. Asset management of the community will be supported by weather data, monitoring of snowfall, timed snow shoveling at specific locations, the condition of roads and 3D Virtual Reality (Hashimoto et al, 2015).

The Ameresco (USA) partnership with Merthyr Tydfil Council in Wales is an example of an area wide energy conservation approach. The company will work with the Council

"....to provide solutions across the council's 31 sites, including upgrades to the town's aging infrastructure, optimizing the lifespan of the existing equipment, installing nine solar pv systems and 30 LED lighting upgrades, and implementing smart heating and hot water systems" (Ameresco, 2021).

The £1.09m contract is forecast to save the Council £136,000 annually and reduce emissions from buildings by 251 tonnes per year.

Net-Zero Cities

The EU has commenced a NetZero Pilot Cities Programme towards climate neutral European Cities by 2030. It plans to cut emissions from combustion of fossil fuels in buildings by decreasing energy use, improving the fabric of buildings and switching to renewable power. The programme also seeks to promote cleaner and safer transport modes and public transport thus significantly reducing fossil fuel emissions. Cutting emissions from waste, changes in land use and chemical processes in industry, and maximising nature-based solutions are also key objectives (NetZeroCities Guidebook, 2022). One hundred 'mission' cities were announced in 2022 plus 12 in associate countries. The pilot cities will be announced in late February 2023.

The language of 'mission' cities, 'mission' platforms, 'co-creation' and 'world-class' practitioners is the repetition of neoliberal terms. The objective of creating some, if not all, the 'mission' cities to be Net Zero by 2030 has good intentions but is extremely optimistic. Even more so when the current economic forecasts for the next few years are taken into account.

The objective appears to be to spread the initiative and funding as widely as possible but achieving fundamental change in a smaller group of cities which can be transferred, developed and applied more widely is likely to have substantially more impact. **A study of climate planning in 50 US cities revealed significant gaps:**

"Most plans have long-term decarbonization goals, but less than one-third (32%) have detailed benchmarks and reporting - only 54% of plans aim to achieve net-zero emissions by 2050.

Only about one-quarter (28%) of plans include detailed, sector-specific strategies for electricity, buildings, and transportation decarbonization - strategies often are not quantifiable, do not set specific deadlines, or do not evaluate progress over time.

Nearly two-thirds of plans provide some detail on who will lead decarbonization efforts, but few offer extensive detail - lack of accountable, shared ownership contributes to fragmentation and lack of effective communication when addressing concerns across the built environment.

Many cities struggle to pay for decarbonization efforts; only 16% of plans identify detailed funding sources or financing approaches - cities have limited budgets to staff and operate their environmental departments and do not identify or secure additional funding beyond traditional revenue sources such as property taxes.

While almost all decarbonization plans identify equity as a goal, nearly three-quarters lack details on how to achieve it - Yet their plans usually only pay lip service to it; they lack details when building equity into different strategies, embedding equity into metrics and evaluation, and engaging community members." (Brookings Metro, 2022)

Recommendations were very basic and included an assessment of capacity to decarbonise; coordinate local and regional networks; develop a skilled workforce; standardise climate data and measurement; negotiate with infrastructure and economic development stakeholders and to identify funding sources!!

Manufacturing and industry

Decarbonisation has profound implications for manufacturing and industrial processes more broadly. Firstly: the conversion of a wide range of factories, plants and workshops to renewable power. Secondly: the future use of factories and plants that are closed because they are considered 'redundant'. Thirdly: manufacture/production/installation of renewable energy infrastructure such as onshore/offshore wind farms (turbines, towers, blades and transformers) solar parks (PV panels), battery storage and supply chains.

The network of nine Catapult technology and innovation centres in the UK has a critical role in the transformation of manufacturing and industrial processes. The Catapult network is an independent non-profit organisation with over 40 research and innovation centres working with private companies and public sector organisations, alongside over 5,000 academic collaborators. Its High Value Manufacturing Research Centre at Broughton scaled up production of ventilators during the Covid-19 pandemic. The Levenmouth Demonstration Turbine testing facility in Fife (Scotland) attracted over 100 small and medium enterprises for technology development (Catapult Network, 2019).

Other examples of the successful role played by Catapult centres includes the Offshore Renewable Energy centre developed with Durham University which used extensive data from LM Wind Power to undertake fatigue tests on their 88m blades. The bi-axial testing methodology reduced fatigue test duration by nearly 50%. The High Value Manufacturing Centre supported Arriba Technologies to develop a solar-powered heat pump for large buildings which was installed at Addenbrookes Hospital in Cambridge indicating energy efficiency savings of up to 80%. Arriba has since installed heat pumps at two hospitals, a technical college, a leisure centre, a corporate headquarters, a swimming pool and a research park (options included battery storage, refrigerant cooling and dedicated solar system) .

The current rate of electrification in the EU28 industrial sector is estimated to be 30% with significant variation between sectors (Figure 11). Reaching a 40% rate by 2030 would imply c.15% in 2021's total power consumption (Goldman Sachs, 2022). There is clearly a long way to go to achieve the 100% target in most industrial sectors.

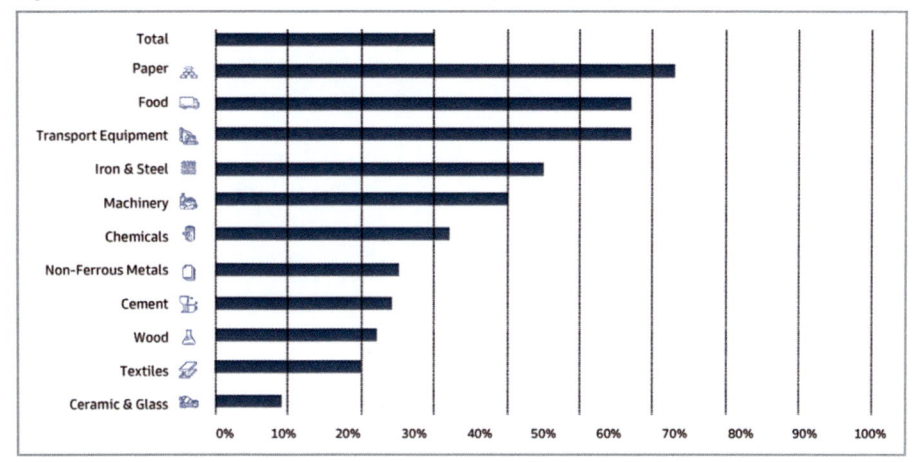

Figure 11: The current rate of electrification in the European industrial sector

Source: Goldman Sachs Global Investment Research, 2022.

The Offshore Renewable Energy Catapult (OREC) established three research hubs - the Wind Blades Research, Electrical Infrastructure Research and Powertrain Research hubs. The latter is a partnership between the OREC and the universities of Sheffield and Warwick to improve reliability, advance condition monitoring and advance the development of next generation turbines.

Catapult's Energy Launchpad undertook a rigorous innovator challenge for small and medium sized companies developing smart heating and cooling systems and selected Ventive, a designer and manufacturer of innovative passive ventilation systems. The company secured a pilot project to trial net zero retrofits in 170 homes by 2022 with Nottingham City Council funded by the Department for Business, Energy and Industrial Strategy (Nottingham City Homes, 2021).

"Ventive is a complete environment management solution, providing balanced ventilation, hot water and comfort by using exhaust air as a source of energy,

combined with a high efficiency heat pump and intelligent connected controls. Actively adapting to each individual home, the system provides outstanding energy performance at a manageable cost" (Ventive, 2022).

Ventive began manufacturing the whole house heat pump and ventilation units in a new manufacturing facility in Worcestershire owned by factory automation company QM Systems starting with 7,500 units and increasing to 100,000 systems by 2025 (H&V News, 2022).

Renewable energy research in Germany

Germany's Fraunhofer-Gesellschaft is an applied research organisation operating through 76 institutes and research units that have made a significant contribution to technological development of solar panels, the development of solar roof systems and developed the world's most effective solar cell with an efficiency of 47.6% in 2022 (Fraunhofer ISE, 2022).

The Fraunhofer Institute for Solar Systems proposed the removal of regulations to permit rooftop solar systems up to 30 kilowatts and an increase in PV home storage systems. At the end of 2021 there were 326,048 battery storage systems (between 5 and 10 kWh) installed in Germany with a third installed in 2021. The Institute worked with three German companies to develop and test a fully automatic device for measuring pollution because operating costs of solar, such as cleaning mirrors and receivers, is increasingly important (Fraunhofer ISE, 2022).

The Institute carried out an analysis of the levelised cost of electricity comparing renewable energy technologies with conventional power plants in Germany in 2021. The costs of renewable energy PV systems and onshore wind are, on average, the lowest cost technology and has reduced dramatically in recent years because of increased efficiency and improvements in materials and system design (Figure 12). It also revealed that offshore wind power plants continue to record a decreasing levelised cost of electricity (Fraunhofer, 2021).

The installation of solar systems is forecast to continue to rise up to and beyond 2100.

*Thus, the **PV market is a great opportunity for the manufacturing industry**. Europe was leading the manufacturing of PV at the beginning of the 21st century and is still leading today in the field of R&D. However, since 2007 China has been much more successful in setting-up PV production capacity since the Chinese government recognised the strategic and political impact which the leadership in a technology with such a gigantic market growth would bring. Chinese companies received strong support while Europe lost its leadership position in PV production. A chance still exists, however, for Europe to play a role in this big future market. **Now is the right time to invest in PV manufacturing in Europe**, especially since* more PV must inevitably be installed in order to fulfil the climate goals agreed upon in Paris. Further cost reduction, new business models and progress in system and battery technologies will lead to more PV installations in Europe (Fraunhofer ISE, 2020).

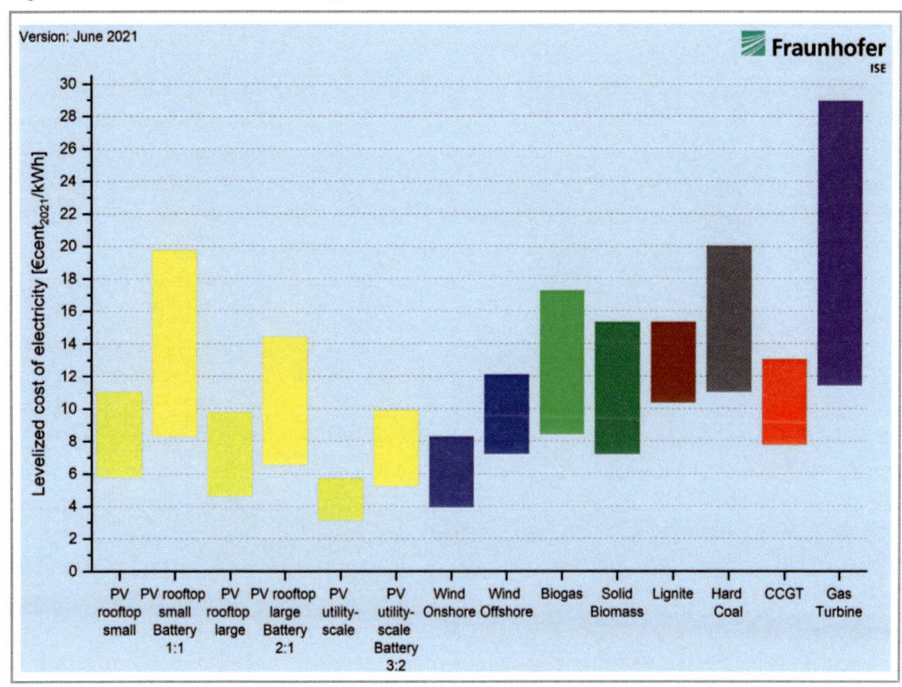

Figure 12: Localised cost of technology

Source: Levelised Cost of Electricity Renewable Energy Technologies, Fraunhofer ISE, 2021.

The European Commission launched the EU Solar Strategy as part of the REPowerEU proposals launched in May 2022. It includes a new EU Solar PV Industry Alliance to achieve 20GW of solar PV manufacturing in Europe in 2025; a Solar Skills Partnership to analyse the skills gap in the solar sector and develop training programmes; a new European Solar Rooftops initiative supported by

> "...a solar mandate on all new public and commercial buildings with useful floor area larger than 250 m² by 2026, on all existing public and commercial buildings with useful floor area larger than 250 m² by 2027, and on all new residential buildings by 2029" (Social Power Europe, 2022).

Manufacture of renewable energy infrastructure

Establishing regional/local supply chains of wind, solar and battery storage equipment, wind pylons, jackets, blades and turbines, solar panels and frames; and the repowering of older wind, solar and battery projects is critical. As are battery production for electric vehicles and application as stand-by power units in case of power cuts in homes, and larger storage units for offices, public buildings, business premises. The development of battery recycling or stringent disposal will be essential.

Several local developments in the UK are in progress. The £300m Teesside offshore wind factory will produce between 100 and 150 monopiles per annum which will be transported to the new South Bank Quay facility and then to the North Sea for installation (Infrastructure Intelligence, 2022). A new £110m offshore wind manufacturing centre is being built at Niggs Energy Park at Cromarty Firth in Ross-shire, Scotland by a joint venture of Global Energy Group and Haizea Wind Group (Spain). It is grant-supported by the UK Government and has financial backing from SSE Renewables (ReNews 2022a). Amite Power is building a Megafactory in Dundee to produce battery cells for energy storage and e-mobility markets which will create 215 high-skilled jobs and 800 more in the supply chain (ReNews, 2022b). The planned government supported Britishvolt electric car battery plant in Blyth, Northumberland, has been stalled for financial reasons (The Guardian, 2022b).

There are many initiatives based on the Factories of the Future, High Performance Centre or Advanced Manufacturing Research Centre concepts. Mitsubishi closed its last Australian car plant at Tonsley, Adelaide in 2008 with the loss of 930 jobs. Tonsley Innovation District now has a Factory of the Future involving the Australian Industrial Transformation Institute (Flinders University), British Aerospace Systems Maritime Australia and funded by the Government of South Australia. It is developing Industry 4.0 technologies, research and training and will provide access to processes and expertise to other companies in the state (AITI, 2021). Belgium has 38 operational Factories of the Future (AGORIA, 2022) and the Fraunhofer Institute has 20 High Performance Centres with research partners in Germany (Fraunhofer, 2022).

The availability of port facilities is critical for the delivery of offshore wind projects, for example the delivery of turbine components and foundations. A study of port facilities in Ireland concluded that Belfast Harbour is the only Irish port with the required capacity. Several ports such as the Port of Cork's Ringaskiddy, Bremore, Cork Dockyard, Moneypoint and Rosslare have development plans which require urgent substantial investment otherwise planned wind farms will have to rely on servicing from UK or European Ports (Wind Energy Ireland, 2022).

Decarbonisation of steel, construction and public transport

Iron and steel production accounts for 7-9% of direct fossil fuel emissions, it has a critical role in the economy in the production of vehicles, the construction of buildings, factories, public transport systems and the sector is expected to have between US$345bn and US$518bn of stranded assets in China, India, Europe, USA and other developed economies (Financial Times, 2022g).

There are 23 trial, pilot and full-scale projects in Europe that inject hydrogen into blast furnaces as a low carbon alternative to coking coal. The plants are operated by the main steel-producing companies such as ArcelorMittal, Thyssenkrupp, TATA, Liberty and H2 Green Steel which plan large scale production commencing in 2025/26. However, as of 2021 there were no plans to use hydrogen to produce primary steel in the UK. A £250m Clean Steel Fund was launched in 2019 to decarbonise steel production but is unlikely to be accessible until 2023 and the government's hydrogen strategy has also been delayed (Energy & Climate Intelligence Unit, 2021).

The International Energy Agency recommended the G7 economies have a responsibility to global industrial decarbonisation by reducing industrial emissions from G7 heavy industry sectors by 25% by 2030 relative to today, compared to 18% for the rest of the world (International Energy Agency, 2022).

Decarbonising construction

Residential and non-residential buildings account for 28% of global energy emissions (direct and indirect) with building construction industry accounting for a further 10%, with other industry 32%, transport 23% and other 7%. The Global Alliance for Buildings and Construction and UN Environment Programme (2021) jointly identified 10 key measures for decarbonising the building sector:

Establish and implement an ambitious energy code for buildings: this includes new and existing buildings and must be performance-based building codes with free-of-cost compliance checks to support implementation of the code.

Support the use of integrated design: Green building standards, certifications and ratings systems establish green and sustainable design standards.

Promote deep energy renovation: activities as leverage to address energy poverty and access to healthy housing for all households.

Lead by example by decarbonizing public buildings: in-depth analysis and audits of exiting buildings and equipment help to define appropriate energy efficiency strategies for individual buildings and building types.

Use energy information and behaviour change to drive energy efficiency; cumulative savings of 7% in average monthly consumption of electricity among 60% of participants.

Promote financing for energy efficiency: demand for cooling is rapidly increasing and the average efficiency of today's cooling systems is low.

Enable easy access to information on the carbon footprint of materials; life cycle assessments underlying carbon calculator tools are critical to understanding the full implications of material choices and vital to decarbonise buildings and infrastructure.

Develop public procurement policies that incentivise materials with low carbon footprints: government leadership in zero-carbon procurement encourages adoption of low-carbon technologies and materials at scale.

Integrate nature-based solutions into urban planning, buildings and construction: adopting a combination of green urban cooling solutions, such as green roofs and street trees at city scale, can reduce outdoor air temperatures by as much as 3ºC.

Develop integrated resilience strategies and plans for the built environment; promotes a holistic view of urban systems, embracing the interconnected and complex nature of cities' spatial configurations, physical assets, socioeconomic functions and organisational structures.

Equally important are projected changes in the global economy, particularly the global material resources outlook to 2060 (OECD, 2019).

"Although global population growth is projected to slowdown, global population is projected to rise to more than 10 billion by 2060. Over the same period, living standards are gradually converging across economies. Thus, emerging and developing economies will grow faster than countries in the OECD region.

Global primary materials use is projected to almost double from 89 gigatonnes (Gt) in 2017 to 167 Gt in 2060. Non-metallic minerals – such as sand, gravel and limestone – represent the largest share of total materials use. These non-metallic minerals are projected to grow from 44 Gt to 86 Gt between 2017 and 2060. Metal use is smaller when measured in weight but is projected to grow more rapidly and metal extraction and processing is associated with large environmental impacts.

Fossil fuel use and the production and use of iron and steel and construction materials lead to large energy-related emissions of greenhouse gases and air pollutants. The volume of concrete use is so large that even relatively low per-kg impacts imply large consequences: concrete production account for 12% of total GHG emissions in 2060, and the production of metals for 12%.

Metals extraction and use have a wide range of environmental consequences, including toxic effects on humans and ecosystems. The overall environmental impacts of extraction and processing of key metals are projected to at least double between 2017 and 2060, mostly driven by the increase in the scale of materials use" (ibid).

Decarbonisation of public bus fleets

Shenzhen (China) was the first and largest city to convert to fully electric bus and taxi fleets in 2018. The city has a population of 12 million and the Shenzhen Bus Group has a fleet of over 6,000 electric buses and since June 2019 has 1,707 fast charging terminals at 104 stations located at bus terminals and depots (World Bank et al, 2021).

A global overview revealed that Denmark, New Zealand and the Netherlands plan to have 100% zero-emission bus fleets by 2025, followed by California (USA) in 2029, Austria in 2032, and Chile, Cape Verde and Columbia in 2035 (Wappelhorst and Rodriguez, 2021). In Australia, New South Wales is committed to 100% zero emissions for their bus fleet by 2030, Queensland by 2032 and all new bus purchases in Victoria will be electric but a fleet target has not been set (Quicke and Parrott, 2022). Many cities have their own targets, such as Mumbai in 2027, Jakarta in 2030 and London in 2034 (Xie and Delgado, 2022). India's state-controlled Convergence Energy Services Ltd is planning a US$10bn order for 50,000 electric public buses (Bloomberg, 2022).

Only a few hundred of the 500,000 school buses in the USA are electric. However, the new Infrastructure Investment and Jobs Act created a US$5bn Clean School Bus Programme with 50% dedicated electric school buses. Some states are planning additional investment, such as California proposing a nearly US$2bn investment. A study by Jobs to Move America reported between 40%-90% savings in fuel and 20%-40% savings on maintenance and expect cost of ownership parity with diesel buses in the next 3-8 years (Elder, 2022).

The US school bus network employs an estimated 409,000 drivers, mechanics and attendants, plus 6,000 employed in manufacturing school buses. Drivers account for threequarters of the workforce and earn a national median of US$34,000-$38,000, well below commercial driver rates, which accounts for school bus fleets being "chronically understaffed" (ibid). Jobs to Move America make a series of recommendations including prioritisation of funding for disadvantaged communities, ensure safe and proper installation of charging infrastructure, promote good jobs and training and domestic manufacturing.

The wide geographic installation of fast-charging facilities in secure locations including the re-use of petrol filling stations and new planning regulations requiring specific level of recharging points in parking garages and high/medium rise apartment buildings should be a priority. Strategic issues for decarbonisation of bus fleets

- The replacement of diesel buses with electric buses should be a priority in all public transport authorities together with the conversion of depots.
- This should be linked to returning privatised bus services into public ownership.
- Private sector coach services for long distance travel, holidays and airport shuttle services.

The further development of hydrogen for commercial vehicles is critically important. The electrification of long-distance trucks, local delivery trucks and vans, private bus operators, mini-buses and taxis is an important part of decarbonisation.

Decarbonisation of Rail

Fourteen hydrogen-powered trains commenced the world's first regular passenger service on 24 August 2022 on a 100 kilometre track in North West Germany (Cuxhaven, Bremerhaven, Bremervoerde to Buxtehude, near Hamburg) replacing diesel trains.

The Coradia iLint emission-free hydrogen fuel cell trains have a range of 1,000 kilometres and can run all day on one tank of hydrogen and have a maximum speed of 140 kilometres per hour (87mph). The trains will save 1.6m litres of diesel fuel and reduce CO_2 emissions by 4,400 tonnes per annum. The trains were designed by Alstom in France and assembled in central Germany and fitted with Cummins (USA) fuel cell systems. The project cost US$92.4m, funded by Germany's National Innovation Programme for Hydrogen and Fuel Cell Technology. A further 27 Coradia iLint will soon be delivered to Frankfurt (Le Monde, 2022 and Matalucci, 2022). In Germany alone *"between 2,500 and 3,000 diesel trains could be replaced by hydrogen models"* - Stefan Schrank, project manager at Alstom.

Birmingham Centre for Railway Research and Education in the UK is working to integrate hydrogen and battery power for the 3,300 diesel passenger rolling stock to meet the 2040 decarbonisation target. Transport Scotland has a 2035 decarbonisation target with a combination of electrification plus alternative traction combined with electrification (Transport Scotland, 2020).

Environmental adaptation and protection

The adaptation and protective environmental works required to prevent flooding and coastal erosion from rising sea levels will require similar planning and production of materials and equipment and organisations to carry out the work. Some relocation to new homes, farms, facilities and business premises may be required together with regulatory changes to ban building on flood plains. Extreme weather events are likely to lead to more frequent power cuts.

Environmental works will be needed to protect coasts and river basins from rising sea levels together with upstream measures to prevent flooding. Carefully planned re-forestation and the integration of agriculture and horticulture is vital to maximise land use and their contribution to preservation of nature and biodiversity.

Building sea walls and river banks will often require heavy equipment and materials, such as green concrete, and materials and rock that are effective and suitable for the specific geology and landscape, including temporary barriers for use in the construction process. Extensive prevention of coastal erosion, flood prevention and tidal energy projects will require the production of electrical heavy equipment for environmental works.

The regulation of forest planting must protect areas of natural significance in the countryside and coastal areas. Where planting is approved it should be with native trees and be linked to conservation and expansion of nature and biodiversity.

In summary, environmental protection and adaptation should include:
- Environmental protection plans prepared with local participation
- Protection of natural landscape and coastal areas
- Flood protection works (rocks, green concrete, heavy equipment)
- Tidal energy projects
- Upland planting of trees

The next section addresses strategic issues for environmental adaptation and protection.

Retrofitting housing, public buildings and business premises

The built environment accounts for 40% of energy related carbon emissions and, therefore, retrofitting existing housing, public buildings and business premises combined with new planning and building regulations, to ensure net zero new buildings have a critical role to play in mitigating climate change. Retrofitting consists of new air or ground source heat pumps and ultra-high level of fabric efficiency, triple glazing, elimination of draughts, wall, floor and roof insulation, passive cooling measures package, water efficiency package of measures plus flood resilience and resistance package of measures. It applies to all types and age of housing and all ownership or tenure models.

To achieve climate targets of reducing global greenhouse emissions by half by 2030 and carbon dioxide emissions to reach net zero by 2050 will be a difficult task given progress to date. The UK building sector will have to:

Reduce the emissions intensity of building use (kgCO2/m2) compared to 2015 levels by 90-95% by 2040 and 95-100% by 2050 (Climate Action Tracker, 2020). *The energy intensity of operations in key countries and regions should decrease by 20–30% in residential buildings and by 10–30% in commercial buildings, relative to 2015 by 2030* (Climate Action Tracker, 2020).

All new buildings should be zero carbon buildings as of now (Climate Action Tracker, 2016, 2020; Kuramochi et al., 2018), which also means no expansion of fossil-fuel infrastructure like gas networks.

Many buildings that exist today will still stand in 2050 or beyond and need to be retrofitted to zero emissions by then at the latest. To reach the emissions and energy intensity goals, 2.5-3.5% of buildings need to be retrofitted every year (Climate Action Tracker, 2022).

New proposals to improve the UK Decent Homes Standard were abandoned by the Conservative government in 2015. A two-part review of the Decent Homes Standard for social housing tenants was launched in 2021. The first part sought 'to understand the case for change to the criteria' with part two examining how 'decent' should be defined due in 2022/23. A Future Homes Standard will come into effect for new homes in 2025!

Limited progress has been made in the installation of heat pumps in UK homes with a mere 54,000 installed in 2021. The government has a target of 600,000 by 2028 with about half this total expected to be in new homes, an easier task than managing the installation of heat pumps in existing homes. The Heat and Buildings strategy requires installation of one million heat pumps annually by 2033 rising to 1.5m per annum to 2048.

A ten-year £3.8bn Social Housing Decarbonisation Fund commenced in 2021 to retrofit the 1.6m of the 4.1m social homes in England that are below Energy Performance Certificate (EPC) Band C (Department for Business, Energy & Industrial Strategy, 2020). The Scottish Housing Quality Standard for social housing had a 37% failure rate in 2017 (Committee on Climate Change, 2019).

In some cases short-term temporary rehousing may be necessary if the process impacts severely on those with pre-existing health conditions and/or the elderly or those who are ill at the time. A coordinated response will be required with social services to maximise use of community centres and transport to day centres. The issue of equalities in housing retrofits was discussed in Chapter 8.

The participation of both tenants and residents will be essential so that there is agreement on the scope of the work to be undertaken, with appropriate action if work is left unfinished or reinstated, or if any damage is caused in the process of retrofitting. Tenants and residents also need to know at the planning stage whether they are responsible for any of the costs. How retrofitting will be carried out is just as important as the contribution it makes to decarbonisation. Coordination of the different works, roles and tasks will be critical.

Retrofitting requires a variety of sizes of triple or double glazed windows, heat pumps for different sized and types of housing, roof and wall insulation and green cement together with trained builders, plumbers and electricians. With the current shortage of construction workers and higher cost of building materials in many countries it is critical that regional production and training is at the core of retrofit strategies.

The idea that a multi-billion retrofitting programme will be delivered successfully and effectively by private contractors is simply not credible given the global evidence of the effects of outsourcing (Whitfield, 2020a, Cohen and Mikaelian, 2021). Production and supply chains have a critical role in the delivery of materials and equipment together with a fully trained workforce to undertake the work to the required standards and to maintain good relations with tenants and residents, workers in public facilities and business owners. If the scale, process, required quality and financial cost of retrofitting is misjudged, it is very likely to be an operational and financial disaster that significantly reduces achieving the climate targets.

Home battery storage and coupling heat pumps with solar panels are in progress (Bellini. 2021). Heat pump developments include an EU supported pilot project at eight sites in Latvia, Germany, Spain and Belgium, which has combined heat pumps with solar systems, using hybrid panels to provide space heating, domestic hot water, power for electrical appliances with excess power fed to the grid (Bellini, 2021).

Areas of large-scale retrofitting could similarly be designated net zero zones to maximise the combined impact of climate action policies. Retrofitting carried out by local Public Building Organisations are to provide trained and multi-skilled staff to implement retrofitting. This will require new design and construction standards for retrofitting and regeneration areas; state planning to ensure production and supply chain of heat pumps, triple glazing and other appliances and equipment.

In addition, there are the production of heat pumps, triple/double glazing, cavity wall, roof and floor insulation, water efficiency measures and flood protection measures where required in retrofitting homes, public buildings and business premises. A UK Public Sector Decarbonisation Scheme operates to retrofit public sector buildings.

The decarbonisation of construction is a priority and must include the production of green cement, steel and aluminium in the construction process, plus electrification of construction equipment to reduce air and noise pollution. Increased offsite fabrication will increase choice and efficiency.

It is essential that retrofitting has four key components:
- Develop a Decent Homes Standard which is inclusive of all aspects of retrofitting together with improvements in the quality of space and storage in homes.
- Prepare a retrofit strategy that takes account of all the different elements of retrofitting and the need for social care support and potential temporary rehousing in some cases.
- Establish new divisions within existing public sector organisations or establish new public organisations to undertake retrofitting of housing and public buildings and to provide a repair, maintenance and upgrade service in future years.
- A lack of strategic planning for retrofitting could result in reliance on commissioning and outsourcing of contracts to cowboy builders that resulting in soaring levels of complaints over shoddy work, failed heating systems and incomplete work.

Adjusted agriculture

Sustainable agriculture must increase the efficiency of arable and livestock farming and promote nature conservation and biodiversity in order to achieve zero emissions by 2040. EU plans a 50% reduction in the use of chemical pesticides and 25% of agricultural land must be organically farmed by 2030 (European Commission, 2020). The EU also proposes a Zero Pollution Action Plan for Air, Water and Soil, a minimum 20% reduction in use of fertilisers, planting 3bn additional trees by 2030 and restored and protected marine ecosystems (Ibid).

There are crude demands to reduce meat consumption from between 30% and 70% (The Guardian, 2022b) and ignore the range of initiatives being undertaken by farming organisations and the agricultural sector in response to the decarbonisation imperative. The complexity of this has been captured in attempts to formulate common positions in the EU, noting:

"Decarbonising European agriculture is challenging as it must be achieved in the context of rapidly growing global food demand (between +50% and +100% by 2050 as estimated by the latest foresights), whilst it must also cope with the growing impacts of climate change" (Dialogue on European Decarbonisation Pathways, 2020).

Strategies to reduce methane emissions from beef production – pasture management, dietary supplementation, breeding (selection of low methane emitting animals) include:

- Improved grassland management; improved fertility performance; periodic pH, nitrogen and phosphorus analysis in soil should be undertaken regularly for each grassland farm. A longer grazing season lowers the Carbon Footprint.

- Adoption of organic farming practices should include that a fertilisation plan be prepared and kept for each grassland farm describing the crop rotation of the farmland and the planned application of manure and other fertilisers.
- The use of red clover with perennial ryegrass and white clover can produce very high yields of multi-cut silage without artificial nitrogen – and greenhouse gas and ammonia emissions are low.
- The growing and finishing of beef cattle should include meeting the requirements for calf sheds; calving at two years of age and identifying and rearing suitable replacement heifer; a younger age at first calving lowers the Carbon Footprint and a higher calving rate also reduces the Carbon Footprint as does slurry management accompanied by a 20% shift to spring application (Teagasc, 2022).

Jobs and quality employment conditions

The broad employment impact of renewable energy and decarbonisation are significant and critically important for local, regional and national economies. The quality, terms and conditions of employment are equally important.

The IMF calculated that public investment could generate between 2 and 8 jobs for every US$1m spent on traditional infrastructure and between 5 and 14 jobs for every US$1m spent on research and development, green electricity and efficient buildings (Gaspar et al, 2020).

Table 12: Estimated direct and indirect jobs in renewable energy worldwide

	World	China	Brazil	India	USA	EU 27
Solar PV	3,975	2,300	68	163.5	231.5	194
Liquid biofuels	2,411	51	871	35	271	229
Hydropower	2,182	813.6	175.8	319.5	71	80
Wind power	1,254	550	40	44	116.8	259
Social heating & cooling	816	670	47.2	21	n/a	21
Solid biomass	765	188		58	44.5	368
Biogas	339	145		85	n/a	76
Geothermal energy	96	3			8	40
CSP	32	11			n/a	6
Total	12,018*	4,732	1202	726	838.4	1,300*

Source: IRENA: Renewable Energy and Jobs, Annual Review 2021
* Includes 39,000 job in waste-to-energy and 1,000 jobs in tide, wave and ocean energy.

An equitable transition will require a rapid rundown of coal mining and fossil fuel exploration and extraction and to secure the permanent stranding of assets in the ground. The transition processes must ensure manufacturing and production, utilities and services are converted to new sources of power. This process will involve significant employment change and retraining.

For example, retrofitting of housing affords the opportunity to create new or revitalised existing organisations to maintain and service new heating systems, linked to training programmes and wider organisation remits to manage, repair, maintain and service for the whole public sector. They have the potential to provide a wide range of public services such as schools, health centres, community centres, including a role in the integrated model of public, primary, medical and social care (Whitfield 2015 and 2021).

It is vital to reject the neoliberal approach of commissioning, outsourcing and privatisation which will simply repeat all the failures and wasted public sector resources endured over the last fifty years. It is also vital to develop inclusive renewable energy development plans for training, production and integrated servicing of assets by public-owned regional organisations plus multi-skilled environmental agencies to take on environmental protection and conservation/development of new areas of nature and biodiversity.

Jobs generated by renewable energy

"....wind-related job totals in the United States increased by 2.9% in 2021 to 120,164 full-time workers-benefitting from continued robust development (DOE 2022) These jobs include, among others, those in construction (43,371) and manufacturing (23,644). (Land-Based Wind Market Report: 2022 Edition, US Department of Energy, 2022a).

The National Renewable Energy Laboratory analysis of direct and indirect jobs in offshore wind energy projects (fixed bottom and Floating projects), assuming 25% domestic content, and 100% domestic content reveals significant variation in the impact on jobs. The differential for fixed bottom projects was 10,630 to 40,500 jobs and 4,103 and 16,415 for floating projects (Table 13).

Quality of jobs is equally important

A survey by the American Council on Renewable Energy and the Clean Energy Leadership Institute found that clean energy jobs paid 25% more than the national median wage in late 2019. Solar workers earned $24.48 an hour whilst wind and grid modernisation jobs paid on average more than $25 an hour. Electricians in clean energy have an average median wage of $29.64 per hour (Table 14).

Table 13: USA Offshore Wind Energy Supply Chain: Direct and Indirect Jobs

Component	Average number of jobs through 2030	
	25% Domestic Content	100% Domestic Content
Fixed-bottom projects		
Nacelle (Turbine pod)	4,600	18,600
Rotor blade	900	3,500
Towers	1,200	4,700
Monopile	1,300	5,400
Transition piece	800	3,100
Jacket	500	2,000
Gravity based foundation	400	1,500
Substation topside	30	100
Array cable	300	1,100
Export cable	600	2,300
Total	**10,630**	**40,500**
Floating projects		
Nacelle (Turbine pod)	1,100	4,600
Rotor blade	200	800
Towers	300	1,100
Floating structure	2,200	8,700
Substation topside	3	15
Dynamic array cable	100	400
Dynamic export cable	200	800
Total	**4,103**	**16,415**

Source: Shields at al, 2022.

"In addition, jobs in many clean energy sectors are more likely to be unionised and come with health care and retirement benefits than the rest of the private sector" (ACORE and Clean Energy leadership Institute, 2019).

Table 14: Wage rates in US Clean Energy Industries

	2019 Median Hourly Wages * ($)	% Above or Below the National Median
U.S. TOTAL	19.14	–
CLEAN ENERGY INDUSTRIES OVERALL	23.89	25
Renewable Energy Generation	23.44	22
Solar	24.48	28
Wind	25.95	36
Energy Efficiency	24.44	28
Energy Star Appliances	24.63	29
Renewable Heating & Cooling	24.91	30
Efficient Lighting	24.21	26
Traditional & High-Efficiency	24.43	28
Grid Modernisation and Storage	25.07	31
Grid Modernisation	25.40	33
Storage	24.82	30
Clean Fuels (Advanced Biofuels)	19.55	2
Clean Vehicles	22.20	16
Other industries		
Retail Trade	13.16	-31
Accommodation	11.64	-39
Food Services & Drinking Places	11.48	-40
Arts, Entertainment & Recreation	13.88	-27

Source: ESSU Global Renewable Energy Secondary Market Transaction Database, 2020.

The Scottish TUC investigation into the low carbon and renewable energy economy concluded that without a domestic renewable industrial strategy:

"...not only will workers in Scotland miss out, but there are serious implications in terms of tax, transparency, economic democracy and meeting climate targets". Furthermore, *"a lack of concern about ownership leads to a plethora of overseas*

financial interests within the Scottish economy. This leads to the offshoring of jobs and tax revenues; limits transparency and lessens the accountability that workers, communities and Government hold over multinational companies" (Scottish TUC, 2017).

Despite the Scottish Government's Low Carbon Strategy 2010 predicting 130,000 jobs by 2020, direct employment in 2018 was 23,100, caused by the sector being *"... dominated private and overseas interests are the primary reason behind this lack of employment"* (Scottish TUC, 2020). The award of 17 contracts in the ScotWind auction in 2022 (Table A1 in Appendix) is likely to have limited impact in increasing local employment.

Renewable energy employment can fully replace coal employment

This is the conclusion of a study by the University of Michigan's School for Environment and Sustainability (Vanatta et al, 2022). The research recognised that coal plant workers have strong community ties which prevent former plant workers from moving to seek employment elsewhere. They developed a model which took account of 256 coal plants in eight regions due for closure by 2030; solar employment usually exceeded wind employment accounting for 46%-74% of replacement jobs, although it offered more cost effective electricity generation in most locations.

The research

"...found investments in wind and solar plants can replace electricity generation and employment on an annual basis for each U.S. coal plant at coal-to-renewable siting limits as low as 50 miles. Siting renewables within 50 instead of 1,000 miles of retiring coal plants, which would keep employment local, would increase replacement costs for the U.S. coal plant fleet by $83 billion, or 24%. These costs are significant in isolation but are small relative to annual power investments ($70 billion (U.S. Energy Information Administration, 2018a, 2018b) and to the total costs of the energy transition (as high as $900 billion by 2030 (National Academies of Sciences Engineering and Medicine, 2021). Thus, our results indicate replacing lost jobs in coal plant communities would modestly increase overall energy transition costs while significantly furthering a just transition for one category of frontline communities. Furthermore, within most regions, coal plants exist with low-cost increases for replacing coal plants with local instead of distant renewables. While a just transition for all U.S. coal plant communities might not be feasible, ample opportunity exists for just transitions for numerous coal communities at small cost increase" (Ibid).

Australia's Million Jobs Plan

The plan covered the production of renewable energy projects, decarbonisation and an equitable transition in the 2021 to 2040 period which resulted in 1.8m job years (Table 15).

Table 15: Australia's One Million Jobs Plan

Activity	Job years
90GW Renewable energy and transmission	200,000
Net-Zero energy buildings	900,000
Modernisation and expanding Australian manufacturing	140,000
100% Renewable mining	75,000
Recycling – 100%	80,000
Electrified transportation	140,000
Land restoration and carbon	200,000
Training, Education and Research	10,000
Total	**1,800,000**

Source: Beyond Zero Emissions, 2021.

The Australian Labour Party produced a Powering Australia plan in 2021 and won the election in May 2022 and the new Government held a Jobs + Skills Summit in September 2022. It agreed immediate action to:

- Implement a Digital and Tech Skills Compact, with business and unions, to deliver 'Digital Apprenticeships' that will support workers to earn while they learn in entry level tech roles, with equity targets for those traditionally under-represented in digital and tech fields.
- Deliver 1,000 digital traineeships in the Australian Public Service over four years, with a focus on opportunities for women, First Nations people, older Australians, and veterans transitioning to civilian life.

in addition to existing commitments which include:
- A$15 billion National Reconstruction Fund to create secure well-paid jobs, drive regional development, and invest in our national sovereign capability.
- Invest in cleaner and cheaper energy through the Powering Australia plan.
- Provide investment certainty to businesses through legislating Australia's emission reductions targets and delivering stable policies like a reformed safeguard mechanism.
- A$20 billion Rewiring the Nation plan to rebuild and modernise the grid.

- New Energy Apprenticeships plan to support 10,000 apprenticeships.
- Work with states and territories on development of a National Energy Workforce Strategy to identify current and future skills gaps in the energy sector, and provide a plan to ensure Australia has the skilled workforce it needs.
- Establish a First Nations Clean Energy Strategy, through the National Energy Transformation Partnership, co-designed with states and territories.
- Partner with the Queensland Government to create a Battery Manufacturing Precinct.
- Improve reporting of climate and nature related financial risks.

Good quality jobs and training

The elimination of insecurity and exploitation of labour must be a prime objective. A 16-part Code of Practice for Quality Employment with terms and conditions, pensions, health and safety, training and rights should be negotiated with trade unions and used to develop protocols to facilitate the implementation of the Code (Whitfield, 2020a). Employment and equality standards must be continuously maintained, with immediate action taken against any employer failing to meet them. Skills development and training in manufacturing and construction industries will be essential if climate action targets are to be achieved. However, few of these objectives will be achieved unless there are strong alliances of political, trade union, civil society and community organisations with well organised activist memberships who are willing to challenge corporate power and conservatism. A trained and skilled workforces with good quality terms and conditions, equality practices, health and safety arrangements and the right to organise and negotiate are vital. Training and educational pathways and apprenticeships should be created for the unemployed, underpaid and marginalised workers.

Technological developments in renewable energy

Technological advances have improved the effectiveness and efficiency of solar panels, battery storage and the use of hydrogen and designed floating wind and solar projects. Research and development continues in several elements which will have a significant impact in accelerating decarbonisation and improving the efficiency and effectiveness of renewable energy. They include:

Green Hydrogen

There are several initiatives for the great hope of decarbonisation in all sectors that cannot be electrified. They vary from ITM Power in England, backed by Royal Dutch Shell; the AquaVentus project in the German North Sea which includes RWE; Shell, Equinor and Gasunie which plan a 10 gigawatt of electrolysis capacity for green hydrogen production from offshore wind power.

In Western Australia Infinite Green Energy is pressing ahead with a commercial-scale hydrogen refuelling station built on the 11 MW Northam Solar Farm. In addition, the ABB Group (Sweden) and Hydrogen Optimized (Canada) have an agreement to accelerate green hydrogen production on a large scale.

However, the International Energy Agency's Global Hydrogen Review (2022) reported *"A significant portion of projects are currently at advanced planning stages, but just a few (4%) are under construction or have reached final investment decision"*.

Combining battery storage with wind and solar

The combination of battery storage with wind and solar projects is likely to accelerate with the need for the continuity and security of supply and the need to minimise peaks and troughs will require further research and development.

Safer, greener, cheaper polymer battery alternative to lithium

Researchers at Deakin University, Australia, have developed new polymer electrolyte chemistries that can be used with high energy metals that are more abundant and less expensive than lithium. They have found that:

"The new materials can contribute to a more sustainable, greener future battery technology, as a well as providing society with safer, high performance energy storage devices" Dr Fangfang Chen, lead researcher, Institute for Frontier Materials, Deakin University, Melbourne (Carroll, 2022b).

Larger wind turbines and rotor blades

The growth of offshore wind projects has led to more powerful turbines with larger blades and a 220 meter rotor. Engineering innovation and technological development of new materials is likely to continue this trend driven by the generation of increased power and reduction in megawatt costs.

Repowering of old wind farms

Replacing older wind turbines with new turbines to increase the power output and improve efficiency will become more frequent.

Waste to energy improvements

Anaerobic digestion requires a consistent type of organic waste such as food waste, bio-solid and slurry waste and a highly controlled environment to produce and combust methane. Mass combustion waste to energy projects take large volumes of waste but without any sorting, separation or treatment. However, some combustion waste to energy projects sort waste into different streams or are shredded (with recycled items removed). Pollution from waste incinerators is a major concern in

Scotland with carbon dioxide emissions from three household waste incinerators increased from 468,000 tonne in 2029 to 575,000 tonnes in 2020. Up to ten new incinerators are either planned or due to begin operating in next few years (Dobson and Edwards, 2022). The failure of some projects in England, the threat to recycling and increased pollution indicates a radical review of the technology.

Predictive maintenance

Many operations and management service providers already use predictive maintenance programmes to assess conditions, confirm damage and schedule maintenance and refurbishment.

This reduces the need for site visits, enables timely ordering of parts and provides valuable performance data.

Increased power demand

Global energy demand is forecast to increase by 50% between 2020 and 2050 (Goldman Sachs, 2022). They note that the purchase of an electric vehicle and a heat pump would triple the electric power consumption of a typical European household. Increased digitalisation of public services will also impact on demand, for example between local healthcare centres and patients and in greater use of distance learning.

The International Energy Agency reported that global demand is expected to grow by 2.4% in 2022 after a 6% increase in 2021 (IEA 2022a). The annual changes in demand are inevitable given changing economic conditions and progress in decarbonisation.

Strategic planning for renewable energy, regeneration and public services

Strategic planning of towns and cities including regeneration plans, local housing development plans, economic development initiatives and public service innovation and improvement plans must be integrated with the planning of renewable energy projects, decarbonisation, retrofitting and national and local adaptation plans and vice versa.

Integration is necessary to maximise the benefits of expanding renewable energy and National Grids and the planning of Net Zero Cities or regional/local Renewable Energy Zones, Energy Parks and Net Zero Economic Zones. They include:

- economic development for the manufacture of battery storage, solar panels, wind farm towers, blades and turbines, heat pumps, double/triple glazing and retrofitting materials
- good quality employment policies, job training and the right to organize to create a workforce capable of fully implementing public policies
- more effective use of resources by co-ordinating implementation and avoiding repetition

- address the equality needs of different equality groups and prevent new inequalities from arising
- communicate progress and performance and the causes of any delays
- maximise impact by achieving multiple objectives
- plan for longer term upgrades, repair and maintenance
- coordinate access to national/local networks for recharging batteries and high-speed fibre network for the digitalisation of public services
- integrate continuous monitoring systems with frequent scrutiny/oversight and review
- align increase in renewable energy generation with the secure stranding of fossil fuel assets

Governments have a critical role in establishing planning and regulatory frameworks that integrate climate, infrastructure, public service and welfare state policies. This must be interventionist to ensure public goods and public values are central in assessing equality impacts, identifying costs and benefits, setting standards, monitoring and scrutiny of implementation, and in achieving environmental, economic, social, labour and democratic rights. There is a compelling need for the integration of public health services, primary, medical and social care services to create a fully unified public healthcare system (Whitfield, 2020).

Democratic accountability, transparency and participation give citizens, communities and trade union organisations belief that they have a significant and effective role in the planning, design and delivery of climate policies, public services and the welfare state to ensure their needs are understood and met. Participation in planning must be genuine, continuous and systematic with information disclosure. Research based analysis should underpin innovation and new methodologies adopted in renewable energy and other processes. Similarly, make your experience available to others.

The impact of climate change and achieving climate targets is paramount but this must be in parallel with regeneration, making progress in achieving sustainable development targets and improvement of and innovation in public services and welfare state functions. Climate policies must not be prioritised over the wide range of important public policies but must be jointly developed and implemented. Otherwise, political opposition is likely to mount against climate policies and could erode support for the provision of core public services.

There is a danger of neoliberal individualism imposing responsibility on individual households to take the initiative and bear the costs of retrofitting out of a 'duty' to personally contribute to achieving the climate change targets. This is not to say that we shouldn't as individuals think globally and act locally. But the reality is that it would be much more effective, equitable, efficient and less costly if planned, programmed and delivered by a trained and resourced public retrofitting agency.

CHAPTER 10
Strategic Opportunities

Chapter 10 explores strategic opportunities for democratising decarbonisation. It begins with an overview of ways in which the corporate domination of renewable energy can be challenged by alternative policies and action. The second section describes how the public sector must and can have a key role in direct investment, ownership and operation of renewable energy systems, in effect translating the broad objective of global public goods into public policy and operational reality. The third section emphasises the need to combine the different methods of decarbonisation to maximise their impact. The final section focuses on economic growth and technological advances to improve lives, living and working conditions up to and after 2050.

Challenging corporate domination of renewable energy

Challenge and replace the obsession with Environment, Social and Governance (ESG): Use the weaknesses in ESG (detailed in Chapter 4) to challenge the claimed performance of private renewable energy companies. ESG should be replaced with a commitment to undertaking rigorous and comprehensive equality impact assessments. This should be modelled on the best practice Section 75 of the Northern Ireland Act 1998 (Equality Commission for Northern Island, 2010). All renewable energy projects should be subjected to comprehensive and rigorous economic, equality, social and environmental impact assessments and cost/benefit analyses and include how human and labour rights will be advanced and evidenced (see Chapter 8).

The adoption of the Core Public Values Framework is essential (Chapter 6).

Challenge the use of tax havens and demand this practice is terminated: Tax avoidance increases corporate profits and shareholder dividends but has little or no benefit for service users or employees. The use of tax havens reduces tax revenue in the host country which is likely to have a small impact in the case of a small renewable energy asset but represents a larger loss revenue when all the projects in a country using this avoidance strategy are taken into account. Tax avoidance means corporate financial secrecy and less local democratic accountability concerning profitability and the ability to challenge claims by companies with regard to employment conditions, activity in the local economy and supply chains.

Companies that persist in retaining offshore registration in a tax haven should be informed that their proposals are not welcome and will incur negative impacts in formal impact assessments and cost/benefits analyses.

Challenge the methods and quality of operational and financial performance monitoring and disclosure: Ensure that monitoring is not limited to power output and renewable energy performance and is inclusive of wider issues such as environmental impact, social and economic equalities, effect on local residents and the local economy, sustainability objectives, quality of employment and meeting public values and policy.

Challenge the corporate track record of private ownership of renewable energy: Have the objectives and performance targets been achieved – compare with company's original statements and describe the reasons for success or failure? The prime objective must be to de-commodify and reverse of the marketisation of the renewable energy sector and to rapidly increase public sector capabilities to plan, develop, own, operate and manage renewable energy projects.

Challenge the policy, justification and process if a company seeks to sell a renewable energy asset: Draw up a set of demands which should be included in a sale agreement drawing on the degree to which the original commitments have been met along with new demands arising from the operation and management of the project. If it is financially driven asset recycling, then who are the potential buyers and are they likely re-sell again soon? In addition, new regulations should be considered such as any sale should require the repayment of subsidies; and the protection of terms and condition for staff on transfer to a new owner.

Challenge the reasons for the planned sale of renewable energy assets and make the case for local, regional or national government acquisition either by negotiation or submission of a bid: This could be a strategic way of acquiring renewable energy assets to increase direct public sector provision of renewable energy. It would depend on the performance of the assets and their lifespan before the need for repowering.

Challenge the commercialisation of nature and biodiversity: Immediately stop the commercialisation of nature and biodiversity, abolish competitive bidding and outsourcing and maximise public management of these assets. Prevent the forestation of land near areas of natural beauty, coastal areas and inland lakes and reduction of food production capacity or productivity.

Challenge the lack of democratic accountability and participation: Democratic accountability is critical at national, regional and city levels for energy policies, long-term planning, repowering and upgrading. Firstly, it must include genuine and continuous participation of community and trade union representatives in the planning and service delivery process. Secondly, it must evidence full monitoring and reporting of the implementation and performance of public sector values (see Chapter 5). Thirdly, a regular scrutiny/oversight review and evaluation by public authorities to include evidence and evaluation from contractors/suppliers and from community organisations, trade unions and other interested organisations. Finally, the scope of the above should include the effectiveness of regulations, progress in the transition from fossil fuels and stranding of assets, and economic development initiatives linked to renewable energy projects.

Challenge failure of local economic development in construction and operation of assets: Identify whether local companies were employed in the construction process and the tasks they were responsible for. Similarly, have any operational activities been outsourced in the planning, construction and operation of wind, solar, hydro or battery storage projects and gather information about any disputes over terms and conditions and trade union recognition?

Challenge level and quality of local employment generated by the project: Gather information about the terms and conditions of workers employed by the company and in work which has been outsourced. Compare with the terms and conditions of comparable workers/skills in other sectors.

Challenge continued use of auctions to allocate renewable energy projects: This has become the common mechanism in the European Union and many other countries. It is very significant that there is little opposition to this methodology from renewable energy companies because it ensures a private sector monopoly by excluding public sector bidders, who are much more experienced in the tendering process which has a degree of negotiation over the details of proposals and costs.

Challenge proposed Public Private Partnership (PPP) projects: Demand a joint public sector model and use the detailed critical assessments of PPPs on the use of private finance, democratic accountability, performance risks, future sale of assets, maximise benefit in local economy, quality of jobs.

Joint public sector projects should be publicly financed, focus exclusively on renewable energy, and be managed and operated by the public sector.

Challenge Private Equity Funds: The Americans for Financial Reform and Private Equity Stakeholder Project has developed the Private Equity Climate Risks Scorecard which has graded eight private equity funds with a combined US$3.6 trillion in assets under management. The Carlyle Group was rated F, KKR, Brookfield, Ares, Apollo, Blackstone and Warburg Pincus were rated D and TPG a B.

"Align with science-based climate targets to limit global warming to 1.5ºC:
- *Immediately cease investments in fossil fuel expansion.*
- *Cease gas flaring and venting by 2025.*
- *Achieve a fossil-free energy portfolio by 2030.*
- *Retire fossil fuel energy assets by 2030*

Disclose fossil fuel exposure, emission and impacts:
- *Disclose all fossil fuel assets and financial estimates and assumptions regarding asset impairment.*
- *Disclose all direct and indirect emissions and climate-related community impacts.*

Report a portfolio-wide energy transition plan:
- *Disclose a portfolio-wide climate transition plan.*
- *Disclose role of voluntary carbon offsets immediately and cease their utilisation by 2025.*
- *Disclose use of carbon removal, carbon utilization and storage, and related technologies.*
- *Disclose comprehensive analyses under various climate warming scenarios and decarbonization timelines.*

Integrate Climate and environmental justice;
- *Establish robust due diligence, verification, and grievance redress mechanisms to ensure that all human rights and land rights are respected.*
- *Require all portfolio companies to adopt no-deforestation, no-peat, and no-exploitation (NDPE) policies.*
- *Develop a just transition program with impacted communities and workers.*

Provide transparency on political spending and climate lobbying:
- *Disclose political spending and climate lobbying at asset manager, portfolio company, and trade association level.*
- *Provide transparency on alignment with global standards on responsible corporate climate lobbying"* (Americans for Financial Reform and Private Equity Stakeholder Project, 2022).

Challenge the repowering of renewable energy assets: Who gains the benefits of increased output and efficiency? How will the work be carried out and are the proposed safeguards acceptable or are more comprehensive safety and other arrangements necessary?

Demand that fossil fuel companies do not make ISDS or Energy Charter Treaty claims against nation states: Nor should they take other forms of legal action over changes in climate policies that are in the public interest.

Promote the need for public ownership, provision and radical public management: Make the case that renewable energy assets should be publicly owned and operated and highlight the benefits for workers, service users, local employment and training and the local/regional economy.

Opportunities for public ownership

Electricity systems have four distinct elements or functions - power generation, national or regional transmission or grid, local distribution networks and retail suppliers. The pattern of public/private ownership varies between countries. It is vital that the public sector develops a joint coordinated strategy to integrate the energy sector and the decarbonisation processes. The impact of climate change is very substantial and will absorb significant public and private resources for the next 27 years or more.

The 2050 target date for decarbonisation, renewable energy, retrofitting and environmental protection is an essential collective target. However, it is often treated as the only meaningful target. This leads to a fixation with 2050 and virtually no public debate about objectives, public policies, political economies and international relations after that date. The reluctance to discuss strategic long-term planning is deeply embedded in capitalist economies where the focus is on here, now and the short-term.

The strategy must be forward looking, creative and innovative and take account of *economic growth and technological advances to improve lives, living and working conditions and the welfare state now, up to and well beyond 2050.*

There are continuing fundamental inadequacies in provision in most countries such as:

- Long delays for health care
- Fractured and failing social care
- Homelessness and failure to build public housing
- Poverty and food insecurity
- Lack of student accommodation
- Failure to provide special educational needs for children
- Lack of local young people centres
- More extensive sports and recreational facilities
- Privatised, financialised and marketised public services
- Increasing flows of refugees fleeing the impact of climate change, war and civil conflicts

The roots of many of these inadequacies lie in the adoption of neoliberal economic policies in the USA, UK and Latin America in the 1970s and austerity policies imposed in response to the 2008 global financial crisis which continue today.

Radically increase public ownership of renewable energy

As Chapter 6 revealed, only 4% of renewable energy projects are publicly owned, hence the importance of increasing public ownership of renewable energy generation and retuning national grids and local distribution networks to public ownership.

- Make the case that renewable energy assets should be publicly owned and operated and highlight the benefits for workers, service users, local employment and training and the local/regional economy.
- Governments should establish a National Renewable Energy Agency to increase direct public investment in new renewable energy projects and to nationalise key renewable energy companies and their assets.
- Municipal authorities should seek to fully acquire renewable projects when they are offered for sale on the secondary market initially targeting small and medium sized projects to build experience and capacity. They should avoid very small stakes in renewable energy projects. This approach was adopted in the latter stages of the UK's failed Private Finance Initiative (PPP) programme when some local authorities became very minority shareholders with real no benefit.
- Government and municipal authorities should consider financing the repowering of renewable energy projects on condition they obtain a majority stake in the project company.
- Draw up a set of demands to be included in a sale agreement drawing on the degree to which the original commitments have been met and make new demands arising from the operation and management of the project.
- Eliminate outsourcing and exploitation of low wage and poor working conditions for employees. Take the initiative for radical improvement in employment terms and conditions in all stages of renewable energy projects. Introduce improved regulations on quality of jobs, employment standards, training and sourcing of supply chains. Trade unions and pension fund trustees should re-examine the scale and type of pension fund investments made in renewable energy projects and the associated risks and alternative investment strategies.
- Governments and public authorities should adopt a comprehensive approach to procurement with specific design and operational specifications and a rigorous evaluation process with detailed criteria.
- Integrate power generation and renewable energy technologies, and increase capacity of grid transmission and distribution

- Integrate environmental protection and adaptation works to ensure that public authorities have all the required equipment.
- A comprehensive approach should be adopted for public utilities combining renewable energy, water and sanitation, waste to energy systems and broadband.

All future public financial support must be conditional on binding agreements that give the public sector the first option to acquire full ownership of a project in any future sale of the project.

Detailed inspection and rigorous due diligence in municipalisation and nationalisation processes is required. The current expected lifetime of solar panels (IEA 2022b), is 30 years. It is necessary to be aware that increasing severe weather conditions are likely to cause more damage than anticipated and reduce the 30-year lifetime. The renewable energy planning and development process should maximise opportunities for public intervention to stop, or significantly reduce, the use of auctions.

Continued reliance and acquiescence to market forces to address climate change is certain to lead to failed projects, missed targets and increased costs. Research and innovation should maximise efficiency and sustainability of wind, solar, tidal, hydro, biomass and other renewable energy techniques such as energy from waste.

Chapter 2 comments on continued growth of renewable energy infrastructure to 2050, therefore, if the current pattern of ownership and provision continues, this infrastructure will largely be in private ownership. Only a concerted and coordinated era of public investment for public ownership and provision together with nationalisation and municipalisation will radically change this situation. Otherwise privatisation, asset recycling and PPPs will be endemic as market forces and private capital dictate the provision of power globally. Takeovers and mergers will result in private sector consolidation into a few global companies.

For example **the State of Queensland** is to build Australia's largest publicly-owned wind farm – a 150 turbine 500MW to be built by the state-owned Stanwell Corporation supported by Renewable Energy Systems (Readfearn, 2022).

The Queensland Premier Annastacia Palaszczuk launched a A$62bn Queensland Energy and Jobs Plan on 27 September 2022 to create a super grid of new wind and solar projects plus the Borumba Pumped Hydro which will deliver 2GW of 24 hour storage together with a new pumped hydro site. The projects will create 4,000 construction jobs a year for over a decade and the overall Plan will support nearly 100,000 more jobs. By 2035 the state is expected to have 80% generation by renewable energy.

An Energy Workers Charter and Jobs Security Guarantee whilst at transmission and training hubs in Gladstone and Townsville will support 570 workers each year. A Regional Economic Futures Fund will support local communities to develop economic futures strategies for regions where existing coal plants are located. The super grid will include new 500 kilovolt transmission lines to power new manufacturing jobs in the regions (Queensland Government, 2022). It will connect 22GW of new renewable projects.

The Labour controlled Welsh Government has agreed to establish a publicly-owned company to develop and operate renewable energy projects starting in April 2024 (BBC, 2022). The Trades Union Congress proposed the formation of a National Energy Agency and Regional Energy Agencies that *"...could build and control between 27 GW – 77 GW of new clean generation by 2040"* and act as 'a public sector champion' (TUC, 2022). The UK Labour Party announced that 'Great British Energy' would be launched in the first year of a Labour government with £8bn funding from a new National Wealth Fund to co-invest in renewable energy with the private sector. A spokesperson said it is *"not about nationalisation, this is a new player into the market"* (The Guardian, 2022c).

The talk of champions, wealth funds, markets, and co-investment with the private sector is using neoliberal language which should not be applicable to a new national publicly-owned renewable energy developer and operator. The organisational structure, functions, values, objectives, powers, resources and democratic accountability must be rigorous to avoid the fate of the Green Investment Bank which was privatised by the previous Conservative government to the Macquarie Bank in 2017 (Whitfield, 2020a).

New public sector organisations

Local authorities should establish or expand existing organisations to undertake retrofitting of housing and public buildings and environmental protection projects, such as flood prevention work, sea wall and river basin works, and to provide a continuing maintenance, repair and improvement/upgrade service. These organisations must attract good quality public managers, adopt radical public management practice and have training programmes to ensure they have a fully skilled workforce (Whitfield, 2020a). Arms-length companies or privatised direct works departments should be returned to direct public provision.

Retrofitting will require area wide initiatives with housing and social services support because tenants and owners who have long-term illnesses or are elderly may depend on social care; others may have health problems and would be affected by the high level of disruption and dust if a full refit is required. Municipal direct works departments should be revitalised with a skilled workforce to undertake retrofitting, longer term whole life maintenance, repowering and upgrading of heat pumps and other equipment.

There is a unique opportunity for new public organisations created by the acquisition or re-municipalisation of facilities management companies previously sold off to the private sector or currently operated as arms-length companies. This approach creates important opportunities for training in new skills and jobs.

Increase skills and capacity of public management

Increased public sector in-house capabilities to plan, develop and operate renewable energy projects. A decommodification process (redesign of services, jobs, regulations, democratic accountability, participation and disclosure) in government and public authorities should be combined with the adoption of radical public management committed to public ownership and provision. This would terminate the financialisation, marketisation, individualisation and privatisation processes and significantly improve the quality of public services and terms and conditions and training of public employees (Whitfield, 2020a).

All the strategies require a radical public management that replaces commissioning, outsourcing and the commodification of public services with strategic planning based on needs, in-house integrated services, public services innovation and improvement plans, democratic accountability and participation and social/economic impact assessment and cost benefit analysis (Whitfield 2020). This includes the implementation, monitoring and review of the public sector values set out in Chapter 6 and Figure 9. It is vital that public organisations are organised and managed on the basis of learning from research and development, long-term planning, implementation, democratic governance and performance scrutiny and review. Finally, the quality of employment including terms and conditions, skills training and the right to organise and recognition of trade union negotiating rights are critical.

Prevent a new surge in asset recycling and privatisation

The assumption of a continuing role for markets and market forces ultimately means a significant expansion of financialisation, marketisation and privatisation. This will result in a surge in the scale of privatisation, specifically in all the aspects of climate action such as renewable energy, decarbonisation, retrofitting, nature and biodiversity, environmental protection, agriculture, transportation, housing, health, education and other public services.

> *"Claims about the apparent 'end' of neoliberalism and austerity are over-optimistic because they can only be terminated when the embedded ideology, policies and processes have been rejected, reversed and replaced"* (Whitfield, 2020b).

Community-owned renewable energy projects

Island communities and very rural or isolated communities in many countries have developed community-owned wind farms or solar projects to secure a supply of energy. Many projects are attracted by the idea of selling surplus energy to the grid to increase revenue and reduce the price of energy for members. Community-owned wind projects in the UK generated 113MW in 2021 (Energy Saving Trust, 2022).

The UK created an energy retail market, but 50 companies exited the market between 2017-2022 (Oxera, 2022). Customers were transferred to existing or new suppliers with the £2.7bn costs mutualised across current and future bill payers - an extra £94 was added to every UK household energy bill. The £6.5bn failure of Bulb Energy Ltd (Office for Budget Responsibility, 2022) could add a further £200 to bills (Thomas, 2022b). Several local authorities set up retail energy companies, but they collapsed with multi-million losses.

Community owned, cooperative or worker ownership organisational models have been established in many European countries for renewable energy projects. The REN21 (2016) reported 2,800 energy cooperatives, although the REScoop organisation currently states a figure of 1,900. Similar projects exist in North America (see detailed studies in Sweeney, Treat and Shen, 2020; Verde and Rossetto, 2020; REN21, 2016; Fairchild and Weinrub, 2017).

The benefits of community energy projects in these locations are substantial – providing a more secure supply of electricity, energy to public spaces which are not currently connected, reducing energy costs and contributing to decarbonisation.

For example, in Scotland South Uist Renewable Energy operates three 2.8MW turbines at Loch Carnan on South Uist island in the Outer Hebrides. Surplus energy is sold to the national grid although the interconnector and grid system on the island limits the transfer of power. A proposed 600 megawatt subsea cable from the Western Islands to the mainland was rejected by the regulator OFGEM, because of the potential cost to customers and because not enough wind power was being generated on the islands to justify the project. However, access to the national grid is a major problem in many countries (see Chapter 9) with long delays to gain access to the grid and significant connector and export meter costs. The siting of small community renewable energy projects in urban areas is more problematic.

The ultimate focus for all renewable energy projects should be on large scale production of renewable energy to maximise the rate of decarbonisation and achieve the 2050 targets. Adopting a policy of sanctioning more and more singular projects which are miniscule in terms of MW is not the solution.

Furthermore, community projects should not focus solely on energy generation. Firstly they should incorporate energy storage, the decarbonising of all forms of transport and the creation of interconnected renewable energy systems that are sustainable well beyond 2050 and can be repowered. Secondly, the retrofitting of housing and community buildings which includes air source heat pumps, high level of building fabric efficiency including, walls, floors and doors, passive cooling measures, water efficiency measures and flood resilience measures must be an integral part of a renewable energy project.

Community projects must avoid contributing to the continued fracturing and fragmentation of public services, utilities and welfare states – stand-alone opted out schools, privatised and fragmented health and social care provision, commercialised parks and open spaces.

Other important policy changes are required

Joint Public Sector Renewable Energy projects that are publicly financed, managed and operated should replace Public Private Partnerships given the detailed critical assessments of PPPs on the use of private finance, democratic accountability, performance risks, future sale of assets and negative impact in the local economy and quality of jobs (Pollock, 2005; Shaoul, 2005; Hall, 2015, Whitfield, 2010, 2017a, 2017b, 2020; European Court of Auditors, 2018, and many others).

This requires the World Bank, Global Infrastructure Hub and development banks to promote joint public sector infrastructure projects and to develop public sector capabilities to undertake projects in a sustainable way. Given the scale of change and investment required to meet the climate targets it would be a major error if a much broader strategy is not adopted to develop a socio-economic-environmental strategy that could produce a much more comprehensive and sustainable transformation.

The opportunity for multinational companies to take legal action for compensation whenever nation states adopt renewable energy policies and the ultimate closure of fossil fuel plants must be prohibited by making fundamental changes in trade agreements and the Energy Charter Treaty.

The planning of Net Zero zones, energy parks and other zonal models should develop at a pace and draw on experience internationally (Australian Energy Market Operator, 2021; Beyond Zero Emissions 2021 and 2022; Cass et al, 2022; Eurowind Energy, 2022).

Oppose all attempts to commercialise nature and biodiversity.

Promote alternative uses for redundant factories, plants and fossil fuel depots. A National Conversion Agency should be established to acquire, convert and adapt factories, plants and depots and to demolish and reclaim land and property for new economic and social use such as the manufacture of electric cars, vans, buses, heat pumps or components for renewable energy systems. This agency must also provide support to local campaigns with alternative plans that oppose closures.

Cancellation of debt in the 20 countries in the Climate Vulnerable Forum.

Decarbonisation of bus fleets, rail and steel as discussed in Chapter 9 must be extended to the decarbonisation of the construction industry and facility management services.

Retrofitting of housing, public buildings and business premises is likely to continue until 2050. It is critical that the regulations governing the construction of new homes, public buildings, offices and factories are revised to incorporate new standards and prohibit the use of gas or fossil fuel heating - New York City and Boston and other towns and cities in Massachusetts already have gas bans (Infrastructure Intelligence, 2022).

Strategic organising and action

Challenging the rise of Corporate Power in Renewable Energy identifies fundamental flaws in the funding and ownership of renewable energy projects in many countries. The financialisation and marketisation of renewable energy via the secondary market has no limits. The demand for electricity is forecast to increase 50% by 2030 in Europe and by the same percentage globally by 2050.

It is commonly propagated that any action that can be perceived to support progress in achieving decarbonisation and meeting the climate targets is justified. This includes privately financed and owned renewable energy projects but ignores who develops and owns projects and how they are subjected to being bought and sold in the secondary market. There is understandably wide public hostility to housing and property developers, but there appears to be little or no questioning of renewable energy developers.

The current structure of renewable energy will inevitably seek to consolidate in a capitalist economy, through larger scale acquisitions and mergers, which will lead to domination by a small number of global companies. This will have a very negative impact on achieving the climate targets, energy policies, prices, jobs, equalities and economic justice.

Socialist and progressive political parties internationally and local level, trade unions, community organisations, energy and public policy NGOs should examine the evidence in this book and decide the appropriate demands and coordinated strategies required nationally and in their locality. The unfolding of a global crisis on so many levels requires a state-wide and international response to act as a democratic expression of societal needs (for the many, not the few) in order to avoid a deepening corporate-driven climate and economic crisis.

Through a political reconstruction of the state and public services, institutions based on public sector values, participatory planning, democratic accountability and transparency can be built, able to develop and implement strategic plans to protect people and the planet – as opposed to encouraging corporate profits and shareholder interests. The need for social, economic and environmental justice and equality over nature/biodiversity and production/distribution for the delivery of basic human needs should be fundamental in driving policy and practice. See additional discussion of strategic issues in Whitfield (2020b pages 50-57).

Appendix

Table A1: Result of the Crown Estate ScotWind 2022 auction

Lead Applicant	Option fees (£m)	Technology	Total capacity (MW)
BP Alternative Energy Investments & EnBW Energie Baden-Württemberg AG (Germany)	85.9	Fixed	2,907
SSE Renewables (UK), Marubeni Corporation (Japan) & Copenhagen Infrastructure Partners (Denmark)	95.9	Floating	2,610
Falck Renewables S.p.A. (Italy) & Blue Float Energy (Spain)	28.0	Floating	1,200
CampionWind Shell New Energies joint venture with Scottish Power (Iberdrola)	86.0	Floating	2,000
Vattenfall (Sweden) & Fred Olsen Seawind 50/50	20.0	Floatin	798
Thistle Wind Partners (TWP) DEME Group (CFE engineering contractor via Ackermans & van Haaren investment, Belgium): Qair (France) and Aspiravi Energy (Belgium)	18.7	Fixed	1,008
Thistle Wind Partners (TWP) (As above)	20.0	Floating	1,008
Falck Renewables S.p.A. (Italy) & Blue Float Energy (Spain)	25.6	Floating	1,000
Caledonian Offshore Wind Farm: Ocean Winds (50/50 joint venture with EDPR (Portugal) and ENGIE (France)	42.9	Fixed	1,000
Falck Renewables S.p.A. (Italy) & Blue Float Energy (Spain) & Orsted (Denmark)	13.4	Floating	500
MarramWind Scottish Power Renewables (Iberdrola, Spain) & Shell New Energies	68.4	Floating	3,000

Table A1: Result of the Crown Estate ScotWind 2022 auction (continued...)

Lead Applicant	Option fees (£m)	Technology	Total capacity (MW)
Floating Energy Allyance BayWa (Germany), Elicio (Belgium) & BW Ideol (France)	33.0	Floating	960
Offshore Wind Power: TotalEnergies SE (France), Macquarie's Green Investment Group, RIDG (Scotland)	65.7	Fixed	2,000
Northland Power Inc. (Canada)	3.9	Floating	1,500
Magnora Offshore Wind AS (Sweden) & TechnipFMC (USA)	10.3	Mixed	495
Northland Power Inc. (Canada)	16.1	Fixed	840
MachairWind Scottish Power Renewables (Iberdrola, Spain)	75.4	Fixed	2,000
Total	699.2		24,826

Source: Scotland Awards 25 GW in ScotWind Auction, offshoreWIND.biz and Company websites.

Table A2: Companies often operate through subsidiaries

Parent	Subsidiary companies
Ardian	Skyline Renewables
Blackstone	Aypa Power
Brookfield Renewables	CEE Group
Canadian Solar	Recurrent Energy
Canada Pension Plan Investment Board	Pattern Energy, Cordelio Power
Carlyle Group	Acadia Renewable Energy LLC, Copia Power
Global Infrastructure Partners	Clearway Energy, NRG Renewable Energy
Iberdrola	Avangrid Renewables Scottish Power
KKR	Virescent Infrastructure, Stellar Renewable Power
Macquarie Group	Green Investment Group, Blueleaf Energy, Acacia Renewables Corio Generation
National Grid Renewables	Geronimo Energy LLC
Nuveen Asset Management	Gennmont Partners
Ontario Municipal Employees Retirement System (OMERS)	Cubico Sustainable Investments, Leeward Renewables
OPSEU Pension Trust	Bruc Energy

Table A2: Companies often operate through subsidiaries (continued...)

Parent	Subsidiary companies
Shell	Savion LLC, Silicon Ranch Corp (43.8%)
Softbank	SB Energy
Stratkraft	Solarcentury
Tetragon Financial Group	Equitix Limited
Total	Sunpower
TPG	Matrix Renewables

Source: Company Annual Reports and websites.

Table A3: Examples of publicly owned energy companies

State Owned Company	% owned	Other public and private shareholders
Statkraft (Norway)	100.0	n/a
Vattenfall (Sweden)	100.0	n/a
China Three Gorges Corp.	100.0	n/a
CGN Energy (China)	100.0	n/a
Masdar, Mubadala Investment Co. (UAE)	100.0	n/a
EnBW Energie Baden Wurttemberg AG (Germany)	100.0	State of Baden 46.75%. Association of regional & local govt 46.75%, others 6.5%
Electricity Supply Board (Republic of Ireland)	96.10	Employee Share Ownership Plan 3.9%
EDF (France)	84.08	Institutional & individual 14.80% (include Vanguard funds, JP Morgan & BlackRock); Employee 1.08%, Treasury shares 0.04%
Hidroelectrica, (Romania)	80.06	Fondul Proprietatea 19.94%
CEZ group (Czech Republic)	69.78	CEZ a.s. 0.47%; other legal entities 17.19%; private individuals 12.56%
Equinor ASA (Norway)	67.00	Norwegian National Insurance Fund 3.63%, Others 29.37%
Fortnum (Finland)	56.72	Finnish corporate/financial 3.66%, households 12.42%
Orsted (Denmark)	50.12	Andel AMBA, Denmark 5.01%: The Capital Group 5.1%, others 39.77%

Table A3: Examples of publicly owned energy companies (continued...)

State Owned Company	% owned	Other public and private shareholders
Minority public sector ownership		
ENI (Italy)	30.33	institutional 50.44%; retail investors 18.1%; ENI Treasury 1.13%.
Engie (France)	23.64	Employee shareholders 3.28%; Groupe CDC & CNP Assurances 4.59%: Treasury stock 0.63%; institution & individual shareholders 67.86% (includes BlackRock 4.44%)
Enel (Italy)	23.60	Institutional investors 59.4% (include BlackRock 5.08%; Capital Research & Management 5.03%); retail investors 17.0%

Source: Company Annual Reports for 2020/2021 n/a – not applicable.

Table A4: Examples of privately-owned energy companies

State Owned Company	Other public and private shareholders
E.ON (Germany)	RWE 15.0%; Canada Pension Plan Investment 5.02%; BlackRock Inc 4.92%; Capital Income Builder USA 4.90%; Capital Group Companies USA 4.82%; DWS Investment 3.02%
American Electric Power	Maple-Brown Abbott Global. 9.8%; Vanguard Group 7.85%; Blackrock 5.36%; SsgA Fund Management 4.88%; T. Rowe Price Associates 4.63%; (59.67% mutual funds)
TotalEnergies (France)	BlackRock 6.2%, Employee shareholders 6.8%, Company mutual fund 4.2%, other shareholders 87%.
Dominion Energy (USA)	Vanguard Group 8.14%, SsgA Funds Management 5.03%, BlackRock 4.82%: Massachusetts Financial 2.50%; two Vanguard Mutual funds 4.92%
Duke Energy (USA)	Vanguard Group 8.06%; BlackRock 5.01%; SsgA Funds Management 4.99%; Wellington Management LP 4.08%; Maple-Brown Abbott Mutual 5.37%; (50.94% mutual funds)
Next Era Energy (owns Florida Power & Light)	Vanguard Group inc 8.61%; SsgA Funds Management 5.06%; BlackRock 4.90%; JPMorgan Investment 1.91%; T. Rowe Price Associates 1.81%; Geode Capital Management LLC 1.59%; Norges Bank Investment 1.55%; Northern Trust Investments 1.23%; Managed Accounts Advisers LLC 1.18%; Wells Fargo Clearing Services LLC 1.08%.
Iberdrola (Spain)	Qatar Investment Authority 8.71%; BlackRock 5.16%; Norges Bank 3.60%. Foreign investors total 69.79%.
Endesa (Spain)	Enel Group (Italy) 70.1%
RWE (Germany)	Blackstock 7.0%; other institutional shareholders 80%

Table A4: Examples of privately-owned energy companies (continued...)

State Owned Company	Other public and private shareholders
EDP (Portugal)	(Germany 24%, rest worldwide), 12% private, 1% employees China Three Gorges Corporation 21.55%, BlackRock 5.06%; Oppidum Capital 7.20%; Norges Bank 3.13%; Qatar Investment Authority 2.27%; Sonatrach 2.19%; Canada Pension Plan Investment Board 2.17%; Bank of America 2.02%; EDP (Treasury stock) 0.49%: others 55.41%
EDP Renewables	EDP 82.6%. others 17.4%
RWE (Germany)	BlackRock Inc 7%, Private shareholders 12%, Empoyees 1%, Institutional shareholders 87%
SSE (UK & Republic of Ireland)	The Capital Group USA 5.19%; BlackRock 5.19%; UBS Investment Bank 4.93%; Invesco Ltd 4.69%; Caisse de depot et placement du Quebec 3.99%
Vestas (Denmark)	BlackRock 5.0%; 159,520 registered shareholders own rest

Source: Company Annual Reports for 2020 or 2021.
Indicates share ownership although the percentage of voting rights may differ.

References

Aalbers, M.B. (2016) The financialisation of Housing: A political economy approach, Routledge, Abingdon.

Agnew, H. (2022) ESG: the next mis-selling scandal? Financial Times, 21 February, https://www.ft.com/content/098131a1-97da-4327-aec3-c2fdc3f61cca?segmentId=114a04fe-353d-37db-f705-204c9a0a157b

AGORIA (2022) Factories of the Future: 12 specific cases, https://acdn.be/enewsv7/upload/whitepaper/FoF_2020_EN.pdf

American Council on Renewable Energy (ACORE) and Clean Energy Leadership Institute (2020) Clean Jobs, Better Jobs, 22 October, https://e2.org/wp-content/uploads/2020/10/Clean-Jobs-Better-Jobs.-October-2020.-E2-ACORE-CELI.pdf

Americans for Financial Reform and Private Equity Stakeholder Project (2022) Private Equity Climate Risks, Scorecard 2022, https://ourfinancialsecurity.org/2022/09/news-release-new-scorecard-shows-private-equitys-race-to-the-bottom-on-climate-2/

Ameresco (2021) Ameresco Announces Energy Conservation Project Partnership with Merthyr Tydfil Council, Press Release, 16 December, https://www.ameresco.com/ameresco-announces-energy-conservation-project-partnership-with-merthyr-tydfil-council/

Anand, P.B. (2004) Financing the Provision of Public Goods, World Economy, Vol. 27(2), 215-237

Andreoni, M. (2022) The climate math just got harder, Climate Forward, New York Times, 30 June, https://www.nytimes.com/2022/06/30/climate/supreme-court-ruling-epa.html

Ardian Infrastructure (2022) Ardian raises record $5.25bn infrastructure secondaries fund, Press Release 22 April, Paris. https://www.ardian.com/press-releases/ardian-raises-record-525bn-infrastructure-secondaries-fund

Armstrong, R. (2021) The ESG investing industry is dangerous: A BlackRock dissident speaks truth, Financial Times, 24 August, https://www.ft.com/content/ec02fd5d-e8bd-45bd-b015-a5799ae820cf

Asian Development Bank (2017) Meeting Asia's Infrastructure Needs, Manila, https://www.adb.org/sites/default/files/publication/227496/special-report-infrastructure.pdf

AusNet Gippsland (2022) Project Update, Issue 1, June, https://admin.grez.com.au/media/G-REZ_Project_Update_-_June_2022.pdf

Australian Energy Market Operator (2018) Integrated System Plan, July, https://aemo.com.au/-/media/files/electricity/nem/planning_and_forecasting/isp/2018/integrated-system-plan-2018_final.pdf?la=en

Australian Energy Market Operator (2021) Appendix 3. Renewable energy zones, Appendix to Draft 2022 ISP for the National Electricity Market, December, https://aemo.com.au/-/media/files/major-publications/isp/2022/appendix-3-renewable-energy-zones.pdf?la=en

Australian Energy Market Operator (2022) Electricity Statement of Opportunities (ESOO), August 2022, https://aemo.com.au/-/media/files/electricity/nem/planning_and_forecasting/nem_esoo/2022/2022-electricity-statement-of-opportunities.pdf?la=en&hash=AED781BE4F1C692F59B1B9CB4EB30C4C

Australian Government (2022) Jobs + Skills Summit: Outcomes, 1-2 September, https://treasury.gov.au/sites/default/files/inline-files/Jobs-and-Skills-Summit-Outcomes-Document.pdf

Australian Industry Energy Transitions Initiative (2022) Setting up industrial regions for net zero, June, https://www.cefc.com.au/media/go4n1v5p/setting-up-industrial-regions-for-net-zero-australian-industry-eti-report-june-2022.pdf

Australian Industrial Transformation Institute (2021) The Factory of the Future, Brochure, https://factoryofthefuture.com.au/wp-content/uploads/2022/03/V8-Factory-of-the-Future-Brochure-WEB.pdf

Australian Industrial Transformation Institute (2021) Manufacturing Transformation: high value manufacturing for the 21st Century. Adelaide: Australian Industrial Transformation Institute, Flinders University of South Australia, https://www.flinders.edu.au/content/dam/documents/research/aiti/manufacturing-transformation-high-value-manufacturing-for-the-21st-century.pdf

Australian Labor Party (2021) Powering Australia: Labor's plan to create jobs, cut power bills and reduce emissions by boosting renewable energy, https://keystone-alp.s3-ap-southeast-2.amazonaws.com/prod/61a9693a3f3c53001f975017-PoweringAustralia.pdf

Azure Power Global Limited (2021) Azure Power Announces Rights Offering for Equity Shares, 27 December, https://www.azurepower.com/sites/default/files/2022-01/Azure Power Announces Rights Offering for Equity Shares.pdf

Azure Power (2022) Announces Final Results of Rights Offering, 27 January, https://www.azurepower.com/sites/default/files/2022-01/01-27-2022-120143895.pdf

Baker, L. (2021) Procurement, finance and the energy transition: Between global processes and territorial realities, Nature and Space, 0(0) 1-27, doi: 10.1177/25148486219

BBC Wales (2022) Climate: Wales to set up publicly-owned renewable energy firm, 26 October, https://www.bbc.com/news/uk-wales-63392646

Bellini, E. (2022) Belgian grid operator expands network to host more solar, heat pumps, EVs, PV Magazine, 10 June, https://www.pv-magazine.com/2022/06/10/belgian-grid-operator-expands-network-to-host-more-solar-heat-pumps-evs/

Berliner Stadtwerke (2021) Berliner Stadtwerke to establish 23-MW of PV systems on public buildings, Press Release, 17 December, https://list.solar/news/berliner-stadtwerke

Berlo, K., Templin, W. and Wagner, O. (2016) Remunicipalisation as an Instrument for Local Climate Strategies in Germany: The Conditions of the Legal Energy Framework as an Obstacle for the Local Energy Transition, Renewable Energy Law and Policy Review, 7 (2016), 2, 113-121.

Beyond Zero Emissions (2021) Renewable Energy Industrial Precincts: Economic Analysis Summary Report, https://bze.org.au/wp-content/uploads/2021/07/EconomicAnaysisSummaryReport.pdf

Beyond Zero Emissions (2022) Hunter Renewable Energy Industrial Precinct, Briefing Paper, April, Melbourne, https://bze.org.au/wp-content/uploads/2022/04/Hunter-REIP-Briefing-Paper-April-2022_v3.pdf

BlackRock (2022) BlackRock and Mubadala to invest $525m in Tata Power Renewables, 20 April, https://www.energylivenews.com/2022/04/20/blackrock-and-mubadala-to-invest-525m-in-tata-power-renewables/ - :~:text=BlackRock Real Assets and Mubadala,Tata Power's renewable energy business.

Blackstone Inc (2022) Invenergy announces approximately $3 billion investment from Blackstone Infrastructure Partners to accelerate renewable development activities, Press Release, 7 January, https://www.blackstone.com/news/press/invenergy-announces-approximately-3-billion-investment-from-blackstone-infrastructure-partners-to-accelerate-renewable-development-activities/

Blazquez, J., Fuentes-Bracamontes, R., Bollino, C.A. and Nezamuddin, N. (2017) The Renewable energy policy Paradox, Renewable and Sustainable Energy Reviews, https://doi.org/10.1016/j.rser.2017.09.002

Bloomberg (2022) India plans US$10 billion investment for 50,000 electric buses, 20 July, https://ieefa.org/articles/india-plans-10-billion-investment-50000-electric-buses?utm_source=Daily+IEEFA+Newsletter&utm_campaign=57733b6589-IEEFA_DailyDigest&utm_medium=email&utm_term=0_e793f87bcc-57733b6589-128765370

BloombergNEF (2021) New Energy Outlook 2021, https://www.bloomberg.com/

BloombergNEF (2022) Energy Transition Investment Trends 2022, January, Summary, https://about.bnef.com/energy-transition-investment/ - toc-report

BloombergNEF and The Business Council for Sustainable Energy (2022) Sustainable Energy in American 2022 Factbook, March, https://bcse.org/2022factbook-top5trends/

Bohm, S., Misoczky, M.C. and Moog, S. (2012) Greening Capitalism? A Marxist Critique of Carbon Markets, Organization Studies, 0(0)- 1-22, doi:10.1177/0170840612463326

Boyd, D. and Hadley Burke, M. (2022) Sacrifice Zones: 50 of the most polluted places on earth: UN Special Rapporteur on Human Rights & Environment, https://www.ohchr.org/Documents/Issues/Environment/Sacrifice Zones-userfriendlyversion.pdf

Boyde, E. (2021) ESG outperformance looks set to end, study suggests, Financial Times, 6 July, https://www.ft.com/content/a3d67827-1f79-4b18-8c36-f26e18ced9cf

Breyer, C. and 22 others (2022) On the History and Future of 100% Renewable Energy Systems Research, IEEE Access, https://ieeexplore.ieee.org/stamp/stamp.jsp?tp=&arnumber=9837910

British Petroleum (2022) BP Statistical Review of World Energy 2022, https://www.bp.com/content/dam/bp/business-sites/en/global/corporate/pdfs/energy-economics/statistical-review/bp-stats-review-2022-full-report.pdf

Brookfield Renewable Partners (2019) Brookfield Renewable Announces 14% Growth in FFO and 5% Distribution Increase, 8 February, https://bep.brookfield.com/press-releases/bep/brookfield-renewable-announces-14-growth-ffo-and-5-distribution-increase

Brookfield Renewable Partners L.P. (2022) Annual Report 2021, Bermuda, https://bep.brookfield.com/sites/bep-brookfield-ir/files/brookfield/bep/reports-and-filings/regulatory-filings/annual-reports/2021/bep-2021-annual-report.pdf

Brookfield Renewables (2022) Brookfield to invest up to US$2 billion in Scout Clean Energy and Standard Solar, Press Release, 29 September, https://bep.brookfield.com/press-releases/bep/brookfield-invest-2-billion-scout-clean-energy-and-standard-solar

Brookings Metro (2022) Not According To Plan: Exploring gaps in City Climate planning and the need for regional action, https://www.brookings.edu/wp-content/uploads/2022/09/Decarbonization_final.pdf

Businesswire (2022) Quinbrook Sells Scout Clean Energy to Brookfield for US$1 billion, 29 September, https://www.businesswire.com/news/home/20220928006126/en/Quinbrook-Sells-Scout-Clean-Energy-to-Brookfield-for-US1-billion

Busshardt, B. (2014) Analysing the Remunicipalisation of Public Services in OECD Countries https://epub.ub.uni-muenchen.de/20883/1/68_Münchener Beiträge zur Politikwissenschaft_Bastian Bußhardt.pdf

California Public Utilities Commission (2022) CPUC Approves Long Term Plans to Meet Electricity Reliability and Climate Goals, 10 February, https://www.cpuc.ca.gov/news-and-updates/all-news/cpuc-approves-long-term-plans-to-meet-electricity-reliability-and-climate-goals

Canadian Solar (2022) Canadian Solar sells to SPIC Brasil 70% stake in 738MWp solar projects, Press Release, 6 June, http://investors.canadiansolar.com/news-releases/news-release-details/canadian-solar-sells-spic-brasil-70-stake-738-mwp-solar-projects

Carbon Action Tracker (2022) Decarbonising buildings: Achieving zero carbon heating and cooling, March, https://climateactiontracker.org/documents/1018/CAT_2022-03-09_Report_DecarbonisingBuildings.pdf

Carlyle Group and GIC (2022) Carlyle and GIC invest in green ammonia development company Eneus Energy to accelerate gigawatt-scale energy security and decarbonization solutions, https://www.carlyle.com/media-room/news-release-archive/carlyle-and-gic-invest-in-green-ammonia-development-company-eneus-energy

Carroll, D. (2022a) Transgrid builds high-voltage interconnector to link Australian states, PV Magazine, 1 June. https://www.pv-magazine.com/2022/06/01/transgrid-builds-high-voltage-interconnector-to-link-australian-states/

Carroll, D. (2022b) New Research shifts sodium batteries from risky liquid to safe solid, PV Magazine, 8 August, https://www.pv-magazine.com/2022/08/08/new-research-shifts-sodium-batteries-from-risky-liquid-to-safe-solid/

Cass, D., Connor, L., Heikkinen and Pearse, R. (2022) Renewables & rural Australia, A study of community experiences in Renewable Energy Zones in NSW and the case for more equity and coordination of the clean energy transformation, Australia Institute and Sydney Environment Institute, https://australiainstitute.org.au/wp-content/uploads/2022/06/P1176-Renewables-and-Rural-Australia-WEB-2.pdf

Catapult Network (2019) Creating the Future Through Innovation, Recovery and Resilience, https://catapult.org.uk/wp-content/uploads/2020/12/Catapult-Network-Impact-Brochure-2020-FINAL.pdf

Catapult Network (2021) Accelerating a UK Hydrogen Economy, https://catapult.org.uk/wp-content/uploads/2021/04/9384_Accelerating-a-UK-Hydrogen-Economy-1.pdf

Catapult Energy Systems (2022) Insights for Smart Local Energy Systems, https://es.catapult.org.uk/report/enabling-smart-local-energy-systems-the-value-of-digitalisation-and-data-best-practice/

Catapult Offshore Renewable Energy and Zero Waste Scotland (2022) End of Life Materials Mapping for Offshore Wind in Scotland, Report from Phase 1 of the Elmwood Project, https://ore.catapult.org.uk/wp-content/uploads/2022/07/FINAL-Catapult_ELMWind_Report-online-version.pdf

Centre for Sustainable Finance, Global Development Policy Center and Heinrich Boll Stiftung (2021) Debt Relief for a Green and Inclusive Recovery: Securing Private-Sector Participation and Creating Policy Space for Sustainable Development, https://eprints.soas.ac.uk/35254/1/DRGR Report 2021.pdf

Climate Action Tracker (2022) Decarbonising buildings: Achieving zero carbon heating and cooling, March, https://climateactiontracker.org/documents/1018/CAT_2022-03-09_Report_DecarbonisingBuildings.pdf

Climate Change Committee (2019) UK housing: Fit for the future? London, https://www.theccc.org.uk/publication/uk-housing-fit-for-the-future/

Climate Change Committee (2022) Independent Assessment: The UK's Heat and Buildings Strategy, March, https://www.theccc.org.uk/publication/independent-assessment-the-uks-heat-and-buildings-strategy/

Climate Policy Initiative (2021) Global Landscape of Climate Finance 2021, December, https://www.climatepolicyinitiative.org/wp-content/uploads/2021/10/Full-report-Global-Landscape-of-Climate-Finance-2021.pdf

Cobham, A. (2019) MauritiusLeaks primer: What to know about corporate tax haven Mauritius, Tax Justice Network, July, https://taxjustice.net/2019/07/23/mauritiusleaks-primer-what-to-know-about-corporate-tax-haven-mauritius/

Cohen, D. and Mikaelian, A. (2021) The Privatization of Everything: How the Plunder of Public Goods Transformed America and How We Can Fight Back, New Press, New York City.

Compliance Week (2021) Global Infrastructure Management fined $4.5m for compliance failures, 21 December, https://www.complianceweek.com/regulatory-enforcement/global-infrastructure-management-fined-45m-for-compliance-failures/31193.article

Construction Skills Queensland (2022) Queensland's Renewable Future: Investment, jobs and skills, August, https://www.csq.org.au/wp-content/uploads/2022/08/CSQ-Queenslands-Renewable-Future-full-report.pdf

Counter Balance (2022) Flattering to Deceive: A reality check for the 'EU Climate Bank', June, https://counter-balance.org/uploads/files/EIB-Climate-Report_w.pdfFlattering to deceive

Dasgupta, Partha (2021) The Economics of Biodiversity: The Dasgupta Review, HM Treasury, London, https://assets.publishing.service.gov.uk/government/uploads/system/uploads/attachment_data/file/962785/The_Economics_of_Biodiversity_The_Dasgupta_Review_Full_Report.pdf

DialoguE on European Decarbonisation Strategies (2020) Research and Innovation to decarbonise the Agriculture and Land-Use sector, Policy Brief Number 5, April, https://agritrop.cirad.fr/596508/1/DEEDS-Policy-Brief-5-Agriculture-and-Land-Use.pdf

Deloitte Africa (2013) PPP Secondary Market, http://deloitteblog.co.za/wp-content/uploads/2013/07/PPP-Secondary-Markets.pdf

Deneulin, S, and Townsend, N. (2007) Public Goods, Global Public Goods and the Common Good, International Journal of Social Economics 34(1/2) 19-36.

Department for Business, Energy & Industrial Strategy (2021) Social Housing Decarbonisation Fund, Launch Webinar, https://assets.publishing.service.gov.uk/government/uploads/system/uploads/attachment_data/file/1011024/shdf-webinar-slides.pdf

Department for Business, Energy & Industrial Strategy (2022) Government hits accelerator on low-cost renewable power, Press Release, 9 February, https://www.gov.uk/government/news/government-hits-accelerator-on-low-cost-renewable-power

Department for Business, Energy & Industrial Strategy (2022) British Energy Security Strategy, April, https://www.gov.uk/government/publications/british-energy-security-strategy

Department for Environment, Food & Rural Affairs (2022) Draft Environmental principles policy statement, May, https://www.gov.uk/government/publications/environmental-principles-policy-statement/draft-environmental-principles-policy-statement

Department for Communities and Local Government (2006) A Decent Home: Definition ad guidance for implementation, June 2006 – Update, https://assets.publishing.service.gov.uk/government/uploads/system/uploads/attachment_data/file/7812/138355.pdf

Department of the Environment, Climate and Communications (2022) National Retrofit Plan, February, Dublin, https://www.gov.ie/en/publication/5052a-national-retrofit-plan/ - :

Dialogue on European Decarbonisation Pathways (2020) Research and Innovation Strategies for Decarbonisation Pathways in Europe and the World, https://deeds.eu/wp-content/uploads/2020/07/D1.3-RI-strategies-for-Europe1-1.pdf

Dobson, P. and Edwards, R. (2022) Carbon pollution from incinerators rises by 100,000 tonnes, The Ferret, 27 April, https://theferret.scot/carbon-pollution-incinerators-rises-100000-tonnes/

Doyle, T.M. (2018) Ratings that Don't Rate: The Subjective World of ESG Ratings Agencies, American Council for Capital Formation, https://accfcorpgov.org/wpcontent/uploads/2018/07/ACCF_RatingsESGReport.pdf

EDF (2022) French government launches public takeover bid to fully control EDF, Euractiv, 20 July, https://www.euractiv.com/section/energy/news/french-government-launches-public-takeover-bid-to-fully-control-edf/

EDPR (2022) EDPR implements new operating model and renews its management team, 11 January, https://www.edpr.com/en/news/2022/01/11/edpr-implements-new-operating-model-and-renews-its-management-team

EirGrid (2021) All-Island Generation Capacity Statement 2021-2030, Dublin, https://www.eirgridgroup.com/site-files/library/EirGrid/208281-All-Island-Generation-Capacity-Statement-LR13A.pdf

Electricity Supply Board (2022) Green Atlantic at Moneypoint, Press Release, 22 August, Dublin, https://esb.ie/what-we-do/generation-and-trading/green-atlantic-at-moneypoint?gclid=CjwKCAjw3qGYBhBSEiwAcnTRLtIPWyvrkSKNZUn1JNQj0BP1ORsvGCstRml6ua2cvZ1oCmhaUJpTFBoCxisQAvD_BwE&gclsrc=aw.ds

Elder, I. (2022) Driving the Future: How to electrify our School Buses and Center Kids, Communities and workers in the Transition, Jobs to Move America, https://jobstomoveamerica.org/resource/driving-the-future-how-to-electrify-our-school-buses-and-center-kids-communities-and-workers-in-the-transition/?emci=b4db7e01-ece0-ec11-b656-281878b85110&emdi=cdfc4391-f0e0-ec11-b656-281878b85110&ceid=4710547

Elliott Management (2016) How Argentina Settled a Billion-Dollar Debt Dispute With Hedge Funds, New York Times, 25 April, https://www.nytimes.com/2016/04/25/business/dealbook/how-argentina-settled-a-billion-dollar-debt-dispute-with-hedge-funds.html - :~:text=Singer of Elliott to his,bonds, according to the ministry.

Elliott Management (2019) Elliott Believes in a Brighter Future for EDP, 14 February, https://www.businesswire.com/news/home/20190213005945/en/Elliott-Believes-in-a-Brighter-Future-for-EDP

Elliott Management (2021) Elliott Investment Management sends letter to Board of Directors of Duke Energy Corporation, https://www.prnewswire.com/news-releases/elliott-investment-management-sends-letter-to-board-of-directors-of-duke-energy-corporation-301292688.html

EnBW (2022) EnBW takes on solar projects in Brandenburg, 23 June, https://www.enbw.com/company/press/enbw-takes-over-solar-projects-in-brandenburg-from-procon-solar.html

Encavis (2022) Annual Report 2021, Encavis_Geschaeftsbericht_2021_EN_geschuetzt.pdf

Energy Cities (2017) Local Energy Ownership in Europe: An Exploratory Study of Local Public Initiatives in France, Germany and the United Kingdom, https://energy-cities.eu/wp-content/uploads/2019/01/local_energy_ownership_study-energycities-en.pdf

Energy Corporation of New South Wales (2022) Illawarra Renewable Energy Zone, https://www.energyco.nsw.gov.au/index.php/renewable-energy-zones/illawarra-renewable-energy-zone

Energy & Climate Intelligence Unit (2021) Stuck on the Starting Line: How the UK is falling behind Europe in the race to clean steel, May, London, https://ca1-eci.edcdn.com/reports/ECIU_stuck_starting_line.pdf?v=1621866013

Energy Saving Trust (2022) What are the benefits of community owned wind power?, 15 June, https://energysavingtrust.org.uk/what-are-the-benefits-of-community-owned-wind-power/

Environment America, Fronter Group & U.S.PIRG Education Fund (2021) Blocking Rooftop Solar: The companies, lobbyists and front groups undermining local clean energy, https://environmentamerica.org/sites/environment/files/Blocking_Rooftop_Solar_2021.pdf?_ga=2.255677519.637776731.1632727395-1502757072.1632727395

Equality Commission for Northern Ireland (2010) Section 75 of the Northern Ireland Act 1998: A Guide for Public Authorities, https://www.equalityni.org/ECNI/media/ECNI/Publications/Employers and Service Providers/S75GuideforPublicAuthoritiesApril2010.pdf?ext=.pdf

Equinor ASA (2022) Equinor acquires energy storage developer in the US, Press Release, 12 July, https://www.equinor.com/news/acquires-energy-storage-developer-us

European Commission (2019) The European Green Deal, COM(2019) 640 final, https://eur-lex.europa.eu/resource.html?uri=cellar:b828d165-1c22-11ea-8c1f-01aa75ed71a1.0002.02/DOC_1&format=PDF

European Commission (2020a) EU taxonomy for sustainable activities, https://ec.europa.eu/info/publications/sustainable-finance-renewed-strategy_en

European Commission (2020b) The new renewable energy financing mechanism of the EU in practice, D6.3-EU August, https://ec.europa.eu/research/participants/documents/downloadPublic?documentIds=080166e5d3146625&appId=PPGMS

European Commission (2021) Next Generation EU - Green Bond Framework, Commission Staff Working Document, SWD(2021) 242 final, 7 September, https://ec.europa.eu/info/sites/default/files/about_the_european_commission/eu_budget/nextgenerationeu_green_bond_framework.pdf

European Commission (2022a) REPowerEU: Joint European action for more affordable and secure energy, 8 March, https://ec.europa.eu/commission/presscorner/detail/en/ip_22_1511

European Commission (2022b) NetZeroCities, Draft Report on City Needs, Drivers and Barriers towards Climate Neutrality, https://netzerocities.eu/wp-content/uploads/2022/04/DRAFT-D13.1-Report-on-city-needs-drivers-and-barriers-towards-climate-neutrality.pdf

European Commission (2022c) Building a European Research Area for clean hydrogen - the role of EU research and innovation investments to deliver on the EU's Hydrogen Strategy, SWD(2022) 15 final, https://ec.europa.eu/info/files/commission-staff-working-document-building-european-research-area-clean-hydrogen_en

European Investment Fund (2021) The European Investment Fund closes a commitment to invest €50 million in Spanish fund Everwood Renewables Europe V FCR focusing on renewable assets in Southern Europe, Press Release, 13 December, https://www.eif.europa.eu/what_we_do/guarantees/news/2021/50-million-in-spanish-fund-everwood-renewables-europe-v-fcr.htm

European Investment Bank (2022) EIB boosts clean energy financing in support of REPowerEU Plan, October, https://www.eib.org/en/press/all/2022-450-eib-boosts-clean-energy-financing-in-support-of-repowereu-plan.htm

European Court of Auditors (2018) Public Private Partnerships in the EU: Widespread shortcomings and limited benefits, Special Report, Luxembourg, https://www.eca.europa.eu/Lists/ECADocuments/SR18_09/ SR_PPP_EN.pdf

Eurowind Energy (2022) Eurowind Energy launches five energy centres, July, https://eurowindenergy.com/insights/eurowind-energy-launches-five-energy-centers

Everwood Capital (2019a) Everwood sells its photovoltaic to Infravia and Euraceo and makes gold to Andbank clients – El Confidencial, 12 September, https://everwoodcapital.com/blog/everwood-vende-su-fotovoltacica—infravia-y-rurzeo-y-hace-de-oro-a-clientes-de-andbank/

Everwood Capital (2019b) Univergy (Macquarie's partner) sells two 75 MW solar projects to Everwood – El Confidencial, 27 September, https://everwoodcapital.com/blog/univergy-macquaries-partner-sells-two-75-MW-solar-projects/

Everwood Capital (2021) Everwood Capital sells a solar plant to Falck Renewables and achieves 25% annual IRR, 29 March, https://everwoodcapital.com/blog/everwood-capital-sells-a-solar-plant-to-falck-renewables-and-achieves-25-annual-irr-el-confidencial/

Export-Impact Bank of the United States (2021) Report to the U.S. Congress on Global Export Credit Competition, June, Washington DC, https://www.exim.gov/sites/default/files/reports/competitiveness_reports/2020/EXIM_2020_CompetitivenessReport_Web-Ready_Single pages.pdf

Fairchild, D. and Weinrub, A. editors (2017) Energy Democracy: Advancing Equity in Clean Energy Solutions, Island Press, Washington DC.

Falck Renewables S.p.A. (2021) Falck Renewables completes the acquisition of an operating solar plant in Spain, Press Release, 20 April, https://www.falckrenewables.com/en/media/documents-detail/falck-renewables-completes-acquisition-operating-solar-plant-spain

Falck (2022) Closing of the acquisition of Falck S.p.A.'s 60 per cent shareholding in Falck Renewables S.p.A. Press Release 24 February, https://www.falckrenewables.com/en/media/documents-detail/closing-acquisition-falck-sps-60-cent-shareholding-falck-renewables-spa

Fernandez, R. (2021) Community Renewable Energy Projects: The Future of the Sustainable Energy Transition?, The International Spectator, 56:3, 87-104, doi:10.1080/03932729.2021.1959755

Financial Times (2022a) Uniper drops coal case as tensions rise over treaty on fossil fuel projects, 15 August, https://www.ft.com/content/0a1406f7-4338-478c-ab11-b0c2c12faac8

Financial Times (2022b) Germany's Uniper on the 'brink of insolvency' after €12bn loss, 18 August, https://www.ft.com/content/2805e7eb-9cef-4756-bd5c-e4f71b699b92

Financial Times (2022c) Brookfield considers spinning off its asset management business, 11 February, https://www.ft.com/content/88aed216-caa0-4097-b6bc-0bdf98e0228a

Financial Times (2022d) BP takes 40% stake in vast $30bn Australian renewables project, 14 June, https://www.ft.com/content/78361493-4ed9-4f63-8f36-1334e44a90dc

Financial Times (2022e) JP Morgan fights nuns and activists over climate disclosure proposals, 27 February, https://www.ft.com/search?q=JP+Morgan+fights+nuns+and+activists+over+climate+disclosure+proposals

Financial Times (2022f) West London faces new homes ban as electricity grid hits capacity, 28 July, h ttps://www.ft.com/content/519f701f-6a05-4cf4-bc46-22cf10c7c2c0

Financial Times (2022g) Global steelmakers face $518bn stranded asset risk, 21 June, https://www.ft.com/content/d1a7ecf0-7f10-4faa-94cf-8a6a8cf3feb7

First Street Foundation (2022) Hazardous Heat: The 6th National Risk Assessment, https://firststreet.org/press/press-release-2022-heat-model-launch/

Fischer, A. (2022) Community Solar: Interconnection bottlenecks and other barriers to growth, PV-Magazine, 14 March, https://pv-magazine-usa.com/2022/03/14/community-solar-interconnection-bottlenecks-and-other-barriers-to-growth

Fitzgibbon, W. (2019) Treasure Island: Leak Reveals How Mauritius Siphons Tax From Poor Nations to Benefit Elites, International Consortium of Investigative Journalists, https://www.icij.org/investigations/mauritius-leaks/treasure-island-leak-reveals-how-mauritius-siphons-tax-from-poor-nations-to-benefit-elites/

Frankfurt School-United Nations Environment Programme Collaborating Centre and Bloomberg New Energy Finance (2020) Global Trends in Renewable Energy Investment 2020, Frankfurt, https://www.fs-unep-centre.org/wp-content/uploads/2020/06/GTR_2020.pdf

Fraunhofer Institute for Solar Systems (2020) Sustainable PV Manufacturing in Europe, https://www.ise.fraunhofer.de/en/renewable-energy-data.html

Fraunhofer Institute for Solar Systems (2021) Levelized Cost of Electricity-Renewable Energy Technologies, https://www.ise.fraunhofer.de/en/publications/studies/cost-of-electricity.html

Fraunhofer Institute for Solar Systems (2022) Fraunhofer ISE develops the world's most efficient solar cell with an efficiency of 47.6 percent, https://www.ise.fraunhofer.de/en/press-media/press-releases/2022/fraunhofer-ise-develops-the-worlds-most-efficient-solar-cell-with-47-comma-6-percent-efficiency.html

G7 countries (2022) G7 Climate, Energy and Environment Ministers' Communique, Berlin, 27 May, https://www.bmwk.de/Redaktion/DE/Downloads/G/g7-konferenz-klima-energie-umweltminister-05-2022-abschlusskommunique.pdf?__blob=publicationFile&v=14

Gabor, D. (2020) The European Green Deal will bypass the poor and go straight to the rich, The Guardian, 19 February, https://www.theguardian.com/commentisfree/2020/feb/19/european-green-deal-polish-miners

Gaspar, V., Mauro, P., Pattillo, C. and Espinoza, R. (2020) Public Investment for the Recovery, IMF Blog, 5 October, https://blogs.imf.org/2020/10/05/public-investment-for-the-recovery/

Global Alliance for Buildings and Construction (2020) GlobalABC Roadmap for Buildings and Construction 2020-2050, https://globalabc.org/our-work/forging-regional-pathways-global-and-regional-roadmap

Global Alliance for Buildings and Construction & UN Environment Programme (2021) 2021 Global Status Report for Buildings and Construction, https://globalabc.org/our-work/tracking-progress-global-status-report

Global Alliance for Tax Justice, Public Services International & Tax Justice Network (2021) The State of Tax Justice 2021, November, https://www.globaltaxjustice.org/sites/default/files/State_of_Tax_Justice_Report_2021_ENGLISH_15-11-2021_v13b.pdf

Global Infrastructure Hub (2021) Infrastructure Monitor 2021, December, https://cdn.gihub.org/umbraco/media/4306/gihub_infrastructuremonitor2021.pdf

Global Infrastructure Hub (2022) Investors are twice as likely to invest in renewable energy in developed markets as in developing markets, June, https://www.gihub.org/infrastructure-monitor/insights/investors-are-twice-as-likely-to-invest-in-renewable-energy-in-developed-markets-as-in-developing-markets/

Global Infrastructure Hub (2021) Infrastructure Monitor 2022, https://cdn.gihub.org/umbraco/media/4806/global-infrastructure-hub_2022-infrastructure-monitor-report_web.pdf

Global Wind Energy Council (2021) Global Wind Energy Manifesto for COP26, https://gwec.net/wp-content/uploads/2021/10/EN-Global-Wind-Energy-Manifesto-for-COP26.pdf

Global Wind Energy Council (2022) Capturing Green Recovery Opportunities from Wind Power in Developing Economies, February, https://gwec.net/wp-content/uploads/2022/02/REPORT_Capturing-Green-Recovery-Opportunities-from-Wind-Power-in-Developing-Economies.pdf

Goedertier, D. (2021) Guest Post: Public energy companies necessary for a fair transition, TUED Bulletin 107, https://web.archive.org/web/20210812023340/https://unionsforenergydemocracy.org/tued-bulletin-107/

Goldman Sachs Equity Research (2022) Electrify Now: The rise of Power in European Economies, 24 January, https://www.goldmansachs.com/insights/pages/gs-research/electrify-now-the-rise-of-power-in-european-economies/report.pdf

Gotham, K.F. (2009) Creating Liquidity out of Spatial Fixity: The Secondary Circuit of Capital and the Subprime Mortgage Crisis, International Journal of Urban and Regional Research Vol.33.2, 355-71.

Government of Ireland (2019) Climate Action Plan, https://www.teagasc.ie/media/website/publications/2019/climate-action-plan.pdf

Greencoat Renewables (2022) RNS Number 0593H, 4 April, Offshore Transaction in German Market, https://otp.tools.investis.com/clients/uk/greencoat_renewables/rns/regulatory-story.aspx?cid=2236&newsid=1570385

Green Investment Group (2022) GIG portfolio company, Corio Generation partners with Ontario Teachers' to pursue global offshore wind development, 12 May, https://www.greeninvestmentgroup.com/en/news/2022/gig-portfolio-company-corio-generation-partners-with-ontario-teachers.html

The Guardian (2022a) France becomes latest country to leave controversial energy charter treaty, 21 October, https://www.theguardian.com/world/2022/oct/21/france-becomes-latest-country-to-leave-controversial-energy-charter-treaty

Heating & Ventilation News (2022) Ventive to build whole-house heat pump and ventilation units in Worcestershire, 10 March, https://www.hvnplus.co.uk/news/ventive-to-build-whole-house-heat-pump-and-ventilation-units-in-worcestershire-10-03-2022/

Hall D. (2015) Why public-private partnerships don't work. The many advantages of the public alternative, PSIRU, http://www.world-psi.org/sites/default/files/rapport_eng_56pages_a4_lr.pdf

Harvey, D. (2003) The New Imperialism, Oxford University Press, Oxford.

Harvey, D. (2006) The Limits to Capital, Verso Books, London.

Hashimoto, K. et al (2015) iKaaS Data Modeling: A Data Model for Community Services and Environmental Monitoring in Smart City, 2015 IEEE International Conference on Autonomic Computing, https://ieeexplore.ieee.org/document/7266984

HM Treasury (2018) Budget 2018, 29 October, https://www.gov.uk/government/publications/budget-2018-documents/budget-2018

House of Commons Business, Energy and Industrial Strategy Committee (2022) Revised (Draft) National Policy Statement for Energy, HC 1151, 25 February, London, https://committees.parliament.uk/committee/365/business-energy-and-industrial-strategy-committee/publications/

House of Commons Committee of Public Accounts (2011) Lessons from PFI and other projects (HC 1201), September https://publications.parliament.uk/pa/cm201012/cmselect/cmpubacc/1201/1201.pdf

House of Commons Committee of Public Accounts (2018) Private Finance Initiative (HC 894) August, https://publications.parliament.uk/pa/cm201719/cmselect/cmpubacc/894/894.pdf

House of Commons Library (2016) Zero Carbon Homes, Briefing Paper No. 6678, 27 April, https://commonslibrary.parliament.uk/research-briefings/sn06678/

House of Commons Treasury Committee (2011) Private Finance Initiative (HC 1146) August, https://publications.parliament.uk/pa/cm201012/cmselect/cmtreasy/1146/1146vw.pdf

House of Lords Industry and Regulators Committee (2022) The net zero transformation: delivery, regulation and the consumer, HL Paper 162, London, 4 March, https://publications.parliament.uk/pa/ld5802/ldselect/ldindreg/162/162.pdf

Hugonnet, R. and 10 others (2021) Accelerated global glacier mass loss in the early twenty-first century, Nature, 592, 726-731 https://www.nature.com/articles/s41586-021-03436-z

Iberdrola S.A. (2020) Diversity and Inclusion Report 2020, https://www.iberdrola.com/documents/20125/41590/IA_ReportDiversityInclusion_2020.pdf/77e612f0-1c34-5e9b-91da-193bf864312b?t=1629440625428

Infrastructure Intelligence (2022) Green light for £300m Teesside offshore wind factory, 20 June, http://www.infrastructure-intelligence.com/article/jun-2022/green-light-£300m-teesside-offshore-wind-factory

Infrastructure Investor (2022) How Quinbrook grew $6m seed platform to $1bn Brookfield sale, 11 October, https://www.infrastructureinvestor.com/how-quinbrook-grew-6m-seed-platform-to-1bn-brookfield-sale/

Infrastructure Partnerships Australia (2022) Decarbonising Construction, August, Sydney, https://apo.org.au/sites/default/files/resource-files/2022-08/apo-nid319240.pdf

Institute for Energy Economics and Financial Analysis (2021) Global Investors Move Into Renewable Infrastructure: Reviewing the World's Top Renewable Energy Financiers, July, https://ieefa.org/wp-content/uploads/2021/07/Global-Investors-Move-Into-Renewable-Infrastructure_July-2021.pdf

Institute for Energy Economics and Financial Analysis (2022) Boston announces plans to restrict natural gas use in new buildings, 17 August, https://ieefa.org/articles/boston-announces-plans-restrict-natural-gas-use-new-buildings?utm_source=Daily+IEEFA+Newsletter&utm_campaign=f9a13f03ce-IEEFA_DailyDigest&utm_medium=email&utm_term=0_e793f87bcc-f9a13f03ce-128765370

Inter-American Development Bank (2014) Study of the Development of the Renewable Energy Market in Latin America and the Caribbean, Working Paper OVE/WP-02/14, https://publications.iadb.org/publications/english/document/Study-on-the-Development-of-the-Renewable-Energy-Market-in-Latin-America-and-the-Caribbean.pdf

Intergovernmental Panel on Climate Change (2021) Climate Change 2021: The Physical Science Basis, https://www.ipcc.ch/report/ar6/wg1/downloads/report/IPCC_AR6_WGI_Full_Report.pdf

Intergovernmental Panel on Climate Change (2022) Climate Change 2022: Impacts, Adaptation and Vulnerability, Summary, March, https://report.ipcc.ch/ar6wg2/pdf/IPCC_AR6_WGII_SummaryForPolicymakers.pdf

Intergovernmental Panel on Climate Change (2022) Climate Change 2022: Mitigation of Climate Change, Sixth Assessment Report, https://report.ipcc.ch/ar6wg3/pdf/IPCC_AR6_WGIII_FinalDraft_FullReport.pdf

International Bank for Reconstruction and Development/The World Bank (2019) The Role of the Public Sector in Mobilizing Commercial Finance for Grid-Connected Solar Projects: Lessons from Developing Countries, Washington DC, http://documents1.worldbank.org/curated/en/266531562798274597/pdf/The-Role-of-the-Public-Sector-in-Mobilizing-Commercial-Finance-for-Grid-Connected-Solar-Projects-Lessons-from-Seven-Developing-Countries.pdf

International Energy Agency (2018) The Future of Cooling, https://iea.blob.core.windows.net/assets/0bb45525-277f-4c9c-8d0c-9c0cb5e7d525/The_Future_of_Cooling.pdf

International Energy Agency (2022a) Global electricity demand growth is slowing, weighed down by economic weakness and high prices, 20 July, https://www.iea.org/news/global-electricity-demand-growth-is-slowing-weighed-down-by-economic-weakness-and-high-prices

International Energy Agency (2022b) Renewable Energy Market Update: Outlook for 2022 and 2023, https://iea.blob.core.windows.net/assets/d6a7300d-7919-4136-b73a-3541c33f8bd7/RenewableEnergyMarketUpdate2022.pdf

International Energy Agency (2022) Achieving Net Zero Heavy Industry Sectors in G7 Members, May, https://iea.blob.core.windows.net/assets/c4d96342-f626-4aea-8dac-df1d1e567135/AchievingNetZeroHeavyIndustrySectorsinG7Members.pdf

International Energy Agency (2022) The value of urgent action on energy efficiency, 7th Annual Global Conference on Energy Efficiency, June, https://iea.blob.core.windows.net/assets/6ed712b4-32a3-4934-9050-d97a83a45a80/Thevalueofurgentaction-7thAnnualGlobalConferenceonEnergyEfficiency.pdf

International Energy Agency (2022) World Energy Investment 2022, https://iea.blob.core.windows.net/assets/cc7fa800-ea94-428c-b2e5-e9890b34509c/WorldEnergyInvestment2022.pdf

International Energy Agency (2022) Global Hydrogen Review 2022, https://iea.blob.core.windows.net/assets/c5bc75b1-9e4d-460d-9056-6e8e626a11c4/GlobalHydrogenReview2022.pdf

International Institute for Environment and Development (2021) Linking sovereign debt to climate and nature outcomes https://pubs.iied.org/sites/default/files/pdfs/2021-11/20651IIED.pdf

International Monetary Fund (2019) Macroeconomic and Financial Policies for Climate Change Mitigation: A Review of the Literature, Working Paper WP/19/185, https://www.imf.org/en/Publications/WP/Issues/2019/09/04/Macroeconomic-and-Financial-Policies-for-Climate-Change-Mitigation-A-Review-of-the-Literature-48612

International Monetary Fund and World Bank Group (2019) PPP Fiscal Risk Assessment Model PFRAM 2.0, https://library.pppknowledgelab.org/documents/5783/download

International Monetary Fund (2021) Still Not Getting Energy Prices Right: A Global and Country Update of Fossil Fuel Subsidies, Working Paper, WP/20/236, September, Washington DC, http://mf.org/en/Publications/staff-climate-notes/Issues/2022/07/26/Mobilizing-Private-Climate-Financing-in-Emerging-Market-and-Developing-Economies-520585?utm_medium=email&utm_source=govdelivery

International Monetary Fund (2022) Special Purpose Entities Shed Light on the Drivers of Foreign Direct Investment, IMF Blog, 25 March, https://blogs.imf.org/2022/03/25/special-purpose-entities-shed-light-on-the-drivers-of-foreign-direct-investment/

International Monetary Fund (2022) IMF DATA ACCESS TO MACROECONOMIC & FINANCIAL DATA: Balance of Payments and International Investment Position Statistics (BOP/IIP) https://data.imf.org/?sk=7A51304B-6426-40C0-83DD-CA473CA1FD52

International Monetary Fund (2022) Mobilizing Private Climate Financing in Emerging Market and Developing Economies, IMF Staff Climate Note 2022/007, https://www.imf.org/en/Publications/staff-climate-notes/Issues/2022/07/26/Mobilizing-Private-Climate-Financing-in-Emerging-Market-and-Developing-Economies-520585?utm_medium=email&utm_source=govdelivery

International Renewable Energy Agency (2017) Renewable Energy Auctions: Analysing 2016, https://www.irena.org/publications/2017/jun/renewable-energy-auctions-analysing-2016

International Renewable Energy Agency (2020) Global Landscape of Renewable Energy Finance 2020, https://www.irena.org/publications/2020/Nov/Global-Landscape-of-Renewable-Energy-Finance-2020

International Renewable Energy Agency and International Labour Organisation (2021) Renewable Energy and Jobs: Annual Review 2021, Abu Dhabi, Geneva, https://www.irena.org/publications/2021/Oct/Renewable-Energy-and-Jobs-Annual-Review-2021

Intrinsic Exchange Group (2022) The Opportunity, https://www.intrinsicexchange.com/solution - :~:text=Natural Asset Company%3A A corporation,in a Natural Asset Company.

Jaeger, J. (2021) Explaining the Exponential Growth of Renewable Energy, World Resources Institute, 20 September, https://www.wri.org/insights/growth-renewable-energy-sector-explained

Johnson, S. (2021) ESG investment favours tax-avoiding tech companies, Financial Times, 23 February, https://www.ft.com/content/486afe00-5347-4f23-ab30-fb2ab901b2cb

Johnson, S. (2022) ETF investing plummets to lowest level since Covid crisis hit, Financial Times, 9 May, https://www.ft.com/content/57d6c725-5d74-4abb-8233-f2a032d14daa

JP Morgan Chase & Co. (2022) Annual Report 2021, April, New York, https://www.jpmorganchase.com/content/dam/jpmc/jpmorgan-chase-and-co/investor-relations/documents/annualreport-2021.pdf

Jubilee Debt Campaign (2018) Don't owe, shouldn't pay, the impact of climate change on debt in vulnerable countries October, London, https://jubileedebt.org.uk/report/dont-owe-shouldnt-pay-the-impact-of-climate-change-on-debt-in-vulnerable-countries

Jubilee Debt Campaign, Jubilee Scotland & six others (2021) Debt and the climate crisis: a perfect storm, September, London, https://jubileedebt.org.uk/wp-content/uploads/2021/09/Debt-and-the-Climate-Crisis-a-Perfect-Storm.pdf

Kaul, I., Grunberg, I. and Stern, M. (1999) Global Public Goods: International Cooperation in the 21st Century, Oxford University Press, Oxford.

KBRA (2021) ESG Global Rating Methodology, 16 June, https://www.kbra.com/documents/report/47746/esg-global-rating-methodology

Keay. M. and Robinson, D. (2019) The Limits of Auctions: reflections on the role of central purchaser auctions for long-term commitments in electricity systems, The Oxford Institute for Energy Studies, April, https://a9w7k6q9.stackpathcdn.com/wpcms/wp-content/uploads/2019/04/The-Limits-of-Auctions-reflections-on-the-role-of-central-purchaser-auctions-for-long-term-contracts-in-electricity-systems-EL34.pdf

KKR (2022) Albioma and KKR reach strategic agreement on a friendly public tender offer, 28 April, Press Release, https://media.kkr.com/news-details/?news_id=96faf866-4d9a-4a80-b50c-5a91d375adaa&type=1

Kolhatkar, S. (2018) Paul Singer, Doomsday Investor, The New Yorker, 27 August, https://www.newyorker.com/magazine/2018/08/27/paul-singer-doomsday-investor

Lawrence Berkeley National Laboratory (2022) Record Amounts of Zero-carbon Electricity Generation and Storage now Seeking Grid Interconnection, 12 April, University of California, https://eta.lbl.gov/news/major-energy-transition-underway

Lefebvre, H. (2003) [1970] The urban process, University of Minnesota Press, Minneapolis, MN.

Le Monde (2022) Germany launches world's first hydrogen train fleet, 24 August, Paris, https://www.lemonde.fr/en/international/article/2022/08/24/germany-launches-world-s-first-hydrogen-train-fleet_5994605_4.html

LexisNexis (2021) Secondary Market in UK Offshore Wind – Spinnakers Out, 24 March, https://bracewell.com/insights/secondary-market-uk-offshore-wind-—-spinnakers-out

McKinsey & Company (2019) Five ways that ESG creates value, McKinsey Quarterly, November, https://www.mckinsey.com/business-functions/strategy-and-corporate-finance/our-insights/five-ways-that-esg-creates-value

McKinsey & Company (2022) Green infrastructure: Could public land unlock private investment? September, https://www.mckinsey.com/industries/public-and-social-sector/our-insights/green-infrastructure-could-public-land-unlock-private-investment?hlkid=417cd5bfddc241e09ca093244464e44c&hctky=2195071&hdpid=bdb774d2-8659-435f-817b-607c11e46ce5

Macquarie Asset Management (2022) Macquarie Asset Management consortium agrees to acquire Reden Solar, Press Release, 7 March, https://www.macquarie.com/au/en/about/news/2022/macquarie-asset-management-consortium-agrees-to-acquire-reden-solar.html

Mainstream and Actis (2022) Mainstream Renewable Power Signs Agreement for the sale of African Renewable Energy IPP, 18 July, https://www.akerhorizons.com/news/mainstream-renewable-power-signs-agreement-for-the-sale-of-african-renewable-energy-ipp

Mainstream and Mitsui (2022) Mainstream announces closing of transaction with Mitsui, 7 April, https://www.mainstreamrp.com/insights/mainstream-announces-closing-of-transaction-with-mitsui/

Mastrucci, A. et al, (2019) Improving the SDG energy poverty targets: Residential cooling needs in the Global South, Energy and Buildings, 186 (405-415).

Matalucci, S. (2022) The Hydrogen Stream: Germany launches world's first operating hydrogen trains, PV Magazine, 26 August, https://www.pv-magazine.com/2022/08/26/the-hydrogen-stream-germany-launches-worlds-first-operating-hydrogen-trains/

Mawji, O. (2022) Canada's Oil and Gas Decommissioning Liability Problem, Institute for Energy Economics and Financial Analysis, May, https://ieefa.org/sites/default/files/2022-05/Canadas Oil and Gas Decommissioning Liability Problem_May 2022.pdf

Meridiam (2022) First ever UK-German energy link moves ahead as €2.8bn NeuConnect project reaches Financial Close, 21 July, https://www.meridiam.com/news/first-ever-uk-german-energy-link-moves-ahead-as-2-4bn-e2-8bn-neuconnect-project-reaches-financial-close/

National Engineering Policy Centre (2021) Decarbonising construction: building a new net zero industry, Royal Academy of Engineering, https://www.raeng.org.uk/publications/reports/decarbonising-construction-building-a-new-net-zero

National Grid (2022) Holistic Network Design: Pathway to 2030, July, https://www.nationalgrideso.com/electricity-transmission/document/262681/download

National Grid (2022) Annual Report and Accounts 2021-2022, https://www.nationalgrid.com/document/146731/download

National Oceanic and Atmospheric Administration (2022) Global and Regional Sea Level Rise Scenarios for the United States, February, Silver Spring, Maryland, https://aambpublicoceanservice.blob.core.windows.net/oceanserviceprod/hazards/sealevelrise/noaa-nos-techrpt01-global-regional-SLR-scenarios-US.pdf

National Renewable Energy Laboratory (2022) The Demand for a Domestic Offshore Wind Energy Supply Chain, Technical Report NREL/TP-5000-81602, June, https://www.nrel.gov/docs/fy22osti/81602.pdf

Net Zero Cities (2021) Net Zero Cities Pilot Cities Programme Guidebook, https://netzerocities.eu/wp-content/uploads/2022/06/Pilot-Cities-Guidebook.pdf

New Zealand Ministry for the Environment (2022) Draft national adaptation plan, April, Wellington, https://environment.govt.nz/assets/publications/Draft-national-adaptation-plan.pdf

Northland Power (2022) Second Quarter 2022 Results, Press Release, 11 August, https://www.northlandpower.com/en/news/northland-power-reports-second-quarter-2022-results.aspx

Nottingham City Homes (2021) Nottingham trials pioneering ventilation system, Press Release, 29 July, https://www.nottinghamcityhomes.org.uk/news/nottingham-trials-pioneering-ventilation-system/

OECD (2016) Business and Finance Outlook 2016, Chapter 5: Fragmentation in clean energy investment and financing, https://www.oecd-ilibrary.org/sites/9789264257573-10-en/index.html?itemId=/content/component/9789264257573-10-en

OECD (2017) Investment governance and the integration of environmental, social and governance factors, Paris, https://www.oecd.org/finance/Investment-Governance-Integration-ESG-Factors.pdf

OECD (2018) Global Material Resources Outlook to 2060: Economic Drivers and Environmental Consequences, OECD Publishing, Paris. https://doi.org/10.1787/9789264307452-en

OECD and The World Bank (2018) G20/OECD/WB Stocktake of Tools and Instruments Related to Infrastructure as an Asset Class – Progress Report (Draft), March, https://www.oecd.org/g20/G20_OECD_WB Stocktake - Progress Report.pdf

OECD/International Energy Agency (2018) The Future of Cooling: Opportunities for energy-efficient air conditioning, https://iea.blob.core.windows.net/assets/0bb45525-277f-4c9c-8d0c-9c0cb5e7d525/The_Future_of_Cooling.pdf

OECD (2019) Investing in Climate, Investing in Growth, Paris, https://www.oecd-ilibrary.org/docserver/9789264273528-en.pdf?expires=1603038813&id=id&accname=guest&checksum=C52BDDAA56C064F0085FF3BC05DF42AE

Offaly Independent (2021) Region to host Ireland's first renewable energy business park, 27 September, https://www.offalyindependent.ie/2021/09/27/region-to-host-irelands-first-renewable-energy-business-park/

Office for Budget Responsibility (2022) Economic and fiscal outlook, November, https://obr.uk/docs/dlm_uploads/CCS0822661240-002_SECURE_OBR_EFO_November_2022_WEB_ACCESSIBLE.pdf

Offshore Wind Industry Council (2022) Offshore Wind Skills Intelligence Report, May, https://www.owic.org.uk/_files/ugd/1c0521_9ffe327ec7da4522b7991226db27fee6.pdf

offshoreWIND.biz (2022) Breaking: Scotland Awards 24GW in ScotWind Auction, More than Half for Floating Wind Farms, Adrijana Buljan, 17 January, https://www.offshorewind.biz/2022/01/17/breaking-scotland-awards-25-gw-in-scotwind-auction-more-than-half-for-floating-wind-farms/

Oluwasanya, G., Perera, D., Qadir, M. and Smakhtin, V. (2022) Water Security in Africa: A Preliminary Assessment, United Nations University, Institute for Water, Environment and Health, Hamilton, Canada, https://inweh.unu.edu/wp-content/uploads/2022/03/State-of-Water-Security-in-Africa-A-Preliminary-Assessment-v5-revised.pdf

Orchard, L. and Stretton, H. (1997) Public Choice, Cambridge Journal of Economics, 21, 409-430

Orsted A/S (2022) Orsted acquires German and French onshore wind platform Ostwind, 22 July, https://orsted.com/en/company-announcement-list/2022/07/2022072254591

Oxera (2022) The energy crisis: where next for the UK energy retail sector? 30 June, https://www.oxera.com/insights/agenda/articles/the-energy-crisis-where-next-for-the-uk-energy-retail-sector/

Peigne, M. (2022) ECT: "ecocide" treaty puts Member States and EU Commission at odds, 22 July, https://www.investigate-europe.eu/en/2022/ect-ecocide-treaty-puts-member-states-and-eu-commission-at-odds/

Pistor, K. (2021) The myth of green capitalism, Social Europe, 27 September, https://socialeurope.eu/the-myth-of-green-capitalism

Plimmer, G. (2022) Renewable projects face 10 year wait to connect to electricity grid, Financial Times, 8 May, https://www.ft.com/content/7c674f56-9028-48a3-8cbf-c1c8b10868ba

Pollock, A. (2004) NHS plc: The Privatisation of our Health Care, Verso, London.

POST (Parliamentary Office of Science and Technology), (2021) POSTbrief 43, Reducing the whole life carbon impact of buildings, UK Parliament, November, https://researchbriefings.files.parliament.uk/documents/POST-PB-0044/POST-PB-0044.pdf

Powershift and Transnational Institute (2022) From Solar dream to legal nightmare, May, https://www.tni.org/files/publication-downloads/english_from_solar_dream_to_legal_nightmare_online.pdf

Public Infrastructure Bulletin (2005) Secondary markets: A natural progression of the PPP market in Australia or simply a UK phenomenon? Vol. 1, Issue 5, http://epublications.bond.edu.au/cgi/viewcontent.cgi?article=1026&context=pib

Public Services International (2020) Taking our Public Services Back In-house https://pop-umbrella.s3.amazonaws.com/uploads/8f22cbc1-0cec-4f32-8691-58b156b9779a_2020_-_EN_Global_Remunicipalisation_full_report_NEW_revised3_26_nov_20.pdf

PV-TECH (2022) Octopus launches AU$10bn renewables platform, acquires Australia's largest PV plant, 20 July, https://www.pv-tech.org/octopus-launches-au10bn-renewables-platform-acquires-australias-largest-pv-plant/

Queensland Government (2022) Energy and Jobs Plan: Premier's 2022 State of the State address, The Honourable Annastacia Palaszczuk, 27 September, https://statements.qld.gov.au/statements/96232

Quicke, A. and Parrott, S. (2022) Next Stop: Zero emissions buses by 2030, Australia Institute, May, Camberra, https://australiainstitute.org.au/wp-content/uploads/2022/05/P1229-Next-stop-for-electric-buses-WEB.pdf

Quiggin, J. (2017) Grid Renationalisation – a discussion paper, Australian Industrial Transformation Institute, Flinders University, Adelaide, http://aiti@flinders.edu.au

Quinbrook Infrastructure Partners (2022) Quinbrook launches $2.5bn 'Supernode' Data Storage Project in Brisbane to be powered by Renewables and Battery Storage, News, 8 July, https://www.quinbrook.com/news-insights/quinbrook-launches-2-5-billion-supernode-data-storage-project-in-brisbane-to-be-powered-by-renewables-and-battery-storage/

Rantanen, M. et al (2022) The Artic has warmed nearly four times faster than the globe since 1979, Communications, Earth & Environment 3:168, https://www.nature.com/articles/s43247-022-00498-3.pdf

Readfearn, G. (2022) 'Field of Dreams': Queensland plans to build Australia's largest publicly owned windfarm, The Guardian, 26 September, https://www.theguardian.com/australia-news/2022/sep/26/field-of-dreams-queensland-plans-to-build-australias-largest-publicly-owned-windfarm

REN21 (2005) Renewables 2005 Global Status Report, https://www.ren21.net/wp-content/uploads/2019/05/GSR2005_Full-Report_English.pdf

REN21 (2010) Renewables 2010 Global Status Report, https://www.ren21.net/wp-content/uploads/2019/05/GSR2010_Full-Report_English.pdf

REN21 (2016) 07 Feature: Community Renewable Energy: Renewables 2016 Global Status Report, https://www.ren21.net/gsr-2016/chapter07.php

REN21 (2021) Renewables 2021: Global Status Report, Paris, https://www.ren21.net/wp-content/uploads/2019/05/GSR2021_Full_Report.pdf

ReNews (2022a) UK backs tower factory for port of Nigg, 6 December, https://renews.biz/74090/uk-backs-new-tower-factory-for-port-of-nigg/

ReNews (2022b) Dundee to host battery Megafactory, https://renews.biz/79488/dundee-to-host-battery-megafactory/

Repsol (2022) Repsol adds EIP and Credit Agricole Assurances as partners to grow its renewables business, Press Release 9 June, https://www.repsol.com/en/press-room/press-releases/2022/repsol-adds-eip-and-credit-agricole-assurances-as-partners-to-grow-its-renewables-business/index.cshtml

Reuters (2022) Brookfield raises $15bn for climate-focused fund, 22 June, https://www.reuters.com/business/sustainable-business/brookfield-raises-15-bln-climate-focused-fund-2022-06-22/

Roberts, M. (2018a) Robots: what do they mean for jobs and incomes, 26 February, Michael Roberts Blog, https://thenextrecession.wordpress.com/2018/02/26/robots-what-do-they-mean-for-jobs-and-incomes

RWE Renewables GmbH (2021) Setting new trends together: RWE and Kerpen municipal utility to jointly develop two wind farms, 3 December, https://www.rwe.com/en/press/rwe-renewables/2021-12-03-setting-new-trends-together-rwe-and-kerpen-municipal-utility-to-jointly-develop-two-wind-farms

RWE AG (2022) RWE agrees to acquire Con Edison Clean Energy Businesses, Inc. and become one of the top leading renewable energy companies in the United States, 1 October, https://www.rwe.com/en/press/rwe-ag/2022-10-01-rwe-acquire-con-edison-clean-energy

Sanzillo, T. (2022) Clean-up Cost for Wells in Guyana, Another Loophole to Benefit ExxonMobil and Partners, Institute for Energy Economics and Financial Analysis, May, https://ieefa.org/sites/default/files/2022-05/Clean-up Costs for Wells in Guyana Benefit ExxonMobil and Partners_May 2022.pdf

Scottish Trade Union Congress (2017) Broken Promises and Offshored Jobs: STUC report on employment in the low-carbon and renewable energy economy, https://stuc.org.uk/files/Policy/Reasearch_Briefings/Broken promises and offshored jobs report.pdf

Scottish Trade Union Congress (2020) Scotland's Renewable Jobs Crisis, https://stuc.org.uk/files/Policy/Research-papers/Renewable_Jobs_Crisis_Covid-19.pdf

Scully, J. (2022) NSW to fast-track renewable energy zones with US$856m grid investment, PVTECH, 10 June, https://www.pv-tech.org/nsw-to-fast-track-renewable-energy-zones-with-us856m-grid-investment/

Securities and Exchange Commission (2021) Investment Advisors Act of 1940: Release No. 5930, December 20, 2021, Administrative Proceedings File No. 3-20683, Global Infrastructure Management LLC.

Securities and Exchange Commission (2022) SEC Proposes to Enhance Private Fund Investor Protection, 9 February, https://www.sec.gov/news/press-release/2022-19

SEI, IISD, ODI, E3G, and UNEP. (2021) The Production Gap Report 2021, http://productiongap.org/2021report

Sekera, J. (2014) Re-thinking the Definition of 'Public Goods', Real-World Economics Review Blog, 9 July, https://rwer.wordpress.com/2014/07/09/re-thinking-the-definition-of-public-goods

Sembcorp Industries (2021) Sembcorp Industries and BCG Energy sign collaborative agreement for up to 1.5GW of Renewable Energy projects in Vietnam, Press Release, 9 December, https://www.sembcorp.com/en/media/media-releases/energy/2021/december/sembcorp-industries-and-bcg-energy-sign-collaboration-agreement-for-up-to-15gw-of-renewable-energy-projects-in-vietnam/

Semieniuk, G. et al (2022) Stranded fossil-fuel assets translate to major losses for investors in advanced economies, Nature Climate Change, https://www.nature.com/articles/s41558-022-01356-y.pdf

Shaoul, J. (2005) A Critical Financial Analysis of the Private Finance Initiative: Selecting a Financing Method or Allocating Economic Wealth, Critical Perspectives on Accounting, 16, 441-471

Shell plc (2022) Shell completes acquisition of renewables platform Sprng Energy group, India, Press Release, 9 August, https://www.shell.com/media/news-and-media-releases/2022/shell-completes-acquisition-of-renewables-platform-sprng-energy-group.html

Shell, Gerdau joint venture on Brazil (2022) solar power joint venture, 7 February, https://www.nasdaq.com/articles/shell-gerdau-to-create-solar-power-joint-venture-in-brazil

Sherry, N.J. and Firzli, M. N. J. (2022) Pensions are poised to power an ESG-driven global economy, Global Infrastructure Hub, 4 February, https://www.gihub.org/articles/pensions-are-poised-to-power-an-esg-driven-global-economy/?utm_source=edm+&utm_medium=email+&utm_campaign=NewsletterFeb

Shields, M. et al (2022) The Demand for a Domestic Offshore Wind Energy Supply Chain, National Renewable Energy Laboratory, NREL/TP-5000-81602, June, https://www.nrel.gov/docs/fy22osti/81602.pdf

Simpson, A. (2021) Rescuing the Green New Deal: Preventing cheap politics from sinking the planet, Spokesman Books, Nottingham.

Spash, C.L. and Hache, F. (2021) The Dasgupta Review deconstructed: an expose of biodiversity economics, Globalizations https://doi.org/10.1080/14747731.2021.1929007

Sol, X. (2021) EU Green Deal is too dependent on private finance, euobserver, 20 October, Brussels, https://euobserver.com/opinion/153272

Solar Power Portal (2019) Pan-European secondary solar market set for 'exciting times' as growth, O&G interest set to continue, 29 January, https://www.solarpowerportal.co.uk/news/pan_european_secondary_solar_market_set_for_exciting_times_as_growth_og_int

Stadtwerke Berlin (2021) Stadtwerke Berlin out together "district package" for solar expansion, 17 December, https://www.energate-messenger.com/news/218621/stadtwerke-berlin-put-together-district-package-for-solar-expansion

Sullivan, S. (2014) The natural capital myth; or will accounting save the world: Preliminary thoughts on nature, finance and values, Leverhulme Centre for the Study of Value, Working Paper Series No. 3, University of Manchester, https://hummedia.manchester.ac.uk/institutes/gdi/publications/workingpapers/archive/lcsv/lcsv-wp3-sullivan.pdf

Sweeney, S. and Treat, J. (2017) Preparing a Public Pathway: Confronting the investment Crisis in Renewable Energy, Working Paper No. 10, Trade Unions for Energy Democracy, New York. https://rosalux.nyc/wp-content/uploads/2021/02/tuedworkingpaper10.pdf

Sweeney, S., Treat, J. and HongPing Shen, I. (2020) Transition in Trouble? The Rise and Fall of 'Community Energy' in Europe, Trade Unions for Energy Democracy, Working Paper No. 13, https://secureservercdn.net/72.167.241.180/f37.96b.mwp.accessdomain.com/wp-content/uploads/2021/10/TUED-WP13-Transition-in-Trouble.pdf?time=1653427253

Tarekegne, B., Kazimierczuk, K. and O'Neil, R. (2022) Communities in energy transition: exploring best practices and decision support tools to provide equitable outcomes, Discover Sustainability, 8 April, https://link.springer.com/content/pdf/10.1007/s43621-022-00080-z.pdf

Tariq Fancy (2021) Tariq Fancy on the failure of green investing and the need for state action, The Economist, 4 November, https://www.economist.com/by-invitation/2021/11/04/tariq-fancy-on-the-failure-of-green-investing-and-the-need-for-state-action

Tax Justice Network Norway (2021) The shadowy side of wind power: Measures against profit shifting and hidden ownership, Oslo, March, (Norwegian only) https://www.taxjustice.no/artikkel/skatteparadis-i-norsk-vindkraft

Teagasc and Bord Bia (2022) Supporting Sustainable Beef Farming and The Beef Carbon Navigator, https://www.teagasc.ie/media/website/publications/2022/Teagasc-Beef-2022-168mm-x-240mm-Friday-240622.pdf

The Economics of Ecosystems and Biodiversity (2010) Mainstreaming the Economics of Nature: A synthesis of the approach, conclusions and recommendations of TEEB, http://www.biodiversity.ru/programs/international/teeb/materials_teeb/TEEB_SynthReport_English.pdf

The Economist (2021) The uses and abuses of green finance, 6 November, https://www.economist.com/leaders/the-uses-and-abuses-of-green-finance/21806111

The Economist (2022a) Climate lawsuits: Habeas carbon – the courts are increasingly important in the fight against climate change, 23 April, https://www.economist.com/international/2022/04/23/lawsuits-aimed-at-greenhouse-gas-emissions-are-a-growing-trend

The Economist (2022b) Private equity may be heading for a fall, 7 July, https://www.economist.com/business/2022/07/07/private-equity-may-be-heading-for-a-fall

The Economist (2022c) Britain's overstretched electricity grid is delaying housing projects, 4 June, https://www.economist.com/britain/2022/06/02/britains-overstretched-electricity-grid-is-delaying-housing-projects

The Ferret (2020) Revealed: Scottish wind farms owned in tax havens, Rob Edwards, 22 November, https://theferret.scot/cayman-tax-haven-ventient-wind/

The Ferret (2021) Windfall: One third of Scotland's biggest wind farms linked to tax havens, Ally Tibbitt & Rob Edwards, 13 July, https://theferret.scot/wind-farms-linked-to-tax-havens/

The Ferret (2022) Tax haven firms own £7.7bn of UK offshore wind power lines, Paul Dobson, 2 January, https://theferret.scot/7-7bn-offshore-wind-cables-owned-tax-haven-firms/

The Guardian (2022a) France becomes latest country to leave controversial energy charter treaty, 21 October, https://www.theguardian.com/world/2022/oct/21/france-becomes-latest-country-to-leave-controversial-energy-charter-treaty

The Guardian (2022b) Huge UK electric car battery factory on 'life support' to cut costs, 12 August, https://www.theguardian.com/environment/2022/aug/12/huge-uk-electric-car-battery-factory-on-life-support-to-cut-costs

The Guardian (2022c) Great British Energy: what is it, what would it do and how would it be funded? 27 September, https://www.theguardian.com/politics/2022/sep/27/great-british-energy-what-is-it-what-would-it-do-and-how-would-it-be-funded

The Rockefeller Foundation (2021) NYSE and Intrinsic Exchange Group Partner to Launch A New Asset Class to Power a Sustainable Future, New York, 14 September, https://www.rockefellerfoundation.org/news/nyse-and-intrinsic-exchange-group-partner-to-launch-a-new-asset-class-to-power-a-sustainable-future/

Thomas, H. (2021) SSE rejects Elliott's call to break-up, Financial Times, 17 November, https://www.ft.com/content/0e8b889e-8c7d-4292-8cb6-08e920053246

Thomas, H. (2022) Why is this £6.5bn Bulb blowout still in the dark, Financial Times, 23 November, https://www.ft.com/content/a3ec2dd2-f443-43e2-b58b-906e42afdc3c

Tibbitt, A. (2022) More than 1,000 Glasgow private lets owned in tax havens, 24 March, The Ferret investigative journalism, https://theferret.scot/1000-glasgow-letting-properties-owned-in-tax-havens/

Tienhaara, K., Thrasher, R., Alexander Simmons, B. and Gallagher, K.P. (2022) Investor-state disputes threaten the global green energy transition, Science, vol. 376, Issue 6594, 13 May, https://www.science.org/doi/epdf/10.1126/science.abo4637

TotalEnergies (2022a) India: TotalEnergies and Adani join forces to create a world-class green hydrogen company, 14 June, https://totalenergies.com/media/news/press-releases/india-totalenergies-and-adani-join-forces-create-world-class-green

TotalEnergies (2022b) United States: TotalEnergies acquires 50% of Clearway, the 5th largest U.S. renewable energy player, https://totalenergies.com/media/news/press-releases/united-states-totalenergies-acquires-50-clearway-5th-largest-us-renewable

Trade Union Congress (2022) Public Ownership of clean power: lower bills, climate action, decent jobs, https://www.tuc.org.uk/sites/default/files/2022-09/TUC_public energy generation_Sept2022.pdf

Trade Unions for Energy Democracy and Transnational Institute (2021) Energy Transition or Energy Expansion, https://www.tni.org/files/publication-downloads/tued-tni-energy-expansion.pdf

Traill, H., Cumbers, A., and Gray, N. (2021) The state of European municipal energy transition: an overview of current trends, Adam Smith Business School, University of Glasgow, https://municipalpower.org/wp-content/uploads/2021/05/State-of-European-municipal-energy-transition-FINAL.pdf

Transnational Institute (2020) The Future is Public: Towards Democratic Ownership of Public Services https://www.tni.org/files/publication-downloads/futureispublic_online_def.pdf

Transparency International (2021) Conflicts of Interest and Undue Influence in Climate Action: Putting a stop to corporate efforts undermining climate policy and decisions, November, https://www.transparency.org/en/publications/conflicts-of-interest-and-undue-influence-in-climate-action

Transport Scotland (2020) Rail Services Decarbonisation Action Plan, https://www.transport.gov.scot/media/47906/rail-services-decarbonisation-action-plan.pdf

Trout, K. et al (2022) Existing fossil fuel extraction would warm the world beyond 1.5 ^{0}C, Environmental Research Letters, 17, 064010, https://iopscience.iop.org/article/10.1088/1748-9326/ac6228/pdf

UK Export Finance (2021) Open spaces, parks and areas of natural significance and biodiversity could also be designated net zero zone, 22 June, London, https://www.gov.uk/government/publications/uk-export-finance-jobs-supported-2020-to-2021/uk-export-finance-jobs-supported-analysis-2020-21

UNCTAD (2021) International Investment Agreements Issues Note, Issue 4, September: Investor-State Dispute Settlement Cases: Facts and Figures 2020, https://unctad.org/system/files/official-document/diaepcbinf2021d7_en.pdf

United Nations (2015) Paris Agreement, United Nations Framework Convention on Climate Change, https://unfccc.int/sites/default/files/english_paris_agreement.pdf

United Nations Environment Programme (2021) The Gathering Storm: Adapting to climate change in a post-pandemic world, Adaptation Gap Report 2021, https://reliefweb.int/sites/reliefweb.int/files/resources/Adaptation Gap Report 2021 - The gathering storm - Adapting to climate change in a post-pandemic world.pdf

United Nations Environment Programme and Cool Coalition (2021) Beating the Heat: A Sustainable Cooling Handbook for Cities, November, https://www.unep.org/resources/report/beating-heat-sustainable-cooling-handbook-cities

United Nations Environment Programme & GRIAD Arendal (2022) Spreading like Wildfire: The Rising Threat of Extraordinary Landscape Fires, February, https://www.grida.no/news/84

United Nation Industrial Development Organization, UNIDO, (2017b). Eco-Industrial Parks Achievements And Key Insights From The Global Recp Programme 2012 – 2018, https://www.unido.org/sites/default/files/files/2019-02/UNIDO_EIP_Achievements_Publication_Final_0.pdf

UrbanLand (2022) Wunder's $650 Million Deal Could Boost Use of Solar in Commercial and Industrial Buildings, Patrick j. Kiger, 14 June, https://urbanland.uli.org/sustainability/wunders-650-million-deal-could-boost-use-of-solar-in-commercial-and-industrial-buildings/

U.S. Department of Energy (2022a) Land-Based Wind Market Report: 2022 Edition, Washington DC. August, https://www.energy.gov/sites/default/files/2022-08/land_based_wind_market_report_2202.pdf

U.S. Department of Energy (2022b) DOE Launches New Initiative from President's Bipartisan Infrastructure Law to Modernise National Grid, 12 January, https://www.energy.gov/oe/articles/doe-launches-new-initiative-president-bidens-bipartisan-infrastructure-law-modernize

U.S. Department of Energy (2022c) Interconnection Innovation e-Xchange (i2X). Washington DC, 31 May, https://www.energy.gov/articles/biden-administration-launches-bipartisan-infrastructure-law-initiative-connect-more-clean

U.S. Federal Energy Regulatory Commission (2022) Presentation: Building for the Future Through Electric Regional Transmission Planning and Cost Allocation and Generator Interconnection (RM21-17-000) https://www.ferc.gov/news-events/news/presentation-building-future-through-electric-regional-transmission-planning-and

Vanatta, M., Craig, M.T., Rathod, B., Florez, J., Bromley-Dulfano, I. and Smith, D. (2022) The costs of replacing coal plant jobs with local instead of distant wind and solar jobs across the United States, iScience, 19 August https://www.cell.com/action/showPdf?pii=S2589-0042%2822%2901089-6

Ventient Energy Holdco Limited (2021) Annual Report and Financial Statements to 31 December 2020, Companies House, UK.

Ventive Ltd (2022) Ventive designs and manufactures the most innovative intelligent building service systems in the UK, https://ventive.co.uk/

Verbund AG (2022) Acquisition of an operational renewables portfolio (82MW) and of a development platform (around 2,100 MW ar an advanced stage) in Spain, News 9 May, https://www.verbund.com/en-at/about-verbund/news-press/press-releases/2022/05/09/corporate-news-labrador

Vestas Wind Systems A/S (2022) Interim Financial Report, Second Quarter 2022, 10 August, https://www.vestas.com/content/dam/vestas-com/global/en/investor/reports-and-presentations/financial/2022/220810_14_company_announcement.pdf.coredownload.inline.pdf

Volz, U. et al (2021) Debt Relief for a Green and Inclusive Recovery: Securing Private-Sector Participation and Creating Policy Space for Sustainable Development, Centre for Sustainable Finance (University of London), Global Development Policy Center (Boston University and Heinrich Boll Stiftung (Berlin) https://www.boell.de/sites/default/files/2021-06/DRGR Report 2021 Endf.pdf

Volz, U. (2022) The debt and climate crises are escalating – it is time to tackle both, Brookings, 8 July, https://www.brookings.edu/blog/future-development/2022/07/08/the-debt-and-climate-crises-are-escalating-it-is-time-to-tackle-both/

Wagner, O. and Berlo, K. (2015) The Wave of Remunicipalisation of Energy Networks and Supply in Germany: The Establishment of 72 New Municipal Power Utilities, Wuppertal Insititute for Climate, Environment and Energy, https://epub.wupperinst.org/frontdoor/deliver/index/docld/5920/file/5920_Wagner.pdf

Wagner, O. and Berlo, K. (2017) Remunicipalisation and Foundation of Municipal Utilities in the German Energy Sector: Details about Newly Established Enterprises, Journal of Sustainable Development of Energy, Water and Environment Systems, Vol.5, Issue 3, 396-407.

Wagner, O., Berlo, K., Herr, C. and Companie, M. (2021) Success Factors for the Foundation of Municipal Utilities in Germany, Energies 14, 981, https://doi.org/10.3390/en14040981

Wall Street Journal Editorial Board (2021) The Green New Deal, in Disguise, 12 April, https://www.wsj.com/articles/the-green-new-deal-in-disguise-11618267156

Wappelhorst, S. and Rodriguez, F. (2021) Decarbonizing Bus Fleets: Global Overview of Targets for Phasing Out Combustion Engine Vehicles, The International Council on Clean Transportation, December, https://theicct.org/decarbonizing-bus-fleets-global-overview-of-targets-for-phasing-out-combustion-engine-vehicles/

Webb, W. (2021) Wall Street's Takeover of Nature Advances with Launch of New Asset Class, 13 October, Unlimited Hangout, https://unlimitedhangout.com/2021/10/investigative-reports/wall-streets-takeover-of-nature-advances-with-launch-of-new-asset-class/

Weghmann, V. (2019) Going Public: A Decarbonised, Affordable and Democratic Energy System for Europe, The failure of energy liberalization, European Public Services Union, https://www.epsu.org/sites/default/files/article/files/Going Public_EPSU-PSIRU Report 2019 - EN.pdf

Welton, S. (2021) Rethinking Grid Governance for the Climate Change Era, California Law Review, Vol. 109, No.1, February, https://www.californialawreview.org/print/rethinking-grid-governance/

Whelan, T., Atz, U., Van Holt, T. and Clark, C. (2021) ESG and Financial Performance: Uncovering the Relationship by Aggregating Evidence from 1,000 plus Studies Published between 2015-2020, NYU Stern Center for Sustainable Business, https://www.stern.nyu.edu/sites/default/files/assets/documents/ESG Paper Aug 2021.pdf

Whitfield, D. (2010) Global Auction of Public Assets: Public sector alternatives to the infrastructure market and Public Private Partnerships, Spokesman Books, Nottingham.

Whitfield, D. (2015) Alternative to Private Finance of the Welfare State: A global analysis of social impact bond, pay-for-success and development impact bond projects, Australian Workplace Innovation and Social Research Centre, University of Adelaide and European Services Strategy Unit, September, http://www.european-services-strategy.org.uk/publications/essu-research-reports/alternative-to-private-finance-of-the-welfare/alternative-to-private-finance-of-the-welfare-state.pdf

Whitfield, D. (2016) The financial commodification of public infrastructure: The growth of offshore PFI/PPP secondary market infrastructure funds, ESSU Research Report No. 8, https://www.european-services-strategy.org.uk/wp-content/uploads/2017/01/financial-commodification-public-infrastructure.pdf

Whitfield, D. (2017a) PPP profiteering and Offshoring: New Evidence, PPP Equity Database 1998-2016 (UK), ESSU Research Report No.10, https://www.european-services-strategy.org.uk/wp-content/uploads/2017/10/PPP-profiteering-Offshoring-New-Evidence.pdf

Whitfield, D. (2017b) PFI/PPP Buyouts, Bailouts, Terminations and Major Problem Contracts, ESSU Research Report No. 9, https://www.european-services-strategy.org.uk/wp-content/uploads/2017/02/pfi-ppp-buyouts-bailouts-and-terminations.pdf

Whitfield, D. (2018) Ownership and Offshoring of NPD and Hub Projects: Scottish Futures Trust, May, https://www.european-services-strategy.org.uk/wp-content/uploads/2018/06/SFT-Offshoring-report.pdf

Whitfield, D. (2020a) Public Alternative to the Privatisation of Life: Strategies for decommodification, public ownership & provision, democratic control, climate action, conserving nature and biodiversity and radical public management, Spokesman Books, Nottingham.

Whitfield, D. (2020b) Equitable Recovery Strategies: Why public ownership and democratic control must be at the heart of Green and Integrated Public Healthcare Deals, European Services Strategy Unit Research Report No. 11, https://www.european-services-strategy.org.uk/wp-content/uploads/2020/07/Equitable-Recovery-Strategies.pdf

Whitfield, D. (2021) Evidence to Select Committee on the Privatisation of Public Services in South Australia, https://www.european-services-strategy.org.uk/publications/public-bodies/evidence-to-select-committee-on-the-privatisation-of-of-public-services-in-south-australia

Williams, A. and Campbell, C. (2022) Climate graphic of the week: Worrying gap in clean energy investment between leading and emerging economies, Financial Times, 24 June, https://www.ft.com/content/fe218353-a395-4fa6-adc9-2decc4c4197d

Wind Energy Ireland (2021) EirGrid grid strategy a step in the right direction, Press Release, 10 November, Naas, https://windenergyireland.com/latest-news/5892-eirgrid-grid-strategy-a-step-in-the-right-direction

Wind Energy Ireland (2022) National Ports Study, September, https://windenergyireland.com/images/files/final-national-ports-study.pdf
WindEurope (2022) Norway announces first offshore wind auction, 18 February, https://windeurope.org/newsroom/news/norway-announces-first-offshore-wind-auction/
Windel Energy (2021) Windel Energy partners again with Canadian Solar Inc., Press release 27 October, https://www.windelenergy.co.uk/windel-energy-partners-again-with-canadian-solar/
Wood, P. (2021) Intact Forests, Safe Communities: Reducing community climate risks through forest protection and a paradigm shift in forest management, Sierra Club BC, Victoria B.C. https://sierraclub.bc.ca/wp-content/uploads/2021-Forest-Climate-Risk-Assessment-Report-final-February.pdf
World Bank Group, ADB & PPIAF (2020a) Global Review of Public Infrastructure Funds: Volume 1 - Identifying key design features and success factors for Public Infrastructure Funds, Washington DC, https://ppiaf.org/documents/5982/download
World Bank Group, ADB & PPIAF (2020b) Global Review of Public Infrastructure Funds: Volume 2 – Case studies, Washington DC, https://ppiaf.org/documents/5983?ref_site=ppiaf
World Bank Group and PPIAF (2019) Who Sponsors Infrastructure Projects? Disentangling public and private contributions, https://ppi.worldbank.org/content/dam/PPI/documents/SPIReport_2017_small_interactive.pdf
World Bank Group (2020) Sustainable Development Bonds & Green Bonds, Washington DC, https://issuu.com/jlim5/docs/world-bank-ibrd-impact-report-2020?mode=window
World Bank Group (2021) Climate Change Action Plan 2021-2025, Washington DC, https://openknowledge.worldbank.org/bitstream/handle/10986/35799/CCAP-2021-25.pdf?sequence=2&isAllowed=y
World Bank Group and PPIAF (2021) Private Participation in Infrastructure (PPI): 2020 Annual Report, https://ppi.worldbank.org/content/dam/PPI/documents/PPI_2020_AnnualReport.pdf
World Bank Group (2021) Catalyzing Investment for Green Growth, Equitable Growth, Finance & Institutions Insight, Washington DC, https://openknowledge.worldbank.org/bitstream/handle/10986/35056/Catalyzing-Investment-for-Green-Growth-The-Role-of-Business-Environment-and-Investment-Climate-Policy-in-Environmentally-Sustainable-Private-Sector-Development.pdf?sequence=1&isAllowed=y
World Bank Group, Shenzhen Bus, UC Davis and China Development Institute (2021) Electrification of Public Transport: A Case Study of the Shenzhen Bus Group, Washington DC, https://documents1.worldbank.org/curated/en/708531625052490238/pdf/Electrification-of-Public-Transport-A-Case-Study-of-the-Shenzhen-Bus-Group.pdf
World Bank Group and PPIAF (2022) Guidance on PPP Legal Frameworks, https://documents1.worldbank.org/curated/en/099440006162228966/pdf/P17521204fa5900710ba160e9613aa44291.pdf
World Business Council for Sustainable Development (2021) Decarbonizing construction: Guidance for investors and developers to reduce embodied carbon, Geneva, https://www.wbcsd.org/contentwbc/download/12455/185688/1
World Meteorological Organization (2022) WMO Global Annual to Decadal Climate Update, May, https://hadleyserver.metoffice.gov.uk/wmolc/WMO_GADCU_2022-2026.pdf
Worrall, L, Gamble, H, Spoehr, J, (2022) The Circular Economy – International Lessons and Directions for Australian Reindustrialisation, Adelaide: Australian Industrial Transformation Institute, Flinders University of South Australia https://www.flinders.edu.au/content/dam/documents/research/aiti/thecirculareconomy.pdf
Xie, Y. and Delgado, O. (2022) Decarbonzing Bus Fleets: How Subnational Targets can aid in Phasing out Combustion Engines, https://theicct.org/decarbonizing-bus-fleets-global-overview-of-targets-for-phasing-out-combustion-engine-vehicles/

About the Author

Dexter Whitfield is Director of the European Services Strategy Unit (continuing the work of Services to Community Action & Trade Unions and the Centre for Public Services (1973-2022). He has undertaken projects for a wide range of public sector organisations, local authorities and agencies and worked extensively with trade unions both in the UK and Ireland at branch, regional and national levels, and internationally. He has worked with many tenants and community organisations on housing, planning and regeneration policies.

He was Adjunct Associate Professor at the Australian Workplace Innovation and Social Research Centre, University of Adelaide (2007-2016) and has been Adjunct Associate Professor at the Australian Industrial Transformation Institute at Flinders University since 2016.

Over 49 years he has carried out extensive research and policy analysis of regional/city economies and public sector provision, jobs and employment strategies, equality impact assessments and evaluation, marketisation and privatisation, public private partnerships, modernisation and public management. This included the national analysis (with Karen Escott) of the Gender Impact of Compulsory Competitive Tendering in Local Government (1995) for the Equal Opportunities Commission which proved discrimination in women's employment compared to men.

A detailed analysis of the Health and Social Care and Sustainable Development in the East of England (with Karen Escott and Alex Nunn) was preceded by a similar analysis for the North West Regional Assembly (2003) and later the New Health and Social Care Economy in Sefton MBC, Liverpool and Greater Manchester City Regions and North West regional economy in 2015.

Dexter developed the ESSU PPP Equity Database 1998-2016 which exposed the profiteering and offshoring of PPP projects and the PPP Database: Strategic Service-Delivery Partnerships for local authority ICT, corporate and technical services in Britain. This included strategic support for Newcastle City UNISON which successfully stopped the outsourcing of central services and the offshoring of the Newcastle-based Prescription Pricing Division of NHS Business Services.

Dexter is the author of 8 books (see inside cover) and was one of the founding members of Community Action Magazine (1972-1995) and Public Service Action (1983-1998). He has contributed chapters in books, articles in journals, conference papers and written 12 ground-breaking ESSU Research Reports.

A full CV is available: https://www.european-services-strategy.org.uk/wp-content/uploads/2022/04/Dexter-Whitfield-cv-2022.pdf

Index

A

ABO Wind, 56
Acciona Energias Renovables, 56
Accumulation, iii, 16–17, 31–32, 72, 98
Actis LLP, 49, 58, 61, 72
Adani Green Energy, 23, 49, 58
Adaptation, iv, 1–2, 5, 8, 16–18, 20, 102–103, 106–107, 122–123, 135, 143
Africa, 16, 20, 45–47, 54, 63, 65, 75, 111
Agriculture, iv, 2, 99, 123, 126, 145
Aker Horizons ASA, 61
Apollo Global Management, 48, 139
Aquila Capital, 56, 72
Ardian Infrastructure, 16, 52, 151
Ares Management Corporation, 49
Argentina, 78
Asset recycling, iii, 16, 33, 47, 75, 138, 143, 145
Auctions, 11, 19, 27, 30, 33, 47, 84–85, 139, 143
Australia, 33, 45, 50-51, 58, 60, 61, 108, 110, 112, 118, 121, 131-133, 134, 143, 147,
Australian Energy Market Operator, 112, 147
Australian Industrial Transformation Institute, viii, 118, 177
Austria, 89, 121
Avangrid Renewables, 151
Azure Power, 77, 78

B

Battery storage, 6–8, 11, 14, 46, 48–49, 59–61, 84, 111, 114–116, 118, 125, 133–135, 139
BayWa, 56, 150
Belgium, ix, 21, 81, 108, 118, 125, 149–15
Bermuda, 71–72, 74–76, 82

Biodiversity, iv, x–1, 8–9, 16–17, 20, 27, 32–33, 40, 90, 92, 97–98, 100–101, 107, 111, 123, 126, 128, 138, 145, 147–148
Biomass, 6, 8, 11, 32, 43, 46, 52, 60, 63–64, 89, 127, 143
BlackRock Real Assets, 41, 60, 85, 153, 154, 155-156
Blackstone, 48, 60, 139, 151
BP, viii, 5, 13, 49, 52–53, 57, 58, 149
Brazil, 21, 45, 60, 64, 79, 86, 127
British Virgin Islands, 71–72, 82
Brookfield Renewable Partners, 47-48, 53–54, 56, 59-60, 74–75, 139, 151
Bulgaria, 21

C

Caisse de dépôt et placement du Québec, 60
California Public Utilities Commission, 61
Canada, 35, 45, 51–52, 56, 60, 134, 150–151, 155–156
Canadian Solar, 49, 59, 61, 151
Capital Dynamics, 74
Carlyle Group, 60, 139, 151
Catapult Centres, 114
Cayman Islands, 50, 61, 71–72, 74–75, 82
CEE Group, 151
Chile, 20, 45–46, 65, 75, 121
China, 1, 13, 22, 45, 59, 61, 64–65, 72, 78, 82, 85–86, 110–111, 116, 119, 121, 127, 153, 156
China Three Gorges (Europe), 72, 78
Chinese National Offshore Company, 36
Clearway Energy, 56, 59, 81, 151
Climate action, 16, 19, 102, 109–110, 124–125, 133, 145

Climate debt, 68-70
Climate litigation, vi, 38-39
Climate Risks Scorecard, 139
Climate targets, 5-6, 31, 35, 54, 92, 123, 125, 130, 136, 140, 147-148
Climate Vulnerable Forum, vi, 69, 147
COP 2021, 98
Columbia, 45, 59, 111, 121
Committee on Climate Change, 30, 124
Community-owned energy projects, 145-146
Contracts for Difference, viii, 30
Copenhagen Infrastructure Partners, 48, 52, 149
Coastal flooding, 2
Cubico Sustainable Investments, 151
Czech Republic, 20, 86, 153

D

Decarbonisation, iv, 1-2, 6, 8, 10, 25-26, 32, 36, 59, 106-107, 111, 114, 118-119, 121-122, 124-127, 131, 133, 135, 137, 141, 145-148
Decarbonising steel, 118
Decarbonising construction, 119
Decarbonising public bus fleets, 121
Decarbonising rail, 122
Decommodification of nature, iv, 1, 100
Democratic accountability, 1, 7-8, 53-54, 62, 71, 84, 92, 101, 106, 136-139, 144-145, 147-148
Denmark, viii, x-1, 21-22, 45, 51-52, 56, 86, 111, 121, 149, 153, 156
DIF Capital Partners, 48
Digitalisation, 109, 135, 136
Dominion Energy, 53, 155
Duke Energy Corporation, 7, 78

E

Eco-Industrial Parks, 111
Economic justice, 148

Economic/social/environmental cost benefit analysis, 91, 145
Ecosystem services, 97-98, 100
EDF, viii, 52-53, 61, 86, 153
EDPR, viii, 55-56, 149, 153
Energiekontor AG, 56
Egypt, 81
EirGrid, 109
Électricité de France, 61
Electric School Buses, 121
Elliott Management, 7, 78-79
Encavis AG, 56
ENEL, ix, 85-86, 154-155
Energy Charter Treaty 18, 35, 37, 141, 147
Energy Parks, 111, 135, 147
Engie, 34, 85-86, 149, 154
ENI, 57, 86, 154
Environmental adaptation, iv, 1, 5, 8, 107, 122-123
Environment, Social & Governance, 7, 8, 9, 17, 38-42, 85, 137
Environmental justice, iv, 7-9, 40, 92, 101, 106, 140, 148
Environmental strategy, 41, 147
Equality, iv, 1, 7-9, 11, 31, 40-42, 44, 57, 90-94, 101-102, 104-106, 124, 133, 136-138, 148, 177
Equinor, 53, 57, 59, 86, 133, 153
Electrification of industry, 115, 122, 125
Electricity Supply Board, Ireland 109
EnBW, 34, 61, 86, 89, 149, 153
Equitable transition, 6, 9, 101, 103, 106-107, 128, 131
Equitix, 50-51, 57, 73, 152
ESSU Global Renewable Energy Secondary Market Database 2019-2021, vii, 6, 9, 28, 47, 55, 84
EU Green Bond Standard, 20
Europe, b, viii, 14, 16, 21, 25, 28, 37, 50, 57, 63, 72, 75, 78, 81, 86, 89, 116-117, 119, 148

European Commission, 16, 19–22, 25, 117, 126
European Investment Bank, ix, 21, 25, 80, 109
European Union, ix, 20, 25, 111, 139
European Union Green New Deal 25
Eurowind Energy, 111, 147
Everwood Capital, 80
Exchange Traded Funds, 17
Exus Management Partners, 60

F

Factory of the Future, 118
Falck Renewables, 56, 61, 80, 149
Fancy, Tariq, 41
Financialisation, iii, 9, 12, 15, 17, 27, 32–33, 43, 54, 97, 145, 148
Finland, 45–46, 153
Floating solar, 7, 128, 129, 133, 149, 150,
Food security, 35, 58, 126, 138, 141
Foresight Group LLP, 48
Fossil Fuel Subsidies, 4
Fossil fuel profits 2022, 55, 57, 58
France, viii, x–1, 21–22, 38, 45, 52–53, 56–61, 73, 81–82, 86, 109, 122, 149–150, 153–155
Fraunhofer Institute, 116, 118

G

G7 Climate Communique, 24
Germany, viii–ix, 1, 4, 13, 21–22, 34, 45–46, 50, 53, 56, 59, 61–62, 82, 85, 88–89, 109–110, 116, 118, 122, 125, 149–150, 153, 155–156
Gippsland Renewable Energy Park, Victoria, 61
Global Infrastructure Partners, 52, 81, 151
Global Public Goods, 9–10, 16, 85, 90, 137
Global temperature, 3
Goldman Sachs Asset Management, 13, 48, 80, 115
Greece, 20, 108
Green Investment Group, 59, 150–151

Green New Deals, 24
Greencoat Renewables, 61
Grid networks, 10, 107
Guernsey, 50–51, 56, 71–73, 82
Guyana, 36–37

H

Harvey, D. 27, 31, 32
Heat Index, 4
Hedge funds, 79
Human rights, 92, 140
Hungary, 20
Hydro, 1, 6, 8–9, 11–12, 14, 16, 28, 43–44, 46, 52, 63–65, 73, 75, 89, 112, 139, 143
Hydrogen, 6, 14, 23, 35, 46, 52, 58, 60–61, 111–112, 119, 122, 133–134

I

Iberdrola, 53, 86, 149–151, 155
Illawarra Renewable Energy Zone, 112
Impact assessment, 7, 30, 79, 91–92, 94, 104–105, 137, 145, 177
India, 20, 23, 45–46, 58, 60, 65, 77, 111, 119, 121, 127
Individualisation, 30–33, 145
Industrial strategy, iv, 8, 30, 107, 115, 124, 130
Infrastructure funds, 12, 15–16, 26, 32, 48–49, 51–52, 65–66, 77, 83, 87
Infrastructure Investments Fund Holding LP (Cayman Islands), 61
Integrated planning of renewable energy, regeneration and public services, 135
Intergovernmental Panel on Climate Change, ix, 2
International Bank for Reconstruction and Development, ix, 19, 63
International Finance Corporation, ix, 15, 63, 65, 85
International Monetary Fund, ix, 1, 4, 17-19, 40, 69-70, 76, 127

Invenergy Renewables, 60
Investment, iii, vi, viii–1, 6, 10–11, 13, 15–21, 23–30, 33, 37–38, 40–43, 46–51, 53–54, 58–59, 61–70, 72–73, 75–76, 78–88, 91–92, 99–101, 109–110, 112, 115, 118, 121, 127, 131–132, 134, 137, 140, 142–144, 147, 149–151, 153, 155–156
Investor-State Dispute Settlements, 37
Ireland, 1, 7, 45–47, 53–54, 61, 74, 78, 86, 104, 109–110, 112, 118, 137, 153, 156, 177
Italy, x, 22, 28, 38, 45, 56–57, 60, 82, 86, 149, 154–155

J

Japan, 3, 13, 45–46, 75, 110, 112, 149
Jersey, 71–75, 82
Jobs, iv, vi, 8, 22, 24, 102–103, 106, 118, 121, 127–129, 131–133, 139, 142–145, 147–148, 177
Jobs and training, 121, 133
JP Morgen, 61, 74, 75, 81, 82, 153

K

KKR & Co, 23, 48, 60, 139
Korea, 22

L

Latvia, 125
Leeward Renewable Energy, 151
Lightsource BP, 49, 52
Lost taxation, 77
Luxembourg, x, 20–21, 71–76, 82

M

Macquarie Asset Management, 59
Macquarie Green Investment Group, 59
Magnora ASA, 150
Mainstream Renewable Power, 61
Malaysia, 53, 67

Manufacturing, iv, 1, 10, 31, 52, 107, 114, 116–118, 121, 128, 132–133, 144
Manufacturing of renewable energy infrastructure, iv
Marguerite Infrastructure Fund, 21
Marketisation, b, iv, 8–9, 12, 16–17, 27, 32–33, 43, 54, 97–98, 138, 145, 148, 177
Markets, iii, 4, 6, 11–12, 15–17, 20, 22, 26–30, 32, 36, 41, 47, 52, 54, 66–67, 69, 76, 78, 99, 107, 118, 144–145
Masdar, 85–86, 153
Mauritius, 76, 78
Mercom Capital Group, 23
Mergers and acquisitions, 8, 23, 66
Mexico, 64
Mirova SA, 73
Morocco, 20, 65, 111
Multilateral and bilateral support, 65
Municipalisation, 88, 110, 143–144

N

National Grid, iv, 74, 107–110, 135, 142, 146, 151
Nationalisation, 34, 143–144
Natural Asset Companies, 98–99
Nature, iv, 1, 8–9, 16, 24, 27–28, 32–33, 40, 54, 92, 97–101, 107, 113, 120, 123, 126, 128, 133, 138, 145, 147–148
Negative impact of tax havens, 84
Neoliberal, 11, 14, 24, 54, 93, 98, 113, 128, 136, 142, 144
Net Zero Economic Zones, 8, 111, 135
Net-Zero Cities, iv, 113
Netherlands, viii–ix, 38, 45, 57, 71, 74–75, 121
New public sector organisations, v, 144
New South Wales, 61, 110, 112, 121
New York Stock Exchange, 77, 98
New Zealand National Adaptation Plan, 102
NextEnergy Capital National, 28, 50
NextEra Energy, 56

NextGenerationEU Green Bonds, 16
Northern Ireland, 46–47, 54, 104, 109, 137
Northland Power, 34–35, 150
Norway, iii, viii, 1, 9, 45, 53, 57, 59, 61, 82–83, 85–86, 153
Nottingham City Council, 115

O

Octopus Investment, 28, 56
Octopus Renewables Infrastructure Trust, 56
Octopus Group, 61
OECD, x, 3, 15, 29, 36, 40, 66, 71, 84, 88, 120
Offshore wind, vi, 7, 11, 14, 21–22, 28, 30, 33, 43, 46, 49, 52, 59, 61, 81–82, 112, 114, 116, 118, 128–129, 133–134, 149–150
Ontario Municipal Employees' Retirement System, x, 77–78, 151
Ontario Teachers' Pension Plan, 59
Orsted, 22, 61, 86, 149, 153
Oversight, 1, 7, 36, 62, 94, 101, 102, 136, 139

P

Partners Group, 48
Pension funds, 7, 11, 15–16, 31, 36, 47–48, 50–51, 77, 79
Peru, 78, 111
Philippines, 20, 65, 67
Poland, 20–21, 38, 45
Political economy or renewable energy framework, 11, 31, 33, 34
Pollution, 2–4, 20, 101, 116, 125–126, 134–135
Portugal, viii, 7, 21, 45, 53, 56, 78, 81, 85, 149, 156
Power generation, 6, 19, 31, 54, 63, 79, 88, 107–108, 141–142
Power Purchase Agreements, 19, 43
PPP secondary market, 65
Private equity funds, 1, 6, 8–9, 11–12, 14–15, 27, 35, 46–48, 53–54, 78, 80, 139

Privatisation, iii, 8–9, 12, 17, 27, 31–33, 43, 50, 63, 85, 97, 128, 143, 145, 177
Public goods, iv, 9–10, 16, 31–32, 55, 85, 90–91, 136–137
Public investment, 29, 33, 87, 91, 100, 110, 127, 142–143
Public management, 26, 92–93, 108, 138, 141, 144–145, 177
Public ownership and provision, b, 97, 143, 145
Public Private Partnership, b, x, 7, 12, 139, 147, 177
Public Sector Equality Duty, iv, 9, 101, 104
Public sector, 1, 6, 8, 10, 12, 17-19, 26, 33, 38, 48-50, 65, 79, 86-95, 107, 114, 125, 126, 128, 137-148, 154,
Public service principles, 11, 41, 91
Public Services International, x
Public Values Framework, iv, 1, 42, 85, 90, 92, 137

Q

Queensland, 121, 133, 143–144
Quinbrook Infrastructure Partners, 60–61, 73

R

Reden Solar, 59
Re-forestation, 123
Re-municipalisation, 88, 110, 144
Relative Sea Level, 2
Renewable energy strategy, 65
Renewable Energy Systems, 10, 35, 56, 88, 137, 143, 146–147
Renewable Energy Zones, iv, 110, 112, 135
REPowerEU, 22, 25, 117
Repsol, 53, 57, 59
Republic of Ireland, 1, 45–46, 53, 74, 86, 110, 112, 153, 156

Retrofitting, iv, 1, 8, 10, 26-27, 30-31, 101, 105-107, 109, 123, 125-126, 128, 135-136, 141, 144-146, 148
Rising sea levels, 2, 9, 27, 102, 107, 122-123
Romania, 1, 46, 153
Royal Dutch Shell, 133
Russian invasion of Ukraine, 4, 24, 58
RWE, 38, 53, 59, 62, 85-86, 89, 133, 155-156

S

Savion LLC, 152
Scotland, iii, 9, 22, 33, 46, 82, 104, 108, 114, 118, 122, 130, 135, 146, 150
Scottish TUC, 130-131
ScotWind, vii, 27, 34, 131, 149-150
Secondary market, 1, 6, 7, 9, 11, 12, 15, 16, 26, 27, 28, 29, 34, 41, 43-48, 52-58, 65, 66, 142, 148
Sembcorp Industries (China), 59
Sempra Infrastructure Partners, 23
Senegal, 20, 65
Shareholder dividends, 55-57, 137
Shell plc, 58
Siemens, 13
Social justice, 11, 84, 90-91, 93-94, 101, 148
Solar, 1, 5-8, 11-14, 16-17, 19-23, 28-30, 32, 35, 43-44, 46, 48-50, 52, 56, 58-65, 67, 73-75, 77, 80-82, 84, 86, 89, 105, 109, 111-118, 125, 127-128, 130-131, 133-135, 139, 143, 145, 151
Sonnedix Power Holdings, 74-75, 82
South Africa, 20, 47, 54, 65, 75, 111
South Australia Grid, 110
Space cooling, 2-3
Spain, x, 21, 28, 37-38, 46, 53, 56-57, 59, 74, 80-82, 118, 125, 149-150, 155
Special Purpose Companies, 75-76
SSE plc, 22
Stadtwerke Berlin, 111
Statkraft, 85-86, 153

Strategic planning, 135-136
Strategic organising, 148
Strathclyde Pension Fund, 50
SUSI Partners, 48, 73
Sustainable Development Bonds, 16-17
Sweden, viii, 1, 34, 46, 56, 85-86, 89, 134, 149-150, 153
Switzerland, 71

T

Taiwan, 22, 46
Tax avoidance, iii, 8, 11, 71, 137
Tax havens, iii, vi, 6, 8-9, 19, 31, 53, 65, 71-75, 77, 82-84, 105, 137
Technological developments, iv, 35, 133
Tetragon Financial Group, 51, 73, 152
The Renewables Infrastructure Group, 56, 73
Three Gorges Asset Management, 72, 78, 85, 86, 153
Thrive Renewables, 57
Tonsley Innovation District, 118
TotalEnergies, 57-59, 150, 155
TPG, 48, 139, 152
Transaction costs, 7, 57-58
Transactions, iii, vi, 1, 6-7, 9, 15, 21, 23, 27-29, 43-48, 51, 53, 55-58, 61-62, 65-66, 71-74, 77-78, 81, 83-84, 87-89, 98
TransAlta Corporation, 75
TUED, x
Turkey, 21-22, 60

U

UAE, x, 85-86, 153
Ukraine, 4, 24, 37, 58
United Kingdom, 7, 9, 12, 22, 25, 28, 30-31, 38, 46, 50-51, 53, 55-57, 59, 60, 65-66, 74-75, 77, 78, 81-83, 85, 92, 97, 104-105, 108-110, 114, 118-119, 122, 123-125, 142, 144, 145-146, 149, 156

United Nations Environment Programme, x, 3, 97, 100
US Export-Import Bank, 22
US Securities and Exchange Commission, 41
USA, vi, x, 3–4, 7, 13, 23, 33, 46, 52–53, 56–57, 59–60, 74–75, 78, 82, 112, 119, 121–122, 127, 129, 142, 150, 155–156

V

Vattenfall, 34, 85–86, 89, 149, 153
Ventient Energy, 50, 61, 74–75, 81–82
Ventive Ltd, 115-116
Verbund AG, 59
Vestas, 156
Vietnam, 59, 67, 111

W

Warburg Pincus, 48, 139
Wildfires, 2, 102, 108
Wind farms, 1, 7, 21, 33, 48, 50, 52, 57, 59, 74, 81–82, 84, 114, 118, 134, 145
World Bank, 7, 12, 15-17, 19, 40, 65, 70, 85, 121, 147
World Bank Private Participation in Infrastructure Database, 63–64
World Bank's Climate Change Action Plan, 16